# MOSES

## *A Sharecropper's Son*

outskirts
press

# ACKNOWLEDGEMENTS

At this point, it gives me great pleasure to express my tremendous appreciation to those individuals who were so instrumental in this writing effort.

First and foremost, I want to cite my favorite granddaughter, Faith Shepherd of Bowie, Maryland. Faith made so many sacrifices in terms of her time and talents, especially when one considers the many activities that a high school student is involved in. She especially honed in on the grammatical aspects of this work.

Roderick Shephard, my nephew, of Statesville, NC also contributed to the reading of the manuscript, and ensuring detail.

And, I'd like to thank my wife, Joyce, for enhancing my writing environment at home. She was always available to assist me in having writing material and resources at hand, and uninterrupted time by fielding phone calls, and taking care of and deflecting other potential distractions.

Rosetta Holmes Nobles was a foot soldier. She took care of mapping and identifying physical landmarks in the Kinston area.

Albert Gaines, of Statesville, NC was an important source for a wide range of information that helped glue pieces together.

Finally, much gratitude is extended to the following: The Kinston Daily Free Press, Lenoir County Community College Library and Security Staff, the Statesville North Carolina Library's History and Genealogy Librarian, and the staff at The Winston Salem North Carolina Library's Genealogy Department.

# TABLE OF CONTENTS

# FOREWORD

The author of this book was born in the nineteen-thirties, at a time when there was much instability for all families and the world at large. Therefore, the writing of this book was a no-brainer. Now imagine, Greene County North Carolina, during that time period. Segregation reigned. Continue to imagine, being black, and poor, living in an environment where tales of the hangings of men and boys of color was the norm. There was nothing to look forward to in terms of doing better. Maybe more succinct, there was no concrete model of what "better" even looked like!!

But time marched on. Things did change—though they didn't become perfect; but moving forward was inevitable. Therefore, the accepted what was presented, worked and "navigated" his way through the morasses that had littered so many possible pathways to surviving. This is not to say that he escaped unscathed; but whatever injuries that were unavoidable, he dealt them, turning them into scars, and incorporating those experiences into positive pieces to make himself an even better person.

Moses Shepherd Junior not only survived all of that, but he managed to see the world (joined the navy), get an education, raise a family, and enjoy life, just a little. And the "good life" was simply that, no more. In the end, he was able to be on equal footing, and to have the opportunity to earn a living on his own terms. Though that kind of progress was in part a function of progressive times, it was still left up to him, to forge ahead with his own choices in terms of how to achieve success.

It is in the pages of this book, Moses: A Sharecropper's Son, where the author boldly, proudly, and most eloquently (countrified and all), shares his trek through the briar patches and dusty fields of life. This took him all the way to the nation's capital. No, he was not on Capitol Hill, but, where he arrived in Washington, he arrived on his own terms.

# PREFACE
*Introduction*

This is an attempt to tell the story of my life growing up in rural eastern North Carolina. I am starting this story from when I was a year old, going on four. However, my personal narrative begins when I was actually four-years old. Some would say that I can't remember that stage of my life. But the truth is that I can remember bits and pieces of events that took place when I was that young. Then they seemed to become progressively more clear by age five. I will, as much as possible, keep events in chronological order.

While the exact year of some events may not be accurate, I have kept them in sequence as best that I remember.

As I approached this project, I realized that my story is only a piece of all that is relevant. But, I feel that the perspective that I bring is an important piece of the whole.

✓ And regarding why I attach importance to this story is that seemingly my off-springs and other young Blacks do not have even the most basic information regarding the trials and tribulations of their ancestors. And consequently, they are not equipped to build on the rich history of what was in place before their arrival.

# INTRODUCTION

In nineteen thirty-seven, the world was fraught with much uncertainty. This was because of two major contributing factors. One was the Great Depression. The other was the unrest that was taking place in Germany.

The Great Depression negatively affected any country where the economy was linked to international finances, and markets of commodities. And, the consequences of the Great Depression in those countries were: businesses folding, workers being laid off, and a drop in spending and investment.

The unrest in Germany led to ripple effects around the world. Even the courts were unable to stop Gestapo activities. Anybody who complained about Hitler was subject to extremely harsh treatment. There were even signs tacked on the walls of businesses, stating that Jews were not to be admitted. *1905*

In South Africa, the Aliens Act was the center of attention. This was a law that targeted Jewish immigration. This law gave a broad power to virtually see to it that Jewish immigrants

*Parliament of the United Kingdom*    v

would not be allowed inside the borders. Of course there were those who did not support such a stance on immigration.

Also, in Canada, there were activities that reflected this same topic. There were confrontations between those for and those against admitting Jewish refugees into their country.

In America, President Franklin Delano Roosevelt, a democrat from New York, was in the first year of his second term as president. And the country was in its eighth year of The Great Depression. This was approximately two years before it ended. So president Roosevelt had a plate full: the Great Depression, war, and other conflicts around the world. Also included was Japan's aggressiveness in attempting to gain dominance in Asia.

And even though race-relations was not on President Roosevelt's agenda, it was still a problematic item that was very visible. However, considering the times, the stance taken by the president was very understandable.

The issue could be broken down to its essence: Blacks being lynched. And in order to attack that, it would mean dealing with lawmakers; and those lawmakers, especially the heads of committees in congress, were headed by the same white men who were championing Jim Crow, and keeping Blacks in their place!

It would be a few years later that, without the help of President Roosevelt, these matters began to come to light in terms of being addressed.

While the president was dealing with the aforementioned matters, in North Carolina, Governor Hoey Clyde Roark, had his own hands full. Along with other matters, he was indeed concerned with the problem of race. However, his was not a pressing concern, as he and the White establishment had concluded sometime previously that in spite of sporadic hangings, the Coloreds in North Carolina were not a problem. It was the conclusion that they had accepted their place and didn't represent a threat to Whites.

But to reduce this discussion to another level, we'll find out that also in nineteen thirty-seven, in Greene County, in the Bull Head community, on Floyd Marshburn's farm, on a Thursday in December, there was quiet; and there was peace.

In that place, there was a birth.

# THE BEGINNING

*1937 to 1942*

I WAS BORN on Thursday, the ninth of December 1937, in the Bullhead section of Greene County, North Carolina. My parents, Moses Shepherd, Sr. (Namon), and his wife, Sarah Pauline Hayes Shepherd (Sack) were sharecroppers.

I learned early that being sharecroppers meant that we would move every two or three years. Near the end of 1938, we moved from Fred Benton's farm to Frank Marshall's farm, less than a quarter of a mile away. That is where my older sister Katie was born.

Daddy had a 1934 Ford with a rumble seat. In today's world, this would be called a trunk. With the lid closed, it looked like a regular car trunk. However, when it was opened, it converted into a seat.

After Christmas in 1940, we moved from Frank Marshall's

farm to a non-farming community in the town of Snow Hill. That place was owned by Louis Holder. I was three years old then, and that's where my memories began to slowly take shape.

The so-called house that we moved into was nothing but a run-down piece of junk. It had loose planks on the walls and ceiling; plus, there were bugs inside. It was located across the road from Greene County Training School, which was the school for coloreds. But this was our new home, so I guess my folks were trying to make the best of it.

Naturally, being in a new place meant that things were different for all of us. With my parents, there was not the urgency to go to the fields and work from dawn 'til dusk. Consequently, they could be at the house more. For me, I didn't have to be alone as much, and I got to play on that real playground at the school.

Mother would take me there at least twice a week. I especially enjoyed playing on those wooden seesaws. And it was even more enjoyable when the weather warmed up. But one of those times when I was having so much fun, I got a splinter stuck in my ass. I was screaming bloody murder. I said, "Oh Lord, please help me! Oh Lord, please save me! Don't let me die!" I had stuck splinters in my finger before, but never in my backside. Mother ran over, trying to calm me down, but I refused to be calm. I just kept screaming. Finally she got me under control. Then she took me home and removed the splinter, but the removal process hurt more than it did when I got stuck.

However, that was nothing compared to the alcohol she applied. So there I was bawling again. But this time she didn't try to get me calm; she just kept on applying that alcohol. Next, she put a cloth on the wound, to "protect it," so she said.

In addition to enjoying the playground, I got to meet people outside of my family. This was quite interesting. The first person I got to know was Louis Holder, the owner of this property that we lived on. Compared to my parents, he appeared to be a giant. Daddy was about five feet and eight inches tall, and weighed maybe a hundred and forty-five pounds. Mother was probably five feet and five inches, weighing about one hundred and fifteen pounds. On the other hand, Mr. Holder was huge, the tallest man I'd ever seen. And he limped when he walked.

He began to stop by periodically. He would pull up in front of the house and limp to the porch, where he and Daddy would talk. While they were talking, I would be staring at him, because in addition to not having ever seen anybody that tall, neither had I ever seen anybody who walked like he did. On one such visit, he asked Mother and Daddy if I could take a ride with him in that red truck that seemed to always have my attention.

They gave their permission, and off we went. Evidently Mr. Holder enjoyed having me ride with him as he went to different houses, probably some that he owned. Plus, we would ride to other houses where the people who lived in them were obviously owners of those houses and they were apparently friends of his. At the latter places, he would be showing me off. Once he took me to an outdoor function, which was at a place that had the prettiest green lawn I had ever seen. And man, there were more white folks in one place than imaginable. They were just oohing and aahing over me. And, yep, I was grinning.

Whenever Mr. Holder drove me around, he'd buy me Pepsi Colas, my favorite soft drink. He thought I was such a great pet that he asked Mother and Daddy to let him have me. He told them that all I would have to do was be his driver, and he would make sure that I finished high school and college.

I guess you know the answer he got.

As well as living across the street from Greene County Training School, we lived less than a block from the pool hall that Daddy operated. At the pool hall, there was an outdoor platform where people danced. One Saturday night, for no reason that I knew, Daddy took me with him. I was supposed to sit quietly on a stool, but it got so hot in there that I decided to go up on the platform, hoping for a breeze. I slipped out and climbed the steps, dodging people who were coming down.

When I reached the platform, I could see people's feet moving and jerking. *This must be dancing,* I thought. I eased my way along the edge, and found a spot near the center of the dance floor. People were pushing and bumping into me as they danced. This definitely was not what I called fun.

One of the men stopped dancing, got me by the hand, and led me back to the stool that Daddy had assigned me to. Then I saw him go talk to Daddy and point in my direction. Daddy didn't even come over where I was. Instead, some fancy-dressed lady came over and said, "Your daddy asked me to walk you back to the house, little man. Come on." I hopped off the stool and followed her out the door and to our house. I found out later that her name was Dasia, and that she was a "loose" woman, and the second prettiest woman in Greene County at that time. The prettiest was my Aunt Erlene, Mother's oldest sister.

It was right after my experience at the pool hall that I began to pay attention to adult conversations. I noticed that Mother and Daddy did a lot of talking about finding someplace else to live. Mother's point was that the current house was too rundown and unfit. They would have discussions about it, and they would argue about it. Mother would complain; but all of this was for naught. Daddy kept promising her somewhere better. But he also continued to carry the excuse that he just had not yet been able to find the right place.

Then the very next month, on August twenty-first, 1941, my sister Marie was born. Apparently, Mother reached the point that she was unwilling to wait any longer for Daddy to find a better place. This was evident because about three weeks after Marie arrived, Mother informed him that she and the children were going to live with her father. She reiterated what she had told him repeatedly, that the conditions where we currently lived were unfit for a newborn.

So, off we went, back to the country, but this time to live with Grandpa. Daddy helped Mother pack what few belongings we had. Then he loaded all of us into his car, and delivered us to Grandpa's house. Meanwhile, he continued to run the pool hall, but he lived somewhere else.

Grandpa lived on Dave Lawrence's farm, about a quarter of

a mile from Nigger Head Swamp. (One of several stories that explained this name was that two black men were lynched, and their heads were chopped off and thrown into that swamp.) Grandpa's house was situated up a short path, approximately fifty yards from the road. And it was just like I'd heard Mother describe: "Fairly large and sturdy." She said that it was like this because Grandpa would do a lot of work on it. Whenever something needed to be repaired, he would immediately take care of it.

Grandpa already had a house full, but he graciously accommodated us. This was Beston E. Hayes' house! The grown ups called him Pa. The grandchildren would come to call him Grandpa. He was a widower, about sixty years old, with a head full of hair that was basic black, but with a noticeable amount of gray sprinkled in. He was a tobacco chewer and a snuff dipper, but he never smoked.

Grandpa's house was like a Travelers' Inn. In addition to him living there, and excluding us, there were: Erlene, his oldest daughter, his youngest daughter, Kathy, and his sons Jack and Bob. Uncle Jack lived there with his wife, Mabel. Uncle Bob lived there with his wife, Ada, son Raymond, and daughter Mattie. They were about two and one year old, respectively.

Daddy visited us on a regular basis, but the one visit that I remembered most vividly was when he drove up to the house really fast, late one afternoon. He got out of the car and was screaming Mother's name as he approached the house. "Sarah! Sarah! …them Japs done bombed Pearl Harbor."

Overall, our time at Grandpa's was mostly uneventful.

The big thing for me was the day he came home with a pretty brown and white puppy in his arms. It was fairly warm on that December afternoon, and some family members were sitting on the front porch as I was playing nearby in the yard.

Grandpa greeted the grown ups and headed toward me. "Look what I got here, boy," he said.

"Hey, Grandpa," I responded, bright-eyed upon seeing the puppy.

"I know you got a birthday coming up, and I know you like dogs, so I brought this little fellow for your birthday present." I was in disbelief as Grandpa handed me the puppy. The grown-ups had stopped talking and were watching me and Grandpa.

I cuddled the puppy and continued smiling. "What are you going to name him?" Mother asked. I barely heard her because I was so much into this little present that I'd just received. This was my first birthday present ever. I eventually caught myself and turned to Mother's question. I simply said, "I don't know yet."

It was the following Tuesday, on my fourth birthday, that I came up with a name: Rascal.

～～

Daddy must have finally gotten his ducks in a row regarding our "family matters," because right into the New Year, we were leaving Grandpa's house. Daddy no longer had his car, so he hired someone to move us.

The man came that morning with a trailer hooked behind the dark green car he was driving. He and Daddy packed all of our belongings in the trailer, making sure to leave enough room for Rascal. Daddy and the driver rode up front. I rode in the backseat with Mother and the girls. Katie sat in the middle, Mother held Marie on her lap behind the driver, and I sat next to the other window.

Duplin County was quite a few miles from Snow Hill. I think we traveled at least half a day. Katie was restless. I was restless, and I think Mother and Daddy were tired, but the baby and the man driving seemed to be the only ones who were not affected.

We finally pulled into the yard of an unpainted plank dwelling. Mother took us kids inside while Daddy and the driver unloaded the trailer. I don't know if the driver was in a hurry or not, but he and Daddy quickly removed our belongings. They placed some on the porch and some on the ground, rather than taking them inside. After the last armful of boxes was on the ground, the man got in his car and drove away. With the trailer now empty, it bounced and squeaked as he pulled onto the road.

Mother had Katie and Marie wrapped in blankets. They were now sound asleep. Me? I was still looking out the kitchen window, trying to see what Daddy was doing.

When Mother was about to go outside to help bring some things in, I asked if I could go too. She said yes, and I was excited. Once I got out there, I started my wandering around the house, looking under the house, just investigating.

While they were making trips in and out of the house, a white lady came over from across the field. She was followed by a small hound and two curious-looking children, a boy, probably a few years older than me, and a girl, who was maybe a couple of years older than the boy.

"Good mornin', Mose," the woman said gleefully as she approached. "I'm sho glad you got here. I saw them clouds this mornin' and didn't figure you could make it without getting a little wet."

"Yes, ma'am," Daddy responded. "I guess we got lucky."

Then the woman began an introduction: "These here my younguns," she said, motioning toward the children, "Margaret and Herm."

Then a somewhat embarrassed look came over her face. Evidently, she realized that she hadn't spoken to Mother; that was apparently due in part to the stare that Mother was putting on her.

"Well, golly be, honey," she said as she walked over to Mother and extended her hand. "I'm Ermine, Ermine Morris. Folks 'round here call me Erma. Mose done told me 'bout you—said I'd love having you here, and I do already."

Mother responded with a chilly "How you?"

Miss Erma continued: "Can I talk to you for a minute, honey?" She and Mother walked a few steps away, obviously to ensure privacy. But I could hear them talking as they moved away. "I'm so sorry," she said before they got out of earshot. After they stopped a few yards away, we children were left standing there, quietly looking at each other, as Daddy picked up another armful of items to take in the house.

Miss Erma and Mother talked for about five minutes. Then

they both came back smiling and still talking. "I'm gon git outta your way," she said to Daddy, as she turned to leave, "but I'm right 'cross the field if you need anything." Margaret and Herm followed her the same way they had come, and stared back as they left.

After Miss Erma and her children had gone, I continued to look around. The house appeared to be okay from the outside. Yet, I could not get my thoughts away from what might be a problem on the inside. When we arrived, I entered and did a brief inspection. From that, I determined that the inside was okay. But I still held reservations, mainly about what I didn't find.

My thoughts kept leading me to compare this place to the one we'd moved from in Snow Hill. *It could be just like the one Marie was born in,* I thought. Since before we moved in with Grandpa, those loose planks on the wall continued to haunt me. I had envisioned them falling on my head at night when I was sleeping. But after a complete tour, my fears subsided. Not a single plank was loose. My conclusion was that this was a palace compared to where we used to call home. Now, it was time to consider the big picture. The front porch stretched the length of the house, but there was no back porch. The back door was in the kitchen. When exiting from there, you had to jump down a couple of feet onto the ground.

Inside, the kitchen was very small, but it was big enough for the table and three chairs that we had. In other words, it was at least large enough for two grownups to turn around in at the same time.

Mother and Daddy got everything into the house and set up in no time. Considering the fact that there was not much to bring in and set up, it all worked out perfectly.

The next day, about an hour after breakfast, Daddy was preparing to take Mother out to show her the fields. They told me to keep an eye on the baby, who was napping, and not to let Katie near the heater. As they were about to leave, since the sun was shining and it wasn't very cold, I asked if Katie and I could go play in the yard if I would come back in periodically and check on the baby. They both said that it would be okay. Mother put a sweater on Katie, and I put on an extra shirt. We went out when they did.

Having moved from Snow Hill, I had never seen nor heard a train. Our house was located about a hundred yards from the railroad track. Once outside, Katie and I went our separate ways. But I could see where she was and what she was doing. Therefore, I could make sure that she was safe at all times.

I was across the yard from her when suddenly this black smoke-belching, screaming monster came hurtling down the tracks. I didn't know what that thing was, and I had no idea what it might do to us. I took off running toward Katie. I grabbed her by the hand and pretty much dragged her as I continued running into the house as fast as I could. That thing went on by without harming us. But it took me a while to get myself composed and convince Katie that we were safe. I also checked on the baby. She was still sound asleep.

Mother and Daddy returned sooner than I expected, and found us back in the house. "Why aren't you outside?" Mother asked. I told her what had happened, and both she and Daddy explained to me what that thing was, where it traveled to, and the possibility that we might ride on it one day.

Even though Daddy had gotten his family back together, our life was still not all peaches and cream. As it turned out, my final conclusion about our new residence was grossly inaccurate, and my initial reservations were justified. That place was COLD! This being winter, it didn't take long to realize how exposed we were to the elements. The roof leaked, the house didn't hold heat, and it was just plain miserable. But evidently Mother was okay enough to stay; or, she was too far from Grandpa's house to move us back.

Daddy would come to my room each morning and wake me up. For some reason, this room seemed to be especially vulnerable. There was a particular bitter cold night when I was in bed, and in spite of all the covers, I couldn't get warm. I figured that everybody else was in their room, apparently sleeping well. But it was absolutely unbearable to me. So, I got up and went outside to the porch in my long johns and got Rascal. I took him to bed with me, and we both slept, warm.

The kicker was the next morning when Daddy came in the room to wake me up. He actually woke both me and Rascal up. He didn't say a word, but the look on his face was priceless.

In spite of not having been at our new home very long, within a few days we were functioning like we had been there forever. Daddy would be out and about, tending the farm. He knew where everything was and what to do. Of course, I thought that was quite remarkable. Meanwhile, Mother had her share of responsibilities, including milking Miss Erma's cows every morning.

One evening when we were sitting at the dinner table, Daddy began to share information regarding where we stood in the big picture of our being at this particular place. "I'll be taking care of the farm and their yard while your momma will tend to the cows and help me in the fields," he said. Daddy also went on to explain why Miss Erma seemed to be running the farm. I had pondered that very question, but I hadn't bothered to ask. However, from what he'd just said, actually he and Mother would be running the whole place!

"Miss Erma ain't the owner," he continued. "She and her husband own it. His name is Herman Morris. He's the one I talked to about moving here. But he ain't home a whole lot... works for the railroad. So you'll only see him from time to time. Since he'll be in and out, he wants us to take care of everything." This was one of the few times I'd seen Daddy appear so at ease with what was going on in his life.

While he had explained the circumstances and shared information about Miss Erma and Herman, I had my own big picture view. In addition to what Daddy had said, and in contrast, where the Morris family lived was the very opposite of a tenant family residence. They lived in a pretty white frame house. From the outside, it appeared to be quite spacious. And it had nice green trimming on each corner. Their back porch was screened in, and Miss Erma filled it with lots of plants. The veranda was completely enclosed, and it ran half way around the house. From left to right, facing the house, there were hanging plants, and these were evenly spread the entire length. That was one pretty place!

It would be several weeks before I ever saw Herman Morris. It was one afternoon, the last Friday in February. The weather was not as cold as it had been the previous few weeks, but it was breezy. I was at the Morris house with Daddy while he was cleaning some debris from Miss Erma's flowerbed. A pickup truck turned into the yard. Of course I stared, because I'd never seen that truck in the neighborhood and I was just plain curious. But when I saw Margaret and Herm race out the door to greet the driver, I realized who he was.

Herman was a bit taller than most men I'd seen, maybe except for Louis Holder. He walked kind of bent over at the shoulders. He stopped and said a few words to Daddy. Then he went on into the house. After Daddy had removed a few more bushes from the flowerbed, we left.

On the way home, Daddy shared the running story about Herman amongst the neighbors. The story was that whenever Herman came home, he spent more time with his dog than he did with Miss Erma.

This being winter, we had our share of cold days. But I never enjoyed them because I could not go outside and play; it was nice from the standpoint of Mother being at home with us as much as she could. However, a few weeks after the nice weather stabilized, there was constant work to be done in the fields. So both Mother and Daddy would be out the door early each morning, headed off to work.

I would be left to care for my two sisters. Picture this. I, a four-year-old, was put in charge of a two-year-old and an eight-month-old! This meant watching over them, feeding them, and changing their diapers! As one can imagine, this was such a tremendous undertaking. And needless to say, sometimes I didn't get it right according to grownup standards. But I must say that since I survived all that came along as consequences for my missteps, I think I did okay.

When Mother and Daddy would leave for work, as soon as I thought it was warm enough to go outside, I would get the girls wrapped up, get a blanket to lay the baby on, and out we'd go. Then we would begin our own routine. No, what we did wasn't work, but we sure could play pretty good. At least Katie and I did, as Marie would crawl around as much as she could.

Of course, much of my time was not "play-time," as I had to keep an eye on my sisters. But being outside allowed me to have some distance from them, and still see what they were doing, making sure that they didn't put themselves in danger.

The biggest problem for me turned out to be the fact that I couldn't keep Marie from putting chicken shit in her mouth. It wasn't dangerous in any way, so I'd just clean her mouth with a rag and go back to my playing. Daddy would come home periodically during the day to check on us. And on those jaunts, often, he too would spend his fair share of time cleaning Marie's mouth.

Even before it got started, I knew that babysitting my sisters would not be an easy matter. But there was no way on earth I could have anticipated just how bad it would be. Little did I know that the experience with the train would only be the beginning of new and negative situations in which I would find myself.

From time to time as I thought about my situation, I came to realize that my role as a babysitter was not something I would wish on anybody, not even my worst enemy. But here I was. And it was more than a case of having my hands full. It was downright awful. It so happened that not only did I have to deal with Marie crying and eating chicken shit, but Katie began to get into anything she could put her hands on. Or, to be more exact, it wasn't always *what* she got into; all too often, it was what she got into her body as a result of her own actions. She liked to stuff objects into her nose. Buttons, beans, and wads of paper were her favorites.

This particular morning, Mother and Daddy had only been out of the house about forty-five minutes. Marie had gone back to sleep after breakfast, and I knew not to awaken her. Katie and I went on outside. Of course I would go back in periodically to check on Marie. I had just made one of those trips, and the baby was fine, still asleep.

When I returned to the yard, Katie was struggling to breathe. She was taking very short breaths and panicking. What was I supposed to do?! Hell, I panicked too. But I quickly calmed down. After all, it wasn't like I had no idea about what had happened. She had put something up her nose again. Previous times, I'd been able to remove the objects.

I tilted her head back, and I could see that it was a bean this time. I squeezed her nose in an effort to dislodge it, but to no avail, as it only went down further. Then I tried to wedge it out with my finger. This too made the bean go deeper.

So I grabbed her by the hand and took off running down the path to the field where Mother and Daddy were working. I took a shortcut by turning from the path and running across rows of corn. Those rows seemed to be so high though, and hard to cross. Finally, I looked up and saw Mother and Daddy. They saw us coming and hurried to meet us, with scared looks on their faces.

"What's the matter?" Mother asked. I was too tired to answer. But she saw how Katie was struggling, and figured it out. She put Katie across her knee, and was able to force the bean out. What a relief that was! But there was another fear that I had. Not only did I allow Katie to put the bean up her nose, but I also left the baby at the house alone. I knew that this would surely earn me an ass whipping. I was shocked when they sent us back to the house, with nothing being said about either of my concerns. Needless to say, I didn't ask any questions.

However, that episode was nothing compared to the next one that I starred in. Keep in mind that I was four years old, at home babysitting my little sisters. Again, Mother and Daddy were working the fields. They came home for lunch as usual. But this time, one of them said, "I smell something burning." They began walking through the house in different directions, like detectives, and sniffing like bloodhounds, searching for where the smell was coming from.

Finally, Daddy hollered, "Here it is." Of course I followed Mother to where Daddy had made the discovery, because I was curious too. Daddy had opened a dresser drawer, and there was a box of "strike-anywhere" matches. They had completely burned up.

Mother turned to me and asked if I'd been playing with matches. I said, "No, ma'am." She quickly told me to stop lying. But I knew I was telling the truth. She went outside and got a thick switch from the yard broom and came back in the house madder than she was when she went out. With no more questions asked, she told me that she was going to beat the truth out of me.

She commenced to whip my ass unmercifully. I was determined not to say that Katie, obviously had played with the matches. If Daddy had not intervened, I think she would've killed me. My body stayed sore from that whipping for over a week!

But we moved on.

In spite of what seemed like so many negatives, there were some better times. One was when Daddy hired a neighbor, Mr. Jenkins, to take the whole family to the nearby town of Bowden on his mule and wagon. This was so that we could catch the train to Goldsboro and visit his mother (Grandma Mary), his sister (Aunt Rudy), and her fifteen-year-old son, Jerry.

This was really an exciting trip. It was Saturday morning, and Mother had the girls dressed up in Sunday outfits that she had made. I had on a pair of clean overalls and a plaid shirt that was only slightly too small.

Katie was looking around, as usual, and being inquisitive about everything. Meanwhile, Daddy spent several minutes explaining the whole scene to me.

Then he let me go with him to purchase our tickets. "Come on, Junior," he said, as he waved his hand for me to follow. We went across the yard to a small building where a frail-looking white man was standing behind a counter, issuing tickets. Two other people were waiting when we got there, so we lined up behind them.

After a few minutes, it was our turn. Now being up close, I could see that the man behind the counter was a clean-shaven white man, wearing a beige shirt and a green bow tie. "What'd you say, boy?" he greeted Daddy. There was no response. Probably none was expected. "What'd you need?" he asked.

"Round-trip tickets for Goldsboro, two grown folks, two chillun, and a baby," Daddy told him. The man turned to his left, and I heard a clicking sound. I got on my tiptoes, trying to see what was making that noise. But I was not tall enough to see over the counter.

The man tore some tickets off and exchanged them with Daddy for some money. Then we went back to where Mother and the girls were sitting. After waiting there for a short while, we heard several loud horn blasts that sounded familiar. I asked Daddy what it was and he told me it was a whistle that the train blew when it was coming into the station. It was then that I realized I'd heard that sound before, when it scared the hell out of me and my sister.

Several people headed to where the train would stop, I guessed. I guessed right, because when the train arrived, it eased to a stop, right near where the line had formed. We waited, as some people got off, some with suitcases in hand, and some with clothes folded across their arms. Then it was time for us to get aboard. Boy, how exciting, the first time ever I got to ride a train! We boarded. Daddy showed us where we would sit. And, in about twenty minutes, we were headed to Goldsboro.

This ride was different. At first the train chugged along, and the ride seemed awfully bumpy; but as it picked up speed, things became smoother. I looked around to see what it was like inside this big moving thing. However, what I began to notice was how fast those trees seemed to go by outside the windows. After that, our trip to Goldsboro didn't seem to take long at all.

The train slowed down significantly when it reached the city limits. This allowed me to size up this new place. It was a town of both paved and unpaved streets; at least that's what I was seeing thus far. There were a lot of small houses, like the one we lived in, but they were so close together with very little yard space.

Once we arrived at the train station and got off, Daddy said that word "walk." We had to walk a pretty good distance to get to where Grandma lived on Beale Street. Daddy carried Katie, Mother carried Marie, and I walked—didn't matter. I liked to walk.

When we got to the house, Aunt Rudy and Grandma greeted us pleasantly. Jerry spoke as he was headed out the door. We didn't see him again the whole time we were there. Daddy, Mother, and Aunt Rudy went into another room. Katie and I played, and Grandma acted like nobody else mattered except the baby. She latched onto Marie, and I don't think she gave her back until it was time for us to leave. Near the end of our visit, we had dinner; then it was time to go home.

Our return trip home was not nearly as exciting as it was going. And the thought of a future visit never crossed my mind. So, it was back to where we now called home. For Mother and Daddy, they would return to working in the fields. For me, it would be staying around the house with my sisters all day—with me being the babysitter.

True to form, we all continued to do what our roles called for. But in this progression of moving forward, there was a specific item that was becoming more and more apparent: the relationship between Mother and Miss Erma.

I wouldn't say that they were becoming best friends, but their relationship had improved drastically from what it was initially. It improved to the point where they would talk and look out for each other. Whenever Miss Erma had to be away from home for a few days, she would ask Mother to go over to her house and water her plants and feed her cats. And whenever Mother had a perilous situation, Miss Erma would be there for her. In a slanted kind of way, the following example attests to that.

It was late May when Mother went to the garden and picked a mess of butter beans. She got everything set up to do some canning. She had jars, pressure cooker, salt, and a couple of other items that I could not identify. Then she sat down and commenced to shell beans. There were so many that I briefly considered asking if I could help; but I decided against it because if she approved my request, and I did a good job, she might make that another one of my required duties. So, I just continued to watch. She did finally get them shelled though; when she did, she had a lot of hulls to dispose of. Being the smart woman that she was, she put the shelled beans aside and loaded the hulls into a foot tub. Next, she headed to the Morris' cow pasture, which was across the road. Reaching the pasture, Mother poured the hulls on the ground for the cows to eat. One of Miss Erma's cows came over immediately and began munching on that delicious meal. Mother went back to the house and resumed canning. I stayed outside and played. Then I began to hear strange sounds coming from the pasture. I looked up and saw one of Miss Erma's cows acting crazy, like she was dancing. I went half way across the road to get a better look. Then I ran to the house and told Mother that Miss Erma's cow must be sick. I was going to tell her more, but before I could, she had bolted out the door, hurrying to the pasture. She climbed through the wooden fence and began frantically throwing butter bean hulls out. After she had gotten all of the hulls removed, she rushed to Miss Erma's house and banged on the door. "Miss Erma! Miss Erma!" Mother called.

"What in the world is wrong?" Miss Erma asked as she opened the door, still drying her hands with her apron. That's when she looked down to the pasture and saw the situation for herself.

"I thought she could eat bean hulls," Mother breathlessly told Miss Erma, "...but that must be what's making her sick." They both headed back down the path to the pasture. By now, the cow seemed to be calming down. Her eyes still looked funny, but she was drinking water, so maybe she would be all right. We stayed there a while longer; and sure enough, the cow was okay.

While Mother seemed to have a little time away from her assignments for something like canning, Daddy had no such luxury. So it was not surprising that Herman Morris could afford not to be at home much. He had somebody running the farm for him and doing all the other work around there. In addition to working the fields, Daddy's assignments included keeping the Morris's flower garden, and making sure that their lawn was manicured. But the only tool available for this latter task was a swing blade. And after he had finished cutting all the grass, Miss Erma would bring him a bowl of ice cream to the back door, and he would slurp it like it was the best thing he'd ever had.

As the weather got warmer, Mother and Daddy got busier. They began to put in extremely long hours. However, shortly before summer, we got a break. Again, Daddy hired Mr. Jenkins to take us to the train station. This time, it was Saturday around noon. The station was not as crowded as it was before. Daddy had already bought our tickets and was around the corner talking with a couple of friends. I was just people-watching, while Mother and the girls sat on a bench.

Suddenly, a man with blood-soaked clothing rushed up to where they were sitting. He picked up a brick that was lying near Mother's foot. "I'm going back and kill that son-of-a-bitch that stabbed me," he announced to anyone who might be listening. But everyone seemed to be doing more looking at him than listening.

Daddy saw what was happening and rushed over to see if we were safe. "I heard all that racket," he said, "…and then I saw somebody running this way. What happened? What did he say?"

"He said that he was going back to kill the man that stabbed him," Mother replied, answering both questions.

Daddy sort of chuckled and shook his head, with a comment: "Well, if he's gonna do all that, he might need to go back the way he came from, 'cause I just saw him running in the opposite direction." Daddy then returned to where he was before, and continued his conversation.

When it was about time for the train, Daddy came back over to where we were. "They were fighting over a woman," he said. "Some guy bought his girlfriend a slice of watermelon, and he took offense to it; that's what started the whole thing."

The train was there. We boarded. We visited. The routine was the same: We walked to Grandma's house. Jerry was leaving; Grandma got the baby. Daddy, Mother, and Aunt Rudy went and talked. Katie and I played outside; and we ate. Then we returned to our little place in the world.

When we got back home, something felt different. After any of us had been away from home, even for a short period of time, Rascal would run to meet us. I didn't know if anybody else noticed it, and I didn't say anything immediately. But once I looked around outside and in the woods, even across the road at the Morris place, I knew that this was a serious matter.

I told Mother that I couldn't find Rascal. She told me to keep looking, but I assured her that I'd already looked everywhere.

However, Daddy didn't seem to be concerned. This was strange though, because I knew that Daddy loved Rascal. My final thinking was that he'd run away.

As spring had ended, I recognized and appreciated the fact that there was less pressure on me as a babysitter. For one thing, summer helped me deal with the loss of Rascal; and maybe equally important, it meant that rather than all the work being out in the fields for Mother and Daddy, much of it would be just a short distance away, right across the road at the barns. If anything was to go wrong at the house, I had quick access to them. And, often my sisters and I would play at the barn where they worked. This was indeed great, because it meant there would be no major slip-ups on my part, and best of all, no ass whippings.

August came, and we were still barning tobacco. It was a Saturday night, right after darkness had set in. Daddy was not at home yet. Mother, my sisters, and I were just sitting there, with the lamps burning. And we were about to get ready for bed. Suddenly, there came a loud noise, rapid banging at the front porch. Mother went to the door and stood there listening. The banging continued. She cracked the door open to see who it was. Standing there was a frantic-looking young white woman with scraggly blond hair. She didn't wait to be greeted or invited inside. She just rushed in and closed the door, locked it, leaned back against it, and exhaled. Her face was bleeding and her lips and eyes were swollen. Katie and I looked on in horror. "Ma'am, can you help me? Please!" the woman begged. Mother invited her to sit down. "He's beating me," the woman continued. "He's beating me again."

Mother got a couple of towels from the drawer and poured some water in the basin. She then wet one of the towels and dabbed the blood and dirt from the woman's face. "What's your name, honey?" Mother asked.

"I'm Pricilla Cobb, ma'am. I just live down the road a piece." Mother applied salve to places where her skin was broken . "Can I stay here?" the woman desperately asked. "Please let me stay here. He's gon kill me."

Mother told her to go into a closet, that she would be safe there. It was only a few minutes later, when we had returned to acting normal, that we heard footsteps outside. It sounded as if someone was pacing around the house.

After a long while, the sound of pacing stopped, but we continued to act normal. And after an even longer period of time, Mother went to the closet and told the woman that she thought it would be safe for her to leave. I could tell by the look on her face that she was still very much afraid, but evidently, to some degree, she had gotten herself together while in the closet. "You'll be okay," Mother assured her as she straightened the woman's hair, treating her like she was one of her own children. "Are you going back home?" Mother asked.

The woman hesitated, not as if she was unsure of how to answer the question, but measuring her response. "No, ma'am," the woman stammered. "My momma and daddy live not too far from here; that's where I'm going."

The woman hesitated again. The two of them walked to the door. The woman opened the door and looked out, then turned back to Mother. "I want to thank you so much," she said, trying to muster a smile. "You probably saved my life."

Mother returned the smile, and said, "You'll be okay, but do be careful." The woman then hugged Mother real tight and walked out into the darkness.

It was also during this season of harvest that another item was added to my resume. "Putting in tobacco" was a process. Tobacco leaves were removed from the stalks, transported to the shelter via tobacco trucks, removed from the truck in handfuls or bundles, and given to the looper, who tied them onto a tobacco stick (using tobacco twine). They were then taken and hung in racks (temporarily), removed from there, hung in a barn, heated/cured, then removed and taken to a pack house, where it was then graded and prepared for selling. It was the removal of the cured tobacco sticks where I became involved. As a four -year-old, I was assigned to be in line with adults where a stick of tobacco was passed to me, as I was to pass it to the next person in getting it to a truck to be transported to the pack house. Those sticks of cured tobacco were awfully long; and they were still heavy. Since I was so little, in order to accommodate a stick of tobacco, I had to place it under the pit of my arm to hold it up; then I would use my left hand to complete the passing of the stick to the next person.

The remainder of 1942 was pretty much a blur. The continued harvesting of different crops seemed to merge as one huge task. Consequently, my babysitting went right along with it. The highlight for me came on December the ninth. I turned five years old. The only brief, single-day breaks that I recall were Christmas and New Year's, and they weren't really celebratory. They were just days off from the normal routines.

It was downright frigid that Thursday morning, but I was sufficiently wrapped, except for my hands, and they did get cold. So I kept them in my pockets on the way to the barn. Miss Erma was going in the door when I arrived. "Good morning, Junior," she said.

"Good morning ma'am," I replied.

She reached up and got a bucket that was hanging on a nail. "We got a lot to do," she said, opening the bin where the corn was stored. "I'm sure glad you can help me today."

"Yes, ma'am," I answered. But I sensed that Miss Erma wasn't nearly as spry as she usually was. Concluding that she was not herself, I also understood that it was none of my business. Consequently, I tried to keep my mind on helping her fill a couple of barrels with corn like she had asked me to. However, I just couldn't keep from noticing. At one point, I happened to look up. That's when I realized that she was actually weeping while she worked. From that point on, I pretended not to see her. As we worked, I would inevitably get a glimpse of her wiping away tears. When we were finishing, Miss Erma thanked me, and did something most unusual. She gave me a long hug and told me that I could go back home.

Upon returning to the house, I told Mother what I had witnessed, and that Miss Erma had thanked me, then strangely enough, hugged me as if something was wrong. She explained to me that Miss Erma was very upset because she didn't want to lose her good help. I asked her what she meant by that. "We're going to move to another farm," she said. "Oh" was my only response, because I still didn't know what all of that had to do with Miss Erma's behavior.

I could think of some reasons not to move, but I also knew that what I thought didn't matter. Therefore, I tried to get those thoughts out of my mind. And apparently no such competing notions would have made a difference anyway, because a few days later, we were packing up, getting ready to move. Mother and Daddy were busy putting things in bags and stacking other items to be put into boxes. Then an older light-skinned black man came with a beat-up-looking green truck.

When they were loading, my mind was wandering all over the place. For one thing, I couldn't get Miss Erma's crying out of my head. Then there was the sadness I saw from Mother. And why were things this way anyhow? Why did we have to do all the work? But what did I know, being a five-year-old?

I did know, however, that living there, for me, had been both good and bad. Maybe the worst part was that I had to be responsible for my sisters; and one of the good things was that I'd ridden a train.

I also recalled Miss Erma's children, Margaret and Herm. The only thing that stood out about Margaret was that she had brown shoulder-length hair and Miss Erma kept it real neat for her.

But Herm was special. He was older than me and we didn't play together, but I just enjoyed being around him because he was fun to watch. Every time I saw him, he was either eating or looking for something to eat. And wherever he was, he was always doing something that made you take notice. For example, one morning we were down at the barn when it suddenly started raining really hard. Herm took off, running to the house, which was not necessarily unusual, but I looked up again and he was running back with an umbrella. What was so puzzling was the fact that the umbrella was not even open, which meant that he was getting drenched. When he got back to where he'd been playing, he crawled through the wooden fence, opened the umbrella, and held it over two young pigs.

Finally, it was time for us to climb into the cab. Boy, it was crowded. Mother sat in the middle, holding Marie. Daddy sat next to her, holding Katie on one knee, and me on the other.

As I continue to think back, I also remember mostly some interesting things that I had experienced on Miss Erma's farm. One of those was the cow getting sick. I also thought about a few bad experiences, like the ass-whippings that I'd received.

However, now it was time to go. The truck was loaded, and we were pulling out. As we drove away, I pressed my face against the window, trying to see Miss Erma. But there was no movement at her place at all.

# THE MIDDLE YEARS

$1943-1947$

ON THE WAY to our new home, I overheard Daddy explaining to the driver what this move was all about. He said that along with two of Mother's brothers (Uncle Jack and Uncle Bob), they had acquired a five-year lease on a fairly large farm in Lenoir County. And for the first time in their lives, they would be farming on thirds instead of sharecropping. The difference between the two systems is as follows.

Sharecropping is also known as farming on halves. In this system, the owner of the land (the landlord) furnishes the tools, the equipment, and a shack for the tenant (the one who will tend the land) to live in. The landlord also pays for half of the seeds, half of the fertilizer, and half of the insecticide. He or she also furnishes the tenant with a monthly allowance until the coming summer. This allotment is usually about thirty dollars.

The tenant is responsible for all of the labor required to operate the farm. In the fall, the two parties settle up.

And let it be noted that it is the landlord who handles all monetary matters. That makes it understandable that settling up is controlled by the landlord. It is the dividing up of the money that remains after all expenses have been paid. Ostensibly, these profits are split half-and-half between the tenant and the owner. But most of the time, the tenant is given only a few token dollars, with the explanation that expenses had eaten up most of the profits.

To stress this point even more, let it be understood that tenants who sharecrop own nothing. They do not see receipts nor do they keep books. The few times that tenants dared to challenge their landlord, they were kicked off the farm and had to look to another white man to rent from.

When farming on thirds, the tenant handles all monetary matters. The owner pays for one-third of the seeds and fertilizer. The tenant provides or pays for all the labor; and at the fall settlement, the tenant receives two-thirds of the profits and the owner receives one-third. So, seeing that this was a great opportunity, the family made the move from Duplin County to Lenoir County, onto Harriet Townsend's farm.

Daddy went on to say that Miss Harriet Townsend was the owner, and that Alvin Allred was the overseer. He also noted that we would be seeing a lot of Mr. Allred, but not Miss Harriet. He understood that she was a rich old white lady who would sometimes ride by in her Prism automobile. Of course, I did not know what that was.

Uncle Jack and Uncle Bob had already relocated their families to our new farm when we arrived. Both of them had been sharecropping in Greene County. We saw them not too long after we got there. However, it wasn't until Mother and Daddy had finished unloading our belongings and putting them in the house.

The two of them came walking up the road. "It's about time you got here," Uncle Jack said to Daddy. Uncle Bob thought that was funny. He didn't say a word; he just laughed.

"And you timed your visit pretty good," Daddy told him. "You could've come sooner; I wasn't gon ask you for any help."

They both got a kick out of the whole exchange. "Where's my sister?" Uncle Bob asked, as he headed into the house, calling Mother: "Sack! Hey, Sack, where you at?"

He went on in to see the house and visit with Mother and the girls. Their visit was rather brief, because as they both said, there was still a lot of work to be done around their new place. After about a half hour, they were on their way.

From our yard to Uncle Jack's path was about four hundred yards; his house sat back off the road maybe another hundred yards. But where Uncle Bob lived made us virtually next-door neighbors. While going to his house via the road was a couple hundred yards; but if you took the short path through the woods, you could be there in seconds.

The first time our families got together to deal with their shared commitment was at Uncle Jack's house on a Saturday afternoon. Mother told me before we left home that Aunt Mabel was going to have something for us to eat, and that afterwards

I would be watching my sisters and two little cousins outside while they did some planning for the winter months.

We rode to Uncle Jack's house in Uncle Bob's old ragged car. We didn't have one, but Uncle Jack sure had a nice-looking tan car that he kept real clean. When we got to Uncle Jack's house, Aunt Mabel had already made sandwiches for everybody. She even used store-bought bread! She had made some chicken salad, and she gave us some kind of sweetened drink that was colorful. That sure was delicious!

After we'd finished eating, Aunt Mabel told me that it was too cold to go outside, and that I could keep the children in the dining room while they met in the living room. It didn't take them very long. But I found out that they needed to cut a lot of wood for curing tobacco; they made plans to get started on that within a couple of weeks, which would give all of them more time to get settled in.

The information shared about tenant farmers not owning farm equipment and supplies stared Daddy and my uncles square in the face. Two weeks after we moved to our new place, they had to go in debt buying tools, equipment, and teams of mules.

Daddy's spending spree began very interestingly. His first major purchase was a brand-new factory-built outhouse, a two-seater no less. This meant that two people could sit side by side as they pooped. Plus, they would have the luxury of talking to each other, if they so desired.

As time grew near for the outhouse to be delivered, Daddy's focus was on getting the pit completed. He had previously invited his two brothers-in-law to come and assist with that task. But so far, neither of them had taken him up on that offer.

Finally, look who's coming! But this was the day before the delivery. Daddy had been digging for a couple of hours when they arrived. Uncle Bob was eating an apple and sporting his ever-present smile. "Namon, you 'bout through?" he asked.

"Where's your shovel?" was Daddy's response.

"You see what I brought," Uncle Jack intoned.

"It's a good thing I got another shovel under the shed for Bob," Daddy told him.

Daddy stopped and leaned on his shovel. By now, he had worked up a pretty good sweat. He wiped his face and the bald front of his head with his shirttail. Then he lit a cigarette. Uncle Jack, still holding the shovel he'd brought, began digging in the spot that Daddy had just vacated. Uncle Bob got the last bite from his apple and tossed the core across the field.

"Since y'all begged me, I'll help," he said. Uncle Bob got Daddy's shovel and started digging. Then he suddenly stopped and put it down, like something was wrong with it. Next, he looked at the hole. "You got a pick?" he asked Daddy.

"Over yonder by the barn," Daddy told him.

Uncle Bob went the few yards to the barn and came back with the "tool of choice," according to him. "Move, Jack," he insisted after a vicious stab into the ground by Uncle Jack, proving that the ground was very resistant. Uncle Bob commenced to dig there with ease, as he smiled, expressing pleasure with his accurate determination that his choice of tool was correct.

They only worked for a short period of time though. As a

matter of fact, that was all Daddy had been able to do, work sporadically at digging this pit, because there were so many other things that had to be done. But progress was being made. However, since tomorrow was the delivery day, a certain amount of urgency had set in. Daddy continued working well after Uncle Jack and Uncle Bob left, but they had agreed to return the next day for the delivery so that they could aid in setting the toilet.

When Daddy opened the door the next morning, to his surprise, he saw Uncle Jack and Uncle Bob sitting down by the barn. This caused him to quicken his pace. When he got there, he was greeted by another one of Uncle Jack's sarcastic comments. "You must've slept late," Uncle Jack said.

"Yeah, but we're right on time," Uncle Bob commented. "Here comes your delivery now." Sure enough, an over-sized green pickup had just turned in to the yard. The driver obviously saw where the delivery was to be made, so he continued to the back of our house. The truck bounced every time it went over a bump, and the toilet bounced with it.

The truck came to a stop as the dust followed, with some going by and some settling on the truck and everything else around it. "How you boys doing?" the driver drawled. He didn't get out immediately, as it seemed like he wanted a conversation first.

He sat there with his pale arm resting on the rolled-down window. "It sho got warmed up some this morning, didn't it?" Daddy and my uncles were pretty much ignoring him, as they inspected the toilet. "Where you want this thang?" he asked.

"Right over here," Uncle Bob answered, pointing to the obvious spot—where the pit had been dug. The man backed the truck over near the pit. Uncle Jack was the first to start untying the ropes that secured the toilet, I guess because he saw that the driver wasn't going to lend a hand. Daddy and Uncle Bob joined him and they struggled a bit, but finally got the toilet on the ground. The driver now got out of his truck. He and Daddy talked while Uncle Bob and Uncle Jack were trying to figure out the best way to get the toilet to its final spot. The man got back in his truck and drove off, except this time the dust was going in the opposite direction.

"How you want to do this thing, Namon?" Uncle Jack asked. "Do you want the door facing the house, or do you want it in another direction?"

By now, Mother was coming out to see the new purchase. She had the baby in her arms, and Katie skipped behind. That's when Uncle Bob took over. "Sarah, which way you want the door to face?" he asked.

"I want it facing the house," Mother said matter-of-factly.

"Okay, move back," Uncle Bob told her. "Namon, you get that corner, Jack you get on that side, and I got it right here." Uncle Bob positioned everybody. "Now when I say 'lift,' pick it up; when I say 'go,' we'll move it to the pit, and when I say 'okay,' we'll put it down."

Even though he was the youngest of the group, Uncle Bob had a habit of taking charge. I actually thought he was quite bossy. But they followed his instructions, and it got the job done.

In addition to all of that, the toilet really looked good. There were smiles all around as Daddy and Uncle Jack got a spade and a shovel to make the dirt around the toilet smooth and even with the grass. This actually made it quite attractive for an outhouse.

Meanwhile, Uncle Bob was at it again. "Sarah, you know you gotta lay the cornerstone," he said. "Let me hold the baby." Mother did. Then with a gentlemanly wave of arms, they all motioned to Mother and cheered as she walked toward the toilet.

Winter was not very cold this year. There were several days, and even a few weeks that were unusually warm. But in spite of now having two cousins added to my babysitting role, I enjoyed every one of those days as much as I could. I considered those four as "babies that I care for but also playmates." And we all visited each other frequently.

However, there were other children in the neighborhood who I didn't know. And there was something about them that puzzled me. Each weekday morning, I would see two or three different groups of black boys and girls going past our house, carrying bags or packs in their hands. Then about midday, I would see those same groups going back in the opposite direction. But since I was new to the community, I figured it was something that I could find out about later.

Having moved back to Lenoir County also meant that we were much closer to where we used to live. As a matter of fact, according to Mother, Grandpa's place was only a few miles away. Consequently, this meant closer proximity to her sisters: Kathy, Erlene, Arlene, and Della Mae.

The first sister to visit was Aunt Kathy. One Saturday, about noon, we saw this fancy-looking car pull into our yard. It had colorful rims on each wheel, and the hubcaps rotated as the wheels turned! There were two men and a woman inside. When they got out, I recognized Aunt Kathy, but I didn't know either of the men. She seemed so glad to see Mother, with the hugs and all. Of course she also said hello to the children. Finally, she turned to the two men. "You know Saul," she said to Mother, gesturing to one of them. "We're engaged," she said with a big smile.

"How long you been engaged, and when is the wedding?" Mother asked.

"We been engaged three weeks," Aunt Kathy responded. "And we're getting married the first Saturday in June." Then she introduced the other man. "This is Saul's best friend, Willie. I just wanted to come down here and welcome y'all back to the area," she continued. Then she and Mother talked, as the two men mainly stood to the side and talked to each other. Me? I went back outside.

At dinner, Mother shared that Aunt Kathy's wedding would be at the usual place (where Uncle Bob and Aunt Arlene got married)—in Reverend Shull's living room—and that she had agreed to make Aunt Kathy's wedding dress.

## FEBRUARY 1943

Recall that when the families had their first meeting, a major item was that they would need to cut a lot of wood. Well, it was time to get started on that. I thought they mainly met for farm-related things. But there was also something else that was relevant to each family. As well as securing fuel for curing tobacco, there was also the matter of having fuel for cooking and staying warm during the winter. Even though this was nothing that involved me individually, it did impact me otherwise. What stands out as a lasting memory was that each morning, I would wake up to the sound of Daddy sharpening his axe with a file and coughing as he puffed on those non-filtered Camel cigarettes.

One day, as Daddy and my uncles were cutting wood near our house, Mother decided to surprise them with some water and sandwiches (bad move). As she approached the area where they were working, a huge pine tree was about to be felled. When they saw her coming, the tree was beginning to lean and twist in her direction. They yelled: "Run, Sarah, run!" And run she did! They said that the tree missed her by only a few feet. If she had moved a bit slower, it would've been lights out for her.

Over the course of a few months, all three families got settled in, and we spent a lot of time together, working, socializing, and going to church. Consequently, I began to see them somewhat differently. I had only been around my uncles and cousins briefly. That was when we lived together at Grandpa's house for a couple of months in 1941. Plus, I was younger then. But now, I felt that I was able to get a more accurate picture of them.

Uncle Jack was the older brother. He was probably thirty-one or thirty-two years old, and Uncle Bob was perhaps twenty-six or twenty-seven. Uncle Jack also was more sturdy looking than his younger brother. He had muscular arms and shoulders, while Uncle Bob was strong-looking, but he was on the slim side. Plus, Uncle Jack was the quieter brother. When he talked, his voice was deep, and his words were slow to emerge. On the other hand, Uncle Bob was somewhat loud, and he talked much faster.

In addition to those differences, while Uncle Jack did things in a slower fashion, Uncle Bob's movements were anything but. He got from point A to point B in a hurry, and he had a distinct walk. When he moved, it was more of a sashay. And if he took things seriously, it never showed. He seemed to be more into enjoying himself. No matter what was happening, he was able to find humor in it.

Now, let's consider their wives. Aunt Mabel, Uncle Jack's wife, was of medium height, and she was a light-skinned lady. She was basically the opposite of Uncle Jack in that she walked rather briskly, and when she talked, her voice was very loud… and he listened! Uncle Bob's wife, Aunt Ada, was of mild complexion and of medium build. She didn't talk overly loud, but her voice sort of swayed musically when she talked. As for their children, Raymond and Mattie were now three and two years old, respectively.

In spite of all that was going on around me, I was able to continue thinking about the bigger picture of our being here. I began to take stock in things within my family. One of those things included the fact that Daddy made some additional purchases. During this spending spree, Daddy also bought a one-horse cart, a two-horse wagon, two mules, three tobacco trucks, and several rakes, hoes, and other yard tools. Also, there was the gear for the mules: reins, ropes, bridles, bits, and collars. I especially remember how good the new leather smelled. But not long after he started using it, that wonderful smell dissipated.

The purchase that impressed me the most were the two mules. Katie and I were down at the stable with Daddy, admiring them when he told us that each of us could name one. I immediately came up with the name Tom for the male mule. And after pondering for a couple of minutes, Katie announced that she had decided that we would call the female mule Kate.

## SPRING 1943

Being back near Mother's family church was a plus. Even though we would not attend every service, the first time returning there was in March. We rode with Uncle Jack and Aunt Mabel. It wasn't very far, but I guess everywhere seemed like a long ways if it was too far to walk.

This was Saint John Holiness church. It was a small white frame building that sat a few yards from the paved road, and was surrounded on three sides by tall trees.

Also, there were two or three trees in the dirt parking area with their roots above ground. When it was Quarterly Meeting, the parking area on both sides of the church would be full, and cars would be lined up along the road.

On the left side of the church, close to the woods, there was a long piece of twill-woven mesh wire about three feet in diameter that extended (about ten feet long) and was attached to trees at each end. This made it taut; and it served as a table. In the afternoon when service was over, the women would get those boxes of food out of the trunks of their cars, and spread it out on the table. What a feast! Of course, I wasn't sure that anybody washed their hands. But I could vouch for the fact that it was always good food.

With spring having arrived, there was the nuance of colors, sweet music of birds, and clean fresh air. Of course those consistent warmer temperatures didn't hurt. It meant that I didn't have to bring in wood for the heater, and only having to fetch wood for the kitchen stove was pretty easy.

This was also a spring that Mother planted the biggest and most beautiful garden I had ever seen. She had squash, tomatoes, string beans, corn, okra, and butter beans. Katie and I were truly impressed with how that garden looked.

We were in the kitchen, and doing nothing but getting in Mother's way. I had been tossing this idea around in my mind, so I thought this was as good a time as any to ask. "Mother, can Katie and I have our own garden?" She seemed to be taken aback by that request. She didn't answer immediately. I thought she heard me, but maybe she didn't. So I figured I'd try again. "Mother, can…"

She interrupted. "I heard you the first time."

By the way she responded, I was unable to pick up on a clue as to what her answer might be. So all I could do was shut up and wait for her to decide, or at least tell me something. And she finally did. "You can have your own garden, IF you keep it cleared of grass, and IF you keep your plants watered," she said.

That was music to my ears. I had imagined this for a number of days, how nice it would be to have my own stuff. I knew I could tend it because I'd been helping her. Plus, I'd seen Daddy work the fields. I grinned big-time and Katie smiled too; then off we went to look around for a place we wanted this garden to be. We finally found the perfect spot. It was on the corner of the field closest to the house. All we would need was enough space for just a few plants. We didn't want a big garden like Mother had.

We hurried back inside to tell Mother that we had found a place for our garden. She was in the bedroom changing the baby. "Mother," I called to get her attention, "we found the perfect spot for our garden."

"Just a minute." she cautioned. "You asked if you could have your own garden, not including where it would be." I did remember that we had not gotten permission to choose our own site. "Where did you find to put this garden?" she asked.

"Right in the edge of the field," I told her.

"No, that won't work. That's part of your daddy's crop area." Mother headed toward the door. "Come on and let me show you what I've got in mind." She then picked up the baby, and we followed her as she went around to the back porch. She visually surveyed a nearby area. "No, this won't work," she said, "too close to the house." We then walked out near the woods, about seventy-five feet. Again, she visually surveyed an area that was actually in the woods. It wasn't big, but it was clear of trees and bush. However, it did have quite a bit of grass and some roots. "This will be your garden," she told us.

"Thank you, Mother," I said. And Katie was excited too, even though her use of words was still coming around, pronunciation-wise.

"When the baby goes to sleep, we'll come back out here and I'll show you how to plant some seeds that I'll give you," Mother told us. This was really something to behold. I could envision having a garden just like the one she had, all those pretty plants.

Just as she had promised, when the baby went to sleep, Mother summoned us to go back outside to our new garden. Even before going out the door, she reminded us that there was quite a bit of work to be done. But I was confident that it would turn out to be a real garden. Mother reached in the cabinet and got some seeds; then she went on the back porch and got some plants that I'd seen in a foot tub. Once outside, she reached under the back porch and pulled out a hoe. Then we headed to our new garden! When we got there, Mother put the packs of seeds and the plants on the ground. Then she leaned on the hoe and began to talk to us like we were about to embark on a mission that was very special, and we needed to know exactly what we were about to get ourselves into. If we didn't understand this, the results were not likely to be good.

"Here's what this is all about," she began. She went on to stress the importance of tending the garden, chopping to keep weeds and grass out, watering the plants on a regular basis, and so forth and so on. We listened intently; at least I did, because Katie was steadily trying to catch a butterfly that was coming and going, as if it was a game between the two of them. "I got this here hoe because the ground is too hard to grow anything in," Mother said. "So instead of using a plow to clear this area and turn the soil to make it soft, we'll use this hoe." She told us to pick up twigs and sticks, and to throw them out of the way. She then went about the business of digging the small roots up and chopping the grass away. This really took some time. But finally, that part had been completed. Then she handed me the hoe and instructed me on what to do. "I'm going to check on the baby," she said. "While I'm gone, y'all just chop the ground to make it soft for our planting."

She left and I got busy. This was now some real fun.

Mother was only gone a few minutes. When she returned I had finished chopping the ground. "Very good," she told me as she reached for the hoe. "We'll only dig where you want to plant something." She demonstrated, then handed the hoe back to me as she began to decide where I would dig to put the plants and seeds. "Start right here," she said, noting that spot with her foot. Then she identified several other places for me to dig. Obviously, she realized that I wasn't able to keep pace with her, so she told me that she'd put clods of dirt where I was to dig. This worked out much better. "I'll be right back," Mother said, as we all heard crying coming from the house.

Meanwhile Katie tried to dig with a stick she'd found, but it only helped a little because where she was digging, the dirt was just too hard; plus, it was outside of the ground that we'd already prepared. Mother came back, and I was almost through digging where she'd assigned me. She brought a fish box with her and placed the baby inside it on a blanket. Then she got back to working on our new garden.

Mother did seeds first. "We'll plant all the different kind of seeds in this row," she said. "Then we'll set out these plants over there." She pointed to the other row that I'd done. This was definitely exciting. Just thinking of this plot as having rows made me know that this was quite an accomplishment. She got Katie involved by letting her drop the seeds in the hole after she'd used a peg to open a place in that now soft dirt. Katie loved it. Then she showed me how to put the roots of the plants into the ground. Katie was now the spectator, but she still hadn't lost interest. We finished after about ninety minutes, and all was well.

Once I started having to tend our garden, I began to have reservations about the whole idea. Chopping and keeping the weeds out was easy. I would see weeds and simply pull them up and chuck them aside. But it was the watering task that was kicking my ass. In order to water the plants, I had to go to the pump, which was located halfway between the house and our garden. This was a good forty yards. Next, I would have to pump a peck bucket almost full of water, then lug it back to our garden.

I learned quickly. I learned that a five-year-old could not carry half a bucket full of water, and doing less than that was too time-consuming. After a few days of lugging that bucket, I came up with what I thought was a brilliant idea. I recruited my playmates. The very next time Raymond came over, I told him and Katie to gather around, that I wanted to talk to them about our garden. I was reminded of Mother when she leaned on the hoe and educated Katie and me about the responsibilities that went hand-in-hand with having our own garden. I got the hoe from under the porch, but I wasn't tall enough to lean on it, so I just held it off to the side and leaned *against* it.

I started my presentation: "You know that Mother let us have our own garden. In order to keep it, the only thing we gotta do is make sure that weeds don't grow in it, and keep it watered." They were actually attentive, probably thinking I was about to introduce a new game.

I was definitely appreciative to have their attention. So, I continued. "I can keep the weeds out with this here hoe," I told them as I pointed to the hoe, "but it's the watering part that I need some help with. I can't carry that big bucket with enough water to keep the plants and seeds watered. So here's what I want you to do: whenever we're out here playing and you have to pee, I want you go out to our garden and pee on the plants." There were no real excited expressions on their faces, so I realized that I was losing them. But that was okay because I had told them what was needed, and I knew they had heard me. So we turned from that and began playing.

Of course I kept an eye on our garden. As a matter of fact, I would look at the plants whenever I had to go pee. I did notice, however, that they were beginning to turn brown and wither, not to mention the fact that our garden had now become a very smelly place. But I didn't have an answer, and I knew better than to ask Mother, or to even update her on how it was doing.

I didn't have to worry about that very long, because that Friday morning, she caught me by surprise. We had just finished breakfast and she was clearing the dishes. "How's your garden doing?" she casually asked.

*Uh oh,* I said to myself. I could tell by the tone of her voice that she was on to something. It would take me a minute to come up with a good answer. I thought. No answer was forthcoming. And since that was the case, I knew I'd have to tell the truth. Yet I figured that I held the upper hand; she'd have to beat it out of me like she tried to do back in Duplin County. "It's okay," I lied. And, as far as I was concerned, that should've been a sufficient answer. Right? Nope, not for her.

"Are you keeping everything watered?" she continued to probe.

I was so nervous now, I figured I might as well go on and tell the truth, and take that inevitable whipping. "Yes, ma'am," I stammered. "We're keeping everything watered…but since the bucket is too heavy for me to tote when I fill it up, we been watering the plants by peeing on them."

Mother had her back to me, and she stopped in her tracks. I knew that this was it. Then she broke out laughing. I thought, *No ass-whipping? I might as well laugh too.* So I did. We both had a good laugh. And Mother laughed so hard that tears were rolling down her face.

As the days went by, there was another thing that was still puzzling me. I continued to picture in my mind those black children who went back and forth pass our house. Even though I hadn't seen them lately, I kept thinking about them. Maybe they would go someplace and work on a farm. But then again, some of them weren't much bigger than I was, and my experience with my garden ruled that out as a possibility.

But my curiosity would not go away. I had to ask. I approached Mother one morning while she was washing dishes. I guess it was without warning, as I was looking out the window and saw those children again. "Mother, are them children big enough to work? Where they work at?"

She stopped drying plates and turned to me, as if to provide me with her undivided attention and carefully answer these questions. So I figured they must have been important.

"They're schoolchildren," she said as she put a plate in the cabinet. "They walk to school in the morning, and back home in the afternoon." Now folding the dishtowel and placing it on the table, she continued. "You see the school every time we go down the road toward Kinston. It's the little building that sits back in the field, just before the end of our road."

Of course Mother was right; I had seen that building, but didn't know what it was. I actually thought it was somebody's house and nobody was ever at home whenever we passed it. "Will I be going to school too?" I asked.

"Yes, you will be one of those children after they get a summer break and then go back to school," she said, standing there to see if I had any further questions.

"Yes, ma'am," I said, and darted out the door.

Now I felt like two burdens had been lifted. I had found out about the children walking by our house, and I had gotten rid of that damn garden.

But while my effort to have my own garden proved to have been a disaster, the farm work had to go on. This being spring, plants were beginning to grow, and weeds were setting in. To address this matter, the fields were teeming with black women, as chopping was considered to be a woman's job, more specifically, a black woman's job.

Stalling Air Force Base was about three miles from us. It was used for training combat pilots during World War II. My sisters, my cousins, and I enjoyed lying on our backs in the grass, watching the planes maneuver high in the sky.

Apparently some of the pilots would relax and take some time off from their training by scaring the daylights out of those field workers by cutting their engines and gliding at barely treetop level toward those busy women. When their planes got close to them, the pilots would restart the planes and gun the engines. Those women would be startled so badly that they would throw down those hoes and run in all directions. After we youngsters got used to it, we thought it was fun, and we looked forward to this show every day.

But not having a garden didn't mean that I was without anything to do. Daddy made sure of that. Normally, the wives didn't work on weekends. Therefore, they would tend to their children. This meant free time for me, so I thought. Apparently,

Daddy came up with this brilliant idea of taking me to the fields with him on Saturday mornings. There wasn't much I could do except fetch different tools for him and run errands. But apparently he was set on keeping me busy.

He and I were in the cornfield one Saturday morning. He was chopping weeds as I was throwing them aside and playing in the dirt. We were several hundred yards from the path when we saw a car coming, kicking up dust. As it got closer, it slowed down. The car was a pretty, tan, sporty-looking vehicle. I had never seen one like it before. The best I could make out as I squinted was an old white woman driving.

Daddy looked up and went back to work. "That's just Miss Harriet," he said. "I told you about her doing her own driving." I heard him, but I was still looking at that car.

"And that's the car you told me about?" I asked.

"Yeah, that's a Pierce-Arrow."

Within a few minutes, another car came down the road. It looked familiar, but I couldn't recall where I'd seen it before. It turned in to our yard and Daddy told me whose car that was. "That's Willie's car," he intoned. "He and Saul probably brought Kathy for one of her quick visits, and to try on her wedding dress that your momma's making." Sure enough, that was exactly what happened.

It was late March, and I was comfortable in where I was in my life. But with that being my mind-set, there was another awakening experience for me. For the first time in my life, I witnessed how cruel one human being could be to another.

There was a big ditch across the road from our house. It was maintained by the state. In our front yard, there were several oak trees, with the roots above ground. One morning I saw what looked like a medium-size flatbed truck with racks on the sides, towing a trailer. Both were tarp-covered. The driver of the truck was a white man. There were several black men in the back of the truck. They were all dressed in striped clothing. Riding in the trailer were two more white men. They were dressed in grayish-blue uniforms, and wore what appeared to be some kind of military caps.

When the men got out their respective modes of transportation, my attention was drawn to the fact that the white men carried weapons. They each had a shotgun in hand, and leather holsters with revolvers strapped around their waist.

Daddy must've seen how I was staring at the scene because he came over and joined me. "Them's convicts, boy," he announced. "They done something that was against the law. Now, they on the road, serving time. This is called the chain gang. See them chains hooked to them balls and around their ankle? That means that there ain't no way they can escape, and if they crazy enough to try to run, that's what them guns are for."

I didn't know if the pride in Daddy's voice represented the fact that he was so knowledgeable, or the fact that he'd shared that knowledge with me, for future reference, of course. I had no response. And even though I understood, it still seemed to be awfully cruel.

Both the guards and the prisoners were of all sizes and

shapes. There were a couple of small prisoners who appeared to be barely old enough to be in that group. Instead, they looked like they should've been in the group of schoolchildren who walked by our house.

The black men got axes, picks, and shovels out of the truck. Then they started working in the ditch while being watched by those gun-toting white men. The only convict not in the ditch was the "water boy." He came in our yard several times during the day to fetch water for the men. He never spoke, and at no time did he look around. He always looked straight ahead.

At noon, all of them were allowed to come in our yard and lie down on the ground, using those roots for pillows.

I had never heard the term "convict" until Daddy used it. Needless to say, I had never seen a convict before. So being a curious five-year-old, I stared at them for the last half hour of their sleep.

When time came for them to return to work, there was another scene that I will remember for the rest of my life. The guards walked amongst the convicts, cursing and kicking them awake. "All right, get your black ass up!" I heard a guard say as he delivered a swift kick to one of the prone men.

I could hear the men replying, "Yessir, boss, um coming, yessir, cap'n…be right there."

It was mid-April, about noon that Saturday, and Daddy and I had just left the field across the road from our house. We were near the end of the path when we saw a car slowly coming up the road. Since there wasn't much dust, it wasn't hard to get a good look at the car. It was a black Chevrolet. We got to our yard and waited to see where it was headed. It pulled into our yard. A big grin registered on Daddy's face. "That's your Uncle Chad," he said.

I'd never met Daddy's older brother, but I'd been looking forward to it, because on several occasions Daddy had bragged about the nice cars that Uncle Chad drove. At that moment, my heart sank, because what he was driving was not even close to fitting the image that Daddy had portrayed to me. My next thought was that he'd probably left the pretty car at home. But I doubted it. However, my focus regarding this matter changed fairly immediately when I saw the two boys with Uncle Chad. I sized them up as they emerged from the backseat. The taller boy was about my height. He looked around all curious-like, as I always did. He wore a pair of bib overalls with a feed sack shirt that had the sleeves cut off, and he was barefooted. When the other boy was getting out, I noticed that he seemed different. I could tell that he was younger, and he seemed to be reluctant. Plus, he had an impish grin that I interpreted as one saying, *I don't give a damn*.

Uncle Chad and Daddy shook hands and embraced. Then they both turned to us, the boys. "This here is Junior," Daddy said. "How you, Junior?"

Uncle Chad greeted me. He shook my hand before he introduced his boys. "These here my younguns," he said real proud-like. "The one 'bout your size is Chuck, and that's my other boy, Bobby Ray." We all said hey to each other. I could tell that Bobby Ray wasn't interested in what was going on. He just stared and grinned.

Daddy and Uncle Chad went down near the barn and talked. I invited my new cousins to play a running-chasing game with me. They did, and we had fun.

After about an hour, Uncle Chad and Daddy halted our game as they wanted to go inside and visit with the rest of the family. That was brief, as Uncle Chad noted that he had to go back to his place and do some work. But I was real pleased to have met some cousins that I didn't have to babysit.

Speaking of cousins, there was another family of kinship that was a part of my growing up. This was one of Mother's older sisters and her family. Aunt Della and Uncle Ott Franks owned a large farm a long ways from our neighborhood. While we lived in Lenoir County, which adjoined Greene County about five miles away, they lived all the way on the far side of Green County. They were a family of six: two older daughters, Nancy and Betty, who were about twelve and thirteen years old. Their twins, Bobby and Billy, were about my age. We called them Big Bo and Li'l Bo. Then there was Thomas, who was the same age as Katie, and Donald, who was Marie's age. Needless to say, we didn't visit each other very often. However, we did spend time together at church on fourth Sundays.

Aunt Kathy's wedding was upon us. This was THE Saturday. Mother and I got dressed and waited for Uncle Jack to pick us up. Mother had me dressed like we were going to church. With that being the case, and the preacher being in charge, I figured that a wedding must be when the preacher preaches to a couple getting married to each other. And in this instance, Reverend Shull would be preaching to Aunt Kathy and Mr. Saul.

It was only a few minutes before Uncle Jack and Aunt Mable arrived. He blew the horn and we went out. Uncle Jack raised his seat so that we could get in the back. Then we drove for about fifteen minutes, and were at Reverend Shull's house.

Apparently, we arrived too early. Uncle Jack turned the car off and said to the women, "Mabel, you and Sarah go on in and see what's going on." The women got out and went inside as Uncle Jack and I waited. I didn't mind though. I was just glad that they let me tag along.

After about five minutes, Aunt Mabel came back to the car and informed us that it would be about ten more minutes before they were ready. She got back in the car and waited with us. Finally Uncle Jack looked at his watch and said, "Okay, it's time."

We went in and sat on a couch in the living room. There was furniture that had obviously been moved to the side, as the center of the floor was completely vacant, save for a flower-decorated arch.

I could see some movement down the hallway, but couldn't determine who it was. In addition to Aunt Della and Uncle Ott, there were two other couples who came in after we did. I didn't know them. They sat in chairs that were situated around the back and side walls. Uncle Greg was also sitting there, so I assumed that Aunt Arlene was in the back room with Mother and Aunt Kathy.

I don't know what the cue was, but folks began to get quiet. Then the preacher walked in, holding a Bible in his right hand. He was a real light-skinned man who looked to be in his mid-thirties, and about the same height and size of Uncle Bob. He had on a brown suit and a frilly shirt that contrasted with his multicolored bow tie. He was clean and he was cool.

Unlike Reverend Dunn at St. John's, this preacher was very deliberate with all of his movements. In front of the arch, and with his back to us, he opened his Bible and stood. The whole room was as quiet as a mouse. Then Mr. Willie walked in with Mr. Saul. Mr. Saul stood to Reverend Shull's left as Mr. Willie went and sat down. Next, in walked Aunt Kathy with Mother and Aunt Arlene. Aunt Kathy stood at Reverend Shull's right, as Mother and Aunt Arlene went and sat down in reserved chairs.

Just like his movements, the preacher's words were also deliberate. He turned to the side, to face those in the audience. After warmly greeting us, he turned to the couple and reminded them of the purpose of this occasion. Next, he read a passage to the couple from the Bible. He then spoke again, and read another scripture. Finally Aunt Kathy and Mr. Saul were instructed to "Repeat after me." They did. Then he announced that they were husband and wife. They kissed, and it was over. Now I knew what a wedding looked like.

Of course there were congratulations for the newly married couple, now my new "Uncle" Saul. After about an hour of refreshments and visiting with them, we returned home.

## Jul/August 1943

It seemed like Aunt Kathy's wedding was perfectly timed, because it ushered in a new period of keeping busy. There seemed to be an intense focus on the crops, as families were preparing for the beginning of harvest.

When it was time to put in tobacco, I could tell that Daddy was a bit unraveled because he couldn't get all of his positions filled. Of course he eventually did, and the summer tasks went on without a hitch.

I thought that after tobacco had been harvested, things would slow down, maybe just a tad. They didn't. My folks finished putting in tobacco the first week of August. Then it was wild again. With the three-tiered packhouse being the central location (a level for each family), they were all over the place, grading and tying and moving tobacco around as space was cleared when some was sold. But for me, I was still the babysitter, and I tried to keep myself and the kids out of the way.

## September 1943

The first opportunity I had to spend significant time with Aunt Arlene and her family was one Sunday in early September. Previous visits had always been brief and never included the entire family.

Whenever some of them came to our community, they

would stop at our house first, even though we lived in the third house along their route. As I would learn later, the reason for this was because Aunt Arlene and Mother had such a close relationship when they were growing up.

This time, I was in my room trying to finish reading the new comic books that Daddy bought. I heard the knock at the door and knew who it was, but it took me several more minutes to finish my reading. As I approached the front room where they had gathered, it was obvious that the children had made themselves right at home. There was loud talking and a lot of noise of children running and playing. When I got to the door, I just stood and stared, trying to take it all in.

Mother and Aunt Arlene were actually sitting at the kitchen table talking, apparently oblivious to what was going on around them. Then there was Daddy and Uncle Greg standing near the heater talking. None of this was normal. I guess I finally realized that what I was witnessing was indeed real. So I went in and spoke to Aunt Arlene. But I knew better than to interrupt Daddy and Uncle Greg because I had learned that whenever Daddy was in a conversation, it was always too important to be interrupted.

But something did finally happen to interrupt Mother and Aunt Arlene. One of the two running and screaming three-year-olds shot past Mother. Aunt Arlene grabbed that one by the arm. It was Marie. Hazel was the one chasing. When she got near Mother, she was corralled. They were simply asked to slow down so that they wouldn't get hurt. Meanwhile, the two quieter five-year-old girls, Katie and Liz, were in the yard playing. Billy, who was a year younger than me, was waiting so that he and I could find something fun to do. The other boys were Greg Junior, who was almost two years old, and the baby, Willie, who was a year old.

Now let's look at the parents. Aunt Arlene was somewhat of a rapid talker, and Uncle Greg was just the opposite. His speech was slow and sometimes words were stuttered. Also, he was a short man, of about five feet, seven inches. As for Aunt Arlene, she, Mother, and Aunt Kathy were about the same size and had amazingly similar features. The three of them could pass for triplets.

This was indeed a unique visit. After quite a while at our house, we went with them to visit Mother's other nearby siblings; then it was back to our house. This was about one o'clock. After Mother and Aunt Arlene finished preparing the meal that Mother had cooked earlier, we ate dinner. Then we played for another hour before they went home.

The most important thing for me the rest of the year happened on December the ninth. That was when I turned six years old. Christmas came and went. Then the New Year was approaching.

## JANUARY 1944

It was Friday night. I went to bed early, waiting for 1944. At midnight, I was awakened by the sound of gunshots. I jumped up and ran to see what all of that racket was. Katie was up too, following behind, looking very frightened. It was Daddy and some friends who were doing the shooting. They were celebrating two things: the New Year, and the fact that all the debts they had incurred in 1943 were paid off.

In addition to the New Year being a time to look back and express thanks, it also meant that it was time to prepare for the work needed to get new crops underway. That's exactly what they did.

The last Saturday in January, Uncle Greg and Aunt Arlene visited. Uncle Greg asked Daddy if he could borrow one of his mules to break some ground.. Of course Daddy wanted to know why he couldn't get a mule from somebody closer to where he lived, especially from Mr. Marvin, whose farm he was living on. He explained to Daddy that they were not on speaking terms. Daddy didn't bother to ask any more questions. He simply told Uncle Greg which mule to get. His family went back home with Mr. Jordan, who'd brought them in his old beat-up Ford; Uncle Greg rode the mule.

Two weeks later, Uncle Greg and his family were visiting Uncle Jack. Daddy said that since he wasn't sure that Uncle Greg would come by our house, he needed to go find out about his mule that had not been returned. I tagged along and was glad to see my cousins. We did our usual playing and being loud, since we were outdoors. I guess we stayed for about an hour. And sure enough, they left Uncle Jack's the same time we did.

I was listening when Daddy told Mother about the mule that he'd loaned Uncle Greg. Daddy shared that Uncle Greg told him that he'd been finished with the mule for over a week, and that he could come get him whenever he wanted to.

Following the job of cutting wood, Daddy and my uncles did some other required tasks before planting crops. The most basic one was that of getting their ground broken.

Then spring came, and Daddy went on another one of his spending sprees. But the difference between this one and the previous one was that this spree was spread out over several weeks. First, he bought a cow that had a young calf. This meant we could have fresh milk and butter. Also during this time, Mother ordered one hundred baby chicks. For the first time in my life, we had chickens, hogs, and cows at the same time. Life was good!

This was also when my primary cursing skills were being honed. One source of this education was a poor, skinny, young white man who lived two doors down from Uncle Bob. He was as poor as we were. His name was Floyd Sams. He lived with his wife and four-year-old son, and his father owned a local lumberyard, but he never worked there, or anywhere else.

Floyd could spout out some impressive curse words! And I latched onto every one. He only cursed when he was talking to his wife or son though. Otherwise, he didn't cuss.

The other source of my education was the man I now called Uncle Saul. Whenever something didn't go his way, he would deliver a bunch of negative words that I never could have imagined! He was good! And whenever he'd visit, I would do my best to stay near him; I would be praying for him to get riled up over something, anything, so that I could learn more.

## April 1944

During the month of April, Daddy and my uncles did not work together. They went their separate ways to plant their corn, cotton, and soybeans. But in May, it was time to set out tobacco. Consequently, this required teamwork. So, they were back together. I knew right off what I would be doing: babysitting my sisters and cousins. Nope. I was wrong this time. They changed the script on me.

After we finished breakfast that Monday morning, I was prepared for the arrival of my cousins; I would babysit them at our house. But after we ate and they didn't bolt out the door, I knew that something was up. I didn't ask any questions though.

Apparently, it was always Daddy's assignment to break this kind of news to me. I honestly could never figure out if he was being the kind of father he felt he should be, or something else altogether. I knew that he wanted to help me become responsible and dependable. But maybe he was just punishing me in a different way than what Mother always did, as she was straightforward. She would say: "Come here, boy, and bring that switch with you." Daddy was so cool with whatever method he used. But I had no other choices in any of the situations that I was confronted with.

This time, he said to me, "Come with me to the plant bed." We started walking, and he started talking. "You know, we usually start a new job on Monday, but your uncles had some other things to finish up, so we'll start setting out 'bacco tomorrow," he said. "The women will be pulling plants. We menfolk will be setting the plants out, and there's one thing missing in this teamwork." I knew, and he knew that there was no need for me to reply. But by now, I knew that in some way it would include me.

I waited, and he did finally tell me, after a few more steps, and a few more drags off that cigarette. "We'll need somebody to get the plants from the plant bed to the field. And I know you can do it." He paused, I guess because he knew what a herculean task that would be. "And I know you will do a good job." That must've been *up-front praise*. Of course, you know what I thought it was.

Bullshit.

But you also know what I said? "Yessir."

The next morning, when it was time to get started, I went to the plant bed with Mother, Aunt Ada, and a couple of other women who were hired. They had pillows to sit on while pulling plants. They would dig the plants up, wrap them in wet burlap cloth, and put them in baskets for me to take to the fields.

This was not play. This was work! And I don't mean easy work. Plus, some of those fields were a long ways from the plant bed. I would have both arms and both hands full when I made trips to the fields. And this was continuous going and coming; no rest breaks, definitely no time for play! On some trips, I was able to go nonstop. But on others, I just had to stop, put the baskets down, and rest for a few minutes. However, if I was not there with a new batch of plants when the men had finished setting out what they had, nobody complained.

We worked the remainder of the week, including Saturday

morning. Then Monday, we were at it again. We finished about eleven o'clock Tuesday morning. I was beat! Of course I was happy as heck that we had finished. After we ate lunch, Daddy even took some time off. He headed off to the store or wherever he sometimes made jaunts to. And I went down by the barn and played for a long time.

When I was going back to the house, I heard what sounded like puppy yips coming from the other side of the house. Naturally, I stopped walking and focused on the sounds that now I was sure were yips. I sped up to see what was making those noises.

There sat Daddy on the back steps, smiling. Mother, Katie, and Marie were all out there looking at this spectacle. Katie was petting one of the two brown, black, and white bulldog puppies. They sure were pretty. Daddy looked up and said to me, "Whaddya think?" He knew he had scored with me, as much as I loved dogs.

"Yessir," I responded, as I got closer and started rubbing the one that he was holding. He handed him to me, and I cradled the pup in my arms. "Did you name them yet?"

"Can we name them?" Katie asked excitedly.

"Naw, not this time," Daddy replied. "I already got names picked out for both of them." He reached down and got the other dog. "You've heard me talk about General MacArthur…" he said, then paused. "General MacArthur was a great leader." I had heard him talk about General MacArthur, and I was hoping he wouldn't tell any more General MacArthur stories now. Lucky for me, he didn't. "This is Mac," Daddy said as he smiled and looked into the eyes of the speckled one. "…and you have Arthur," he declared.

"Where did you get them from?" I asked.

"Matt Franklin's dog had puppies, and he sold me these two." Mr. Franklin was our neighbor who lived north of the corner store.

From the look on his face, I believe that these two puppies represented a crowning moment for Daddy. And if you ever wanted to find him, and you knew that he wasn't in the fields, all you had to do was find those two dogs. He built them a doghouse and placed it halfway between the woods and the house, and both dogs took to it right away. They were free to roam the yard, but once they wanted a nap, off to their little house they would go.

As Mac and Arthur were becoming a part of our family, we continued to move forward in a normal fashion. And part of that normalcy were Uncle Bob's frequent visits to our house. Usually when he visited, he would come through the wooded area between our houses. But on this particular morning, I was standing in the kitchen door, pissing. Instead of coming through the woods this time, he came down the road. If he had come through the woods, I would've seen him. But when he rounded the corner of our house, I was in mid-stream, pissing as high as my head. He tried to duck, but didn't make it. I got him.

"Uh oh," I said.

"Damn!" he spouted as he rushed out of the line of fire. He hurried over to the pump. "The little bastard pissed on me," he said. While he was putting water on his clothing, I finished my duty and went back inside. When he came in, I was hiding in the back room. "Sarah!" he hollered. Mother went in to where he was.

"I didn't know it was raining," she said to him.

He didn't address the "rain" comment. "Did Junior tell you what happened?" he asked.

"Yeah, he told me that he had an accident, that he couldn't get outdoors in time, so he peed from the back door."

"Yeah, he pissed out the back door all right!" Uncle Bob said. "Right on me." Mother started laughing as she inspected his wet clothes. I was peeking and straining to listen. Then I heard him laughing. "It was funny though," he said, "but I'm washed up now. Where is he?"

"I don't know," Mother told him.

"Boy, come on out here!" he yelled.

Sensing that he was safe to be around, I tiptoed into the kitchen. Nobody said a word. Uncle Bob just stared at me, as Mother looked on with amusement. "Boy, don't you ever piss on me again," he said, as they continued to laugh. I smiled, glad that this one was over.

## May 1944

We were in bed that night when we heard a car drive up. Within a few seconds there was a loud knock at the door. Daddy got up and answered. I didn't go in there but I heard all that was said. Uncle Jack had been to visit Grandpa's ailing father-in-law, Edmonton Jones. He said that while he was there, he took a turn for the worse, and to expect the inevitable.

It was a few days later that he died.

The funeral was scheduled for the following Wednesday. When that day arrived, work in the fields was put on hold in order to lay Grandpa Edmonton to rest. Mother and Daddy were all dressed up in their Sunday best when they summoned us kids so that they could take us over to Uncle Bob's house. That was where Uncle Jack would pick them up, and Miss Agnus, Uncle Bob's mother-in-law, would babysit all of us kids.

Of course I was looking forward to such luxury as play-time in the middle of the week! Uncle Jack and Aunt Mabel were driving up when we arrived. We even walked up the road rather than through the woods. I guess that Mother and Daddy didn't want to get their Sunday clothes messed up. Aunt Ada and Uncle Bob were still getting dressed, so we all went inside. Uncle Jack blew his horn, just to hassle his brother.

Finally, they were dressed and ready to go, but not before last-minute warnings were issued. Aunt Ada turned to Mattie and Raymond. She reminded them to be on their best behavior and to remember that "Grandma Agnus is in charge." Then it was Mother's turn. "Junior, y'all know how to act. Don't let me come back and hear that y'all been cuttin' up!" With that said, they were on their way.

We started out real good. Miss Agnus was in the dining room watching the two-year-olds, Mattie and Marie. Raymond, Katie, and I were just sitting around doing nothing. That was boring. Raymond said to me, "Let's play."

Of course I thought that was a great idea. "What you

wanna play?" I asked.

"Anything," he said. That meant, "You think of something." I guess Katie got tired of waiting, so she went in the next room and got a book off the table and sat down and started thumbing through it.

Meanwhile, as I was trying to figure what kind of indoor game we could play, I hadn't noticed that Raymond had gone outside. When I looked up, he was coming back in with two sticks he'd found. He handed me one and said, "Let's fight." It sounded pretty good to me. So we began trying to hit each other with our sticks. Then we began to get loud. I noticed Katie looking at us with that look on her face that said, "Somebody's going to get in trouble." Of course Raymond and I ignored her and continued to have fun. Raymond's back was to the dining room door, but when I looked up, I got quiet and still. Raymond continued to laugh and swing his stick around above his head. Then he saw me continuing to focus on the doorway behind him, so he got quiet too and looked around.

There stood Miss Agnus, death-staring us down. She simply said, "You know better," and went back to tend to one of the girls who was now crying.

I guess since we didn't get punished, we became emboldened, because as soon as Miss Agnus was out the door, we started all over again. In about ten minutes, as Raymond and I got louder and louder, Miss Agnus returned, and without saying a word, she held her hand out for our weapons. Raymond and I handed them to her and sheepishly backed up, because we didn't know whether she would hit us with them or not.

Meanwhile, Katie only looked at what was happening and went back to her book.

As Raymond and I got louder again, Miss Agnus returned to the room, with Maggie in her arms. She instructed Raymond and me to sit on the floor on opposite sides of the room. Of course we did. When she went back to the kitchen area, I had this brilliant idea. "Let's change places," I suggested to Raymond. He thought that would really be good, so we did, including changing to different walls. Miss Agnus must have heard us moving around because she looked in on us. When she returned to the kitchen, we heard her talking to a boy. All we could hear was when he said: "Yes ma'am, Miss Agnus." Meanwhile, Raymond and I continued to act the fool. After about twenty minutes, Miss Agnus came through the house and went out the front door. Raymond and I got up and looked out the window to see where she was going. There was an older boy standing by the roadside. He gave her a brown paper bag and went on. When Miss Agnus headed back to the house, Raymond and I rushed to reclaim our places on the floor. When she came back in, she put the bag on the end table, and turned to Katie. "Katie, now move your chair around to face me," she said. "Raymond, you and Junior can get up now, from where you're sitting. I want you to both go sit next to each other on that wall over there, so that you can look over here" she said, pointing to the spot near the window. Then she turned to Katie and said, "Sweetheart, I was going to send to the store and get some goodies for the three of y'all for not misbehaving. And that's what I did. Bobby went and got it for me." Miss Agnus paused and looked at Raymond and me; then she began opening the brown paper bag and pulling out items as she continued talking. "But since you're the only one that acted like you got good sense, you go ahead and eat everything in the bag while you're reading."

As for Raymond and I, our mouths dropped open and our eyes got wide and we began to salivate. There was chocolate candy, vanilla cookies, a piece of strawberry cake, a popsicle, and a cup of ice cream!

Needless to say, Raymond and I did not give Miss Agnus any more grief the rest of the while that we were in her care.

The following week, Mother had taken us kids with her to visit Uncle Jack. On our way back home, Katie was several paces ahead, playing some kind of counting-skipping game. Mother had Marie cradled in her left arm. I was walking directly behind her. I guess I had my own game going, as I was trying to walk exactly in her footprints. As we neared Uncle Bob's house, I saw Miss Agnus sitting on the front porch. When we were passing by, Mother said, "Good morning, Miss Agnus."

Miss Agnus returned the pleasantry. "Good morning, Sarah. Sure is nice and warm out here," she said.

It was at this point where I said, "Good morning, old Agnus." As soon as I got the words out of my mouth, without even looking back to get me in her sight, Mother backhanded me, right in the mouth. I went down hurting. As I slowly got back to my feet, I tasted blood. Mother never missed a step. I looked over at Miss Agnus; she was smiling.

It had been a few weeks since Daddy brought Mac and Arthur home. They were eating everything and growing like wildfire. Then one evening when we were having dinner, Mac and Arthur took their regular places by the back door in order to get any scraps or a bone that might eventually be available to them. And this happened to be one of those rare days when something was available, even before we sat down. We had been eating for about five minutes when suddenly we were interrupted by the sound of growling.

When we went to the door to investigate, we saw a strange dog. He was eating food that was meant for Mac and Arthur. Instead of eating, they sat cowardly at the edge of the yard. And I was shocked when Daddy didn't run that dog off, as I had seen him do with many other strays. He let that dog stay, because according to him, there was "something about that dog" that he liked.

It took about a week before the stray would let Mac and Arthur eat with him. And after about the second week, he didn't want anybody to come in our yard except family. Daddy loved it. He said that because that dog was so mean, he was going to name him Bilbo, after Senator Bilbo of Mississippi. He said that Senator Bilbo was the meanest, the most racist, and most rubbish white man in America.

## JUNE 1944

Daddy came to love Bilbo as much as he did Mac and Arthur. But Daddy was also still quite busy on all fronts. The third week in June, he bought a 1935 Ford four-door for a hundred dollars. He once owned an old piece of a car, but this was the first car that I can remember him buying. Apparently Mother didn't know that Daddy was going to come home with it. But it happened.

As per usual, Daddy had gone to the corner store, so we thought. After a couple of hours, we heard the sound of a car. Then the sound got closer and closer. Mother went to the window and looked out as the girls and I headed to the door to see what all that noise was. Mother came to the door and stood behind us to get a better view. It was a black car, with wide running boards on each side. It came to a stop near the door. That was when we recognized the man driving the car. It was Daddy. We all ran out. By the time we got down the steps, we were behind Mother. "What in the world have you done?" she demanded. Daddy didn't answer. He just grinned real wide.

Meanwhile, the girls and I walked around it and touched it. Mother and Daddy continued talking. He turned to us. "You wanna get in?" he asked as he opened the door on the driver's side and put Marie in. I went to the other side while he hoisted Katie into the car. Mother's resistance quickly dissipated. "Wanna go for a ride?" he asked. Mother got in with the rest of us.

After we were all seated, Daddy told us to wait. He said that he had to go start it. This was amazing. I had no clue as to how to start a car, train, plane, or anything that had a motor. I only knew how to start a mule. I never imagined that starting a car was done the way that I was about to witness.

This car didn't have a key or a starter button, so a hand crank was required to get the engine going. And the hand crank was a double-L-shaped metal rod that was inserted into the front of the car, in the center just below the radiator; it was then turned or wound up, thus providing for the engine to eventually become engaged.

We only rode to the store in Hugo, but it was such a joyful ride. I noticed that Mother stopped fussing at Daddy, and she enjoyed the ride as much as we children did.

Apparently Daddy was at a good place in his life because he wasn't just doing good things for his family. He was also looking out for his less fortunate neighbors. As I understood it, with the war going on, rationing stamps were required to make purchases, including alcohol. Daddy, being a non-drinker, decided to spread some goodwill in the neighborhood by buying liquor and giving the local drunks one drink at a time. He started off with two drunks. Within a few weeks, he had about eight drunks. Mother put a stop to it.

## July 1944

The first week in July, tobacco harvesting began. This was one of several areas where families swapped labor to minimize expenses. Daddy only had to hire four people, three to work at the shelter, and one in the field as a cropper. The cropper was a tall, skinny man named Leman. Daddy said that he was almost seven feet tall.

The other three people were an elderly Native American man named Dan, and a mother and daughter team. Estelle was the mother, and Ellen was the daughter. I thought the mother was old, even though she was probably in her early forties. My guess was that the daughter was about nineteen or twenty. She was the prettiest female I had ever seen. I was only six years old, but I stared at her nonstop.

During the weeks that they worked, Leman and Estelle became romantically involved. On the third weekend, they got married and made plans to move to New York.

It was now the last week of July, and our car wasn't running anymore. Consequently, we found ourselves walking again. It was the third weekend of July, and on that hot Saturday morning, the whole family walked to the general store. Daddy wanted to go before it really got hot, and we all wanted to tag along.

Other families must've had the same idea because they were coming from all directions. Mother and Daddy seemed to know all the colored folks there. This was just the second trip up there for my sisters and me.

"Sarah, I'll take the girls with me while I pick up the food," Daddy said as we approached the store. "And you said that you want Junior to go with you and pick out some material for school clothes that you gon make." Mother nodded her agreement as Daddy got Katie's hand, and took Marie in his arms. Then we went in different directions. I was so excited. However, I didn't know that Mother was planning to make new school clothes for me.

She and I went to the Material Section, where she told me to select from three possibilities. Once she got the material and some thread, we went back and met up with Daddy and the girls. And it was a good thing that we didn't stay in the Material Section long, because with holding Marie, watching Katie, and picking up items to purchase, Daddy had his arms and hands full. So, Mother and I helped with getting everything to the counter. Before long, we were on our way back home.

## AUGUST 1944/ FIRST WEEK

It was right before noon on Thursday when the work was finished for the week. Daddy was across the road in one of the fields. My sisters and I were playing in the yard, and Mother was in the house. I heard a roaring sound coming from down the road, but couldn't make out what kind of vehicle it was because of all the dust it was kicking up. As the dust was set-tling, I saw that it was Mr. Willie's car. But he was not driving. It was a woman who looked familiar. The car came to a stop near our porch, and Aunt Kathy jumped out and ran in the house. She was wearing a coat and a nightgown, but no shoes. Whenever I'd seen her in the past, she was always dressed up. I gathered my sisters and we went in the house, because I wanted to know what was happening. Aunt Kathy was crying and out of control. Mother had her arms around her shoulder, trying to calm her down. Aunt Kathy was sobbing as she tried to tell Mother what was wrong, but to me it wasn't making a lot of sense. From what I could tell, as Aunt Kathy was talking and crying at the same time, it involved Uncle Saul and his friend Willie. Apparently, Mother understood that much too, because that was when Mother also began to cry.

Then Daddy came in. Mother and Aunt Kathy were pretty

much oblivious to his entrance. He only observed while wearing that *Uh huh, I told you so* look on his face. Based on that, I knew that Daddy would get to the bottom of it; then I would overhear him talking to some of his men friends about it. As a matter of fact, I did recall hearing him and some of the other men talk about Saul before he got married. The gist was that "Saul needs to be careful riding around with Willie and having Kathy in the car." And I recalled Aunt Kathy getting Willie to bring her to our neighborhood several times when Uncle Saul was at work.

When Daddy went back outside, I got the girls and we followed.

A few days after the situation with Aunt Kathy, things around our house got back to normal. Each day, after Mother finished her farming chores, she would make her way to her sewing area, which was in a corner of the dining room. After a while, I got used to her routine. "Junior, come here and let me measure you." Or "Junior, come here and try this on." She had been making our clothes for as long as I could remember, and she never used a pattern. But whatever she made would always fit perfectly.

In addition to this process serving as a reminder that I would be going to school in a couple of weeks, everybody else was reminding me too. They must not have known that I was nervous enough about it already. Or maybe they just didn't give a flip either way. One day, even Uncle Bob got involved. He was over for a visit, and he looked at me sort of sideways and said, "Boy, I reckon you think you 'bout grown now that you'll be going to school." Of course, I said nothing. Then Daddy had his share of comments. One in particular was "It's gon be strange, not having but one man around the house." That comment I could kind of appreciate, but I still couldn't tell if it meant that he would miss my labor or if he was happy for me to be going to school and learning something besides how to work on the farm. Anyway, I tried not to let it bother me.

But the closer that time came for me to go to school, the more scared I became. Then it was the day before. After dinner, Mother called me to the front porch. I must have been too slow in getting there this time because she called again, in her no-nonsense voice, "Junior, get on out here." When I finally got there, she was standing by a chair, holding one of Daddy's long-sleeve shirts in her hand. I had no idea what she wanted, 'cause I knew I couldn't wear that big thing. But once I saw the scissors in her other hand, I knew that I was about to get an off-to-school haircut. I sat down and she tied the sleeves around my shoulders to keep the hair from going everywhere. Yes, there were two spectators: Katie and Marie. She clipped away on my head for about twenty minutes. Then she removed the shirt, put the hair in the trash, and shook the shirt over the side of the porch.

Katie and Marie looked at me and grinned, while pretending not wanting to be noticed by covering their mouths with their hands. It was okay with me that they enjoyed it. But for some reason, this made me feel ready for the day ahead. I was no longer as scared or nervous. I never knew that a haircut could do so much. I was completely relaxed now. And I slept well that night.

## AUGUST 1944/ SECOND WEEK

Yep, this was it. A new school year was about to begin; and, sure enough, I would be one of those children who walked to and fro. I was about to embark on my education experience. It was on a Monday. I woke up to the sound of Daddy making the slop jar ring, as he did every morning. I knew that it was time for me to get up and prepare for my first day of school. In addition to the homemade pants, Mother had also made me a shirt out of fertilizer bags. When I got up, she had them both neatly placed on the settee. And this being August, shoes were not needed.

After I ate, Mother dressed me, and gave me a molasses biscuit for lunch. Then she waited with me on the porch, looking for the older boy with whom she had prearranged to walk with me. Finally, she saw him in the group that I would be in. She waved to him, and sent me on.

The walk to school was probably the easiest and best part of my day. The older children talked to each other, and those of us who were new seemed to be wide-eyed.

The distance from my house to the school wasn't really that far. I saw children ahead of us turn off the road to the right and head for the school. Once we reached the schoolyard, the boy I was walking with looked at me and said, "This is it." This was Heath Chapel, named after a local church. And it was just as run-down as any of the houses we had ever lived in. It was a two-roomer, a faded building that was situated several yards off the road and fairly close to the woods on three sides.

There was a single toilet in the edge of the woods. I would later learn that it was so unbearable to use that everybody went straight to the woods to take care of private needs. I would also discover that there were two teachers who taught primary through eighth grade.

When we reached the building, the boy told me, "This is where you start. This is Mrs. Matthews' room. She teaches primary through third grade." I thought that he would wait there with me until I got checked in or whatever I needed to do in order to become a part of the new class. Instead, he was off to talk with some of the other big kids.

I just stood there, trying to figure out what I was supposed to do next. Mrs. Matthews' desk was almost in the corner, to the right as you entered. I noticed that a line was formed at her desk, so I went and got behind other kids.

While waiting, I began to look around. The first thing I noticed were some decorations on the walls with posters that the teacher had obviously made. But they were all neat. The second thing I noticed was that there were five rows of student desks, with seven or eight in each row. Finally, I saw several switches standing in a corner near her desk, and I wondered why. Boy, did I find out later!

Eventually, Mrs. Matthews finished with the new students who were ahead of me. Now, it was my turn. Before she said a word, she just looked at me, up and down, seemingly with much disdain; then she said, "Boy, what's your name?"

I said, "Junior."

Then she asked, "What else?"

I told her, "Nothing else."

At that point, she seemed even more disgusted. She paused and rolled her eyes back before instructing me, "When you get home, tell your mammy to write your name down and send it to me; and you'd better not forget!" She then assigned me a seat and turned to the next new student.

When Mrs. Matthews had gotten everybody seated, she explained how our day would be structured. She said that she had three grades in there, and that she would spend an equal amount of time with each grade. She explained her rules and what the consequences would be for violating them. Now I had a better picture of what this place would be like. I was certain that those switches standing in the corners were her weapons of enforcement.

Mrs. Matthews was a Native American. She had light skin and waist-length hair. And her way of talking to us showed me that there was a lot of dislike for us, her students.

She followed through on how she would teach each class, allotting her prescribed amount of time to each grade level. And at the end of school that day, sure enough, she had taken some names of students who had broken rules.

After she finished teaching the last class, she stood in front of the room and looked out over her subjects. To me, this amounted to a show of force. It let us know that we were a group of nobodies. Of course, I'd gotten the message that morning when I first met her. It seemed like she stood there for at least three minutes, with none of us uttering a sound.

Then she went to the corner and picked out two switches. Next, she got a folded sheet of paper from her desk. After she returned to her position on the floor, she resumed staring at us. She unfolded the sheet of paper and looked at it. Still silent, she continued her staring. Finally, she spoke. "When I call your name, you need to come forward and line up over here." She pointed to the spot. Of course the students who were in her room last year knew what she was doing. I had no clue.

Altogether, she read the names of six boys. This whole thing was so dramatic. And based on how it was done, it seemed rehearsed. After she read a name, that boy would get up from his seat and slowly move to the front of the room. After she finished reading all names, she paused and placed the list back on her desk. Then it was time to begin what I came to call the "next phase." She explained to the first student why his name was on the list. Then she told him to bend over. At that point, she slid her left hand up and down the switch a couple of times like she was warming it up. Finally, she commenced to lay switch to that boy's backside. I think he received six licks. Each boy was afforded the same courtesy as the first one. She would tell him what his transgression was but not the number of whacks he would get.

I concluded that she had a system to this part of her madness too, and that I would never be able to figure it out. But I believe that the number of whacks a student got was a function of the severity or type of transgression that was committed, along with the level of her hatred at the time toward a particular student, or the world in general.

On my way home, the realization set in with me that it was official. I was now one of those children I saw last year, going and coming. Based on my first day experience with school, as bad as things sometimes got at home, I figured I'd rather be home than at Heath Chapel.

Before I got to the house, I could see Mother and my sisters sitting on the porch. Katie ran to meet me. Boy, she was excited, like she had been the one with an opportunity to have gone somewhere, and I bet she thought it was fun too. But Mother sat there and waited. "How was it?" she asked, with a half smile. It seemed that she was not too confident in how I would handle things. Of course she was right, as I told her what Mrs. Matthews needed. She informed me that my name was Moses Shepherd, Jr. She even went in the house, got a piece of paper, and wrote it down for me. The rest of the day, I went around the house pronouncing my name so that I wouldn't forget it. "Moses Shepherd, Jr. Moses Shepherd, Jr. Moses Shepherd, Jr. Moses Shepherd, Jr.

When I returned to school the next day and gave the paper with my name on it to Mrs. Matthews, she informed me, "You will be called Moses, unless I decide to call you something else."

It took me a long time to get accustomed to folks calling me Moses. All I had ever known my name to be was Junior.

The first week of school, I learned a useful survival behavior from other students. Consequently, I wasn't surprised when I had to employ that maneuver. White students rode to school on school buses. Black students walked. I learned to run into the woods when the white bus passed by us, because if it was dry and dusty, they would try to see how much dirt and dust they could put on you. And if it was raining, they would try to cover you with as much mud and water as they could.

Sure enough, the second week of school, it happened. I was walking along and looking down at the gravel. I heard somebody yell, "Here it comes!" It didn't immediately dawn on me what was about to happen, but I saw everybody take off into the woods, so I ran behind them. You could hear the white kids hysterically laughing as they rode by. I thought back to the white men guarding the black men who were on the chain gang. This seemed to be in some way related to that, but I couldn't figure out exactly how.

I had already concluded that Mrs. Matthews didn't like students, but as the year progressed, I found out that she particularly didn't care for students with dark skin. She was the teacher from hell. And, there was nothing I could do about it. However, that combined with my working on the farm proved to be a positive of sorts. As long as I concentrated on doing my best in both settings, I figured that things would be fine. Then along came a distraction, a positive one that helped me get my mind off of the negative,

I vividly remember that it was on a Monday, the twenty-first of August, Marie's birthday. Early that evening, Dr. Collins brought Raymond and Mattie a baby brother from Hookerton. I saw him get out of his car with a black bag in his hand and go into the house. He stayed in there for a short while, and when he came out, I heard a baby crying. It was then that I knew for sure where babies came from. They named him Johnny Wayne. Mother took us over there before bedtime, to see the new baby. He didn't cry at all while we were visiting. He just lay there, and Aunt Ada let us kids gather around and watch as he slept.

## September 1944/First Week

Johnny Wayne had arrived. And Uncle Bob was extra ecstatic. But he didn't just have a new baby son. He also had a niece next door. As a four-year-old, Katie loved Uncle Bob. Whenever he'd come for a visit, she'd jump up on his lap because she knew that he'd entertain her by acting silly and telling her funny stories.

The only way to continue sharing this scenario is to say that Uncle Bob was not just a comedian; he was also a *farter*. And he didn't entertain just Katie; he entertained everybody.

Uncle Bob also had a special knock. Whenever he came to our house, he would knock and walk on in. By recognizing his knock, you didn't have to go to the door to see who it was. On this particular Saturday evening, there was that knock. Of course Katie had come to recognize it too. When she heard it, she ran to meet him. He sat down and she hopped on his lap. Mother, Marie, and I made up the rest of his audience.

Uncle Bob had barely gotten started when Mother had to go to the bedroom for something. Uncle Bob was telling Katie a story about some fierce animal, and when he got to the animal part, he'd growl and tickle Katie like he was that animal.

Suddenly, he farted real loud. Katie hopped off his lap and ran to Mother, who was now returning from the bedroom. "Uncle Bob pooted," she complained. "Can you make him stop?" But Mother thought it was funny too. She told Katie that it was okay, and that Uncle Bob just needed to "let some wind out." Of course Uncle Bob was enjoying the uproar from his darling niece. Katie didn't return to his lap, but he finished the story from afar, as we all continued to laugh.

Before he left, he and Mother sat down at the kitchen table and talked. The girls and I went outside to play. We had been playing for about fifteen minutes when I realized that there was a toy I'd made in my room. I went to retrieve it and stumbled onto some new information. I overheard Mother and Uncle Bob talking about Aunt Kathy. I didn't get any details, but I surmised that she and Uncle Saul had gotten back together.

## September 1944/Second Week

Understanding that the passage of time can serve as a healing agent is a good thing. It seemed apparent that Katie had gotten over what happened with Uncle Bob, because the following Wednesday afternoon, there was that knock at the front door; Uncle Bob came in. As usual, Katie ran to meet him. When he sat down, she jumped onto his lap. So, things were back to normal.

Uncle Bob was playing a game with her, and they both were laughing and having fun. Suddenly, there was a loud expulsion of gas. "Uh-oh," I said. "Uncle Bob just farted again."

He was still laughing when he interrupted his own roaring

enjoyment with "Ouch! Aw shit!" Katie hopped off his lap and left the room. That was the end of their loving relationship. Katie had gone to that session armed with one of Mother's sewing needles. And her poking it into Uncle Bob was her response to his farting around her.

### September 1944/Third Week

Another thing that happened in September was that Daddy got our car running. Yep, we had transportation again.

With tobacco having been harvested, folks were now busy working that cured tobacco in the packhouse. This included grading, tying, and bundling it in sheets. The latter was the final step in this process before taking it to the warehouse in Kinston to sell.

This was the year that Daddy introduced me to tobacco tyings. He invited people from the neighborhood. To me, this was nothing but a work party. Those who were invited came and worked, with their compensation being the opportunity to socialize and get fed.

The first ones to arrive were Mr. Amos Frye and his family. He and his wife were friends of my parents. They regularly socialized together. And Amos Junior and I were friends from school. In addition, there were four other children. Charlene was the oldest.

Daddy had bought drinks, chips, peanuts, and cookies. And he had cordoned off a small area in the packhouse to serve refreshments. It was simple. There were two chairs with about eight tobacco sticks put close together and spread across the chairs. This served as a table.

With three other cars arriving, plus people walking, it wasn't long until there was a pretty good crowd. And with some other children arriving with their parents, it was a play party for the children.

At times, the grown-ups were louder than we were. And, there was a point when they called the kids to get snacks and drinks. Boy, I loved tobacco tyings!

Incidentally, there was a sidebar to this gathering. I overheard Daddy and Mr. Amos talking about Aunt Kathy's and Uncle Saul's situation. Daddy was speaking as if he had the facts, and I had no doubt that he did. According to Daddy's report, Uncle Saul had gotten a job in Goldsboro. He rode to the job with his neighbor, Jeb. Sometimes they would get off early because there would not be enough work for a full day. So getting off early meant getting home early.

On that particular Wednesday, he and Jeb were on their way back home. About a tenth of a mile from his house, Uncle Saul told Jeb to stop at the next wooded area and let him out because he needed to relieve himself, and he would walk the rest of the way home. Jeb stopped, let Uncle Saul out, and drove off.

When Uncle Saul stepped out of the woods at his house, he saw Willie's car parked in his yard. Needless to say, he became livid. As he neared the house, he began to tiptoe. He eased the front door open and heard Aunt Kathy and Willie in his bedroom. He got his shotgun from over the door, but as careful as he was being, he accidentally kicked the trash can. Then there was silence. Uncle Saul rushed in with his shotgun at the ready. With the surprised, partially covered couple lying frozen-like, he aimed and pulled the trigger. Nothing happened. They both jumped out of bed, buck naked, and ran. Willie got past Uncle Saul while he was trying to figure out what had happened to his gun. He dropped the shotgun and began chasing Willie. Willie ran past his car and into the woods. Uncle Saul then turned and went back inside, looking for Aunt Kathy. She wasn't in the bedroom, so he began searching the rest of the house. He found her in the kitchen, hiding in the pantry. He yanked her out and began beating the crap out of her with his fists. She was yelling and screaming, but somehow managed to escape. Now partially dressed, she ran through the living room, picked Willie's car keys up from the couch, and jumped in his car and drove away. That's how she ended up at our house. The problem with Uncle Saul's shotgun was that Aunt Kathy had removed the shells.

**NOVEMBER 1944**

With the exception of some corn left to be reaped, harvest season was virtually over. November was special to me for a special reason. Mother invited Uncle Saul and Aunt Kathy to Thanksgiving dinner. Yep, they were really back together. In spite of their issues, they both had become two of my favorite people. I guess this was due to the fact that Aunt Kathy was Mother's baby sister, and Uncle Saul merely for the fact that he was her husband.

They arrived about mid-afternoon, allowing them time

to visit before we had dinner at four o'clock. Even though I'd learned as much about cussing as I could from Uncle Saul, I wanted to be certain that I hadn't missed anything. Therefore, I pretty much glued myself to him during this visit.

And speaking of "special," since we moved to this farm, living next door to our cousins was something I'd considered as being most special from day one. But all of that began to unravel Saturday after Thanksgiving. We were eating dinner (Thanksgiving leftovers) when I heard the news. Mother and Daddy were talking, and based on what I was hearing, I had to ask, to make sure that I was hearing what I thought I was hearing. Right before dinner, Daddy had been feeding the live-stock. So what he shared must have slipped his mind, because whenever there was new information, he shared it immediately. He had just cut into his meat when he suddenly stopped. "Oh, I forgot to tell you," he said, looking at Mother. I didn't bother to listen because I was so much into my food. Plus, sometimes they talked about stuff that I had no interest in. The only thing I heard was something about somebody moving. Then I noticed that they both had stopped eating and were heavy into the exchange of information.

"Why is he moving?" Mother asked. "Had he mentioned it before? He never said a word to me."

Daddy patiently waited for Mother to finish her litany of questions. "No, he didn't tell me nothing except he's moving," Daddy said.

"Did he say when he's moving?" Mother asked.

I'm sure my ears lit up. "Who's moving where?" I asked.

"Your Uncle Bob," Mother answered.

"Uncle Bob? Moving?" I inquired in disbelief.

Daddy addressed that. "He's moving back to Greene County after Christmas," he said. "He's gon move back into the house where his mother died…the house that he grew up in."

I was speechless. Suddenly my mind began to race with memories of our times together, doing fun stuff, visiting each other's house, eating at each other's house, and watering my garden. Oh, it was such a sad day.

Even when I returned to school following the holiday, I would sometimes lose focus. Knowing that Uncle Bob and his family would be moving meant Katie and I would be losing our two next-door playmates.

## December 1944

I moped around for days before the news sank in. With it now being December and so much happening so fast at home and at school, distractions proved to be very helpful. But after a couple of weeks, I began to shake myself out of that funk.

There had been several real chilly days before, but now cold days were more frequent. As a result, some of the older boys would light those coal-burning stoves in the classrooms. As the rooms warmed up, the stench of drying urine would permeate the air. That was because most kids only had one pair of underwear, and when they urinated in the bed the night before, they didn't have enough time the next morning for their underclothes to be washed and dried before coming to school. But such was only one of many nuances to be navigated in our daily educational environment.

I had no inkling that my own personal issue would be forthcoming, one which I could not avoid. Overall, school was going okay. I had managed to stay out of trouble with my mean-ass teacher. I had tried my best to not make her angry, but it didn't work. One morning, the week before we were to get out for Christmas, it was extremely cold, and when I reached school, my hands were numb and aching. Mrs. Matthews told me to go to the board and write my lesson. I went to the board, and I knew my lesson, but my hands were so cold that I couldn't grip the chalk. Each time I tried to write, the chalk would fall to the floor.

Every time I dropped it, that bitch would crack me across my back with a switch. This went on for a number of minutes. I don't remember why she stopped beating me, but I think it was because her arms got tired. I never told Mother or Daddy about that experience because I was sure that they would've blamed me and whipped my ass again. Plus, that kind of stuff was the norm, not the exception.

As it turned out, December of 1944 ended on a good note. We had the best Christmas ever. Mother baked at least three cakes—chocolate, coconut, and lemon—and I don't know how many different kinds of pies. Both my sisters got dolls that closed their eyes when they were laid on their back. And they got toy tea sets and toy cook stoves. For me, there was a set of Roy Rogers cap pistols, including the two holsters. I had a pistol on each hip. I also got a Daisy air rifle and a brand-new pair of store-bought overalls!

Christmas was on Monday. Uncle Bob and his family moved Thursday afternoon. Katie and I went over to their house about mid-morning. Raymond and Mattie looked just as sad as we did. This was absolutely a *no-fun* visit. None of us were smiling. Uncle Bob was not even joking around. He was busy packing their belongings. After a short visit, Katie and I left, walking back through the woods to our house.

## JANUARY 1945

In 1945, with New Year's Day being on Monday, it felt like an extra Sunday in the week. But since there was no church service, and no gospel music on the radio, we all just lazed around. This was an opportunity for me to consider how good this year could be for me. With that as a backdrop, I felt quite optimistic. I put my experience with Mrs. Matthews behind me and thought of all of the good things that had happened to me, especially Christmas. Consequently, being back in school was turned into a positive.

On the fourth Thursday afternoon, shortly after I got home from school, a car drove up. Of course we looked out the window to see who was coming to visit. We didn't recognize the car, but we sure did recognize the gentleman who got out with his suitcase. My sisters and I rushed out to greet Grandpa as the car drove away. "What you doing here, Grandpa?" Katie asked excitedly.

"I'm gon spend the weekend with you," he told her as he

handed her a lollipop that he pulled from his jacket pocket. Marie had her hand out, knowing that she would get one too. Me? I could wait, and I did. I took his bag, which was somewhat heavy, but I managed. Once in the house, Grandpa gave me his coat to hang up. That's when he also gave me a bigger piece of candy.

Mother and Daddy came in; they welcomed Grandpa and then Daddy asked: "What you doing here, Pa?"

Grandpa took his time answering, as he usually did. "I came for the weekend. How y'all doing?"

"Things going pretty good," Daddy responded. "As soon as the weather breaks, we'll be working in the fields, getting them ready for planting." There was the familiar small talk, as Mother helped Grandpa get settled in for his short visit.

My sisters and I always enjoyed Grandpa, and whenever he was around I would think about how much he meant to all of us, but especially to the children.

The next day when I got home from school, Grandpa said that he had walked down the road in both directions and that he liked what he saw in the makeup of the community. Then he began to ask me about being in school and the children I'd met. What I gathered from our conversation was that Grandpa had found another reason to spend more time with us in this little community.

I don't know if pork chops and gravy was Grandpa's favorite meal, but that's what we had for breakfast that Sunday morning. Normally, it would be rice with ham or something similar. But Grandpa really raved about that meal. After breakfast, it was time to get dressed for church. When I was dressed, I went and asked Grandpa if he wanted me to carry his suitcase to the car.

Mother was passing by the door and heard his answer. "No. Leave the suitcase. I decided to stay a little longer."

This was really exciting to me. "What did you say, Pa?" Mother asked as she turned around and came into the room, obviously not believing what she'd just heard.

"Yeah, I think I'll stay a while longer," he repeated. "I want to stay long enough to see if this is the right area for me."

Mother looked a little down but okay with Grandpa's decision. Daddy, having walked up on the conversation, looked confused or disappointed. I was unable to discern which. It was obvious that he didn't like it, but he just kept walking as if he hadn't heard a thing.

## FEBRUARY 1945

Even though Grandpa was visiting, it still didn't replace the void in my play options after Uncle Bob moved. Raymond and I could always come up with some fun things to do. And Katie would be there to participate, if she was invited. Now for me, it was back to figuring out stuff to do by myself, unless it was a game or activity that Katie could participate in. But it wasn't just a void that was left in my life. There was also a vacant house a short distance through the woods.

One afternoon, Katie and I were playing in our yard. Eventually, we ended up in the edge of the woods. I told Katie, "Come on, let's go see Uncle Bob's house." When we got there, it felt so strange that there was no liveliness emanating, like Aunt Ada's hollering for Raymond to stop playing so rough, or Uncle Bob laughing.

As we walked around the house, I picked up a few rocks and threw them into the trees, trying to see if I could get one to the top. I was having no success. Katie was playing out by the barn where we had spent a lot of time.

Then the windows got my attention. I picked up a medium-size rock and hurled it with all my might. "Kapowyaw!"

I had never broken a window before, and I had not imagined that the shattering sounded like that! It sounded good! Plus, I considered my accuracy to be outstanding. I tried another one. Same result.

Katie and I returned home, with her not knowing what I had done. I went back over there by myself a couple of times after that and finished breaking out the remaining windows.

It was the third Saturday in February around noon when Daddy came out with his rifle. "Hey, Junior," he said. "Git that box of cans and take them across the road. Then turn the box upside down and put the cans on top of it." I stopped what I was doing and obeyed. I had no idea what he wanted me to do that for. But I followed instructions and returned to the yard to make sure that I got out of the line of fire.

"Now, come here," he said as he placed the rifle in a shooting position and looked over the barrel. "I'm gon teach you how to shoot this thing." He smiled. Daddy then handed the rifle to me. "Aw, don't be scared of it," he said. "It ain't gon hurt you. It's that shotgun that kicks. This rifle is smooth as silk."

I reluctantly got the gun and tried to remember what position he held it in. I put the stock on my shoulder and tried to look across the barrel. He corrected me by getting the butt of the rifle off my shoulder and placing it against the inside pit of my right arm instead.

When he realized that I couldn't reach the trigger from that position, he placed the gun back where I had it. Then he told me to "Hold it where it's comfortable." I did, and again I peered across the barrel.

"You got to line the target up with these two pieces here," he said, pointing to the places on top of the rifle. I practiced holding the rifle, and I practiced lining the tin cans up as my targets. "Now let me load it for you," he said. I handed him the gun. He got some bullets from his pocket and loaded the rifle. Then he gave it back to me with the instructions to be very careful. Once he thought I had the target in my sights, he told me to pull the trigger. I did. The gun fired.

I didn't hit a thing.

"That's okay," he said. "That was your first time." I fired a couple more rounds before I hit a can. After two more misses, I knocked the other four cans off the box. "Atta boy!" Daddy exclaimed as he took the gun and headed to the woods. I was on a cloud! I'd just learned how to shoot a gun!

As luck would have it, the following Wednesday, on his way from Kinston, Uncle Saul stopped by our house. He invited me to go squirrel hunting with him early Saturday morning. When he asked, Mother and Daddy were listening. I looked at them, and they nodded their approval. Uncle Saul said he'd be there at nine o'clock.

When Saturday came, I was up and ready to go by eight o'clock. I waited and waited. This would be my first time going hunting. I had been in the edge of the woods a few times with Uncle Jack and Uncle Bob when they headed out to hunt. Though it wasn't deep into the woods, I thought it ought to count for something.

It was real cold that morning, so Mother made sure that I was dressed appropriately by insisting that I put on layers of clothing. She said that it would be warming up, and that I could peel off one piece at a time, and thereby not get too hot, but still be warm enough.

Nine o'clock came and went. I was peeling off layers before I left. Ten o'clock came and went. At ten forty-five, Uncle Saul showed up. He always had his share of excuses. "My neighbor's cows got out last night and I helped him round them up. Two were all the way over at the Madison farm," he said. I didn't know how far that was, and it didn't matter. Plus, there was no reason for me to balk about it.

"I'm ready," I said. And in spite of being so late, Uncle Saul still seemed excited. But I couldn't tell if the excitement was because he was going hunting, or that he thought he'd have a chance to show off his hunting knowledge and skills, or even brag about them, which he'd never been shy about.

We went across the field behind our house, which was probably one-eighth of a mile. As we walked, Uncle Saul shared some of his hunting prowess. Seemingly, he thought that hunting was totally foreign to me. Then we went into the woods.

That's when he began giving me specific pointers about hunting. "When you spot one that you want, you gotta stay real quiet; you don't even wanna hear yourself breathe," he cautioned. We walked a few more paces, and Uncle Saul said, "I see one," as he pointed to a treetop. There, sitting on a limb, was what appeared to be a squirrel, holding something with its paws.

Uncle Saul put his finger to his lips to make sure that I stayed silent. Then he stepped on a twig. The snapping was so loud that it scared me and the squirrel. Of course Uncle Saul cussed. "Gotdammit! He got away!" The squirrel had jumped to another tree, and by now was surely safe from any impending danger from Uncle Saul.

"Let's go this way," Uncle Saul said, and I followed him amongst a few pine trees until we reached a grove of huge oaks. A few yards in, Uncle Saul began to tiptoe again. I didn't see any squirrels, but I continued to tiptoe behind him. Then I saw Uncle Saul looking up in a tree, so I looked up too. Yep, there was another squirrel, obviously believing that it was well-hidden; it didn't budge, just sat there.

Uncle Saul raised his gun, aimed, and fired. "I got him! I got him!" He shouted as the squirrel tumbled from its perch on the limb.

But a problem occurred in the process. The squirrel got stuck between a couple of branches and never made it all the way down. When Uncle Saul realized what had happened, he cussed again. However, he apparently already had a solution. He fired and hit the squirrel a second time. The squirrel still didn't fall. He fired and hit the squirrel a third time, and a fourth. That was the shot that did the trick. The poor squirrel completed its journey to the ground, at least what remained of that which was once a squirrel. Its body was riddled with so many holes and covered with so much blood that it was beyond recognition.

Yep. What Uncle Saul did to that squirrel was ridiculous. My decision was made. I would never go hunting again.

The next day when we were getting ready for church, I paid close attention to my parents. I noticed that Grandpa didn't have his suitcase, and I noticed that they didn't have an extra bag with Grandpa's clothes.

While the focus for me was on whether Grandpa remained with us or not, it turned out that there was something else that happened at church that took my focus off of that situation. We arrived at church and everything was normal, until there was a special visitor to our service. Reverend Dare did the preliminaries, introduced the topic of his sermon, and was a few minutes into delivering his message.

Then he really got settled in, feeling it. "No matter what your friends tell you, it's between you and God. No matter how many times your friends tell you, it's between you and God!"

I heard a commotion at the door and looked around. A white man was trying to enter the church, and the ushers seemed to be objecting. The commotion got louder, and other people looked back. By this time, the ushers had allowed the man to enter. They had seated him on a back pew. Reverend Dare never missed a beat.

At the center of all this was a local white farmer who owned the farm down the road. He was dressed in bib overalls and was wearing a straw hat. And he was obviously drunk. Instead of sitting, he lay down on the pew. Again, Reverend Dare was never distracted. "So when the day of reckoning come, when the Lord come down for judgment…"

The white man stood up, snatched off his hat, and waved it to and fro, shouting, "Preach, nigger, preach! Preach, nigger!"

Reverend Dare continued, and the congregation continued worshiping as if nothing had happened. I guess that our visitor had gotten his worship experience, because he went on back out the door.

In the end, two things were certain this particular Sunday. Church service was different, thanks to our visitor, and Grandpa would continue living with us.

It was on a Friday morning that I first noticed Daddy was acting somewhat different. He seemed to be nicer to us, and he especially seemed to talk more to Grandpa than he had previously. Maybe it was a hangover from the success he had with his crops last year, or some optimism about his crops for the coming year. Or maybe, just maybe it was because he now realized that Grandpa was not going back home, if he still had his home. But for whatever the reasoning was, Daddy did something that was absolutely astounding. Talk about good deeds!

Apparently he and Mother had already discussed it, and of course I wouldn't know that for sure, nor much of anything else. But at the dinner table that night, Mother brought it up. "Pa, you said that you wanted something to do so you would have some income; I talked with Namon, and he said that he'll give you some chicken and one of his six acres that he was going to use for tobacco. So, along with being able to sell chicken and eggs, you'll also be able to sell vegetables from your garden."

That's when Daddy spoke up. "Yeah, Pa. That'll really keep you busy."

Without hesitation, Grandpa had a reply: "But you know I ain't got no mule, and no equipment."

Daddy interrupted him. "Pa, you know you can use my equipment and mules."

Grandpa was hesitant, but he finally said, "Well, allright, and I thank you both."

The next Wednesday evening, Mother, the girls, Grandpa, and I were sitting by the heater when Daddy came in. It was just as the sun was going down. I could tell that he was unhappy about something.

"Sarah, have you been over to Bob's old house lately?" he asked.

"No. I haven't," she answered. "What's wrong with it?"

I looked at him again, and he seemed to be getting madder and madder. I could've told him, but I wasn't in the conversation.

"Every window in that house done been broke out," he told her. "…probably them younguns that come 'long here going to the store." I was relieved that he was thinking that way. But then he turned to me. "Do you know anything about that,

Junior?"

Without hesitating, I lied. "No, sir," I told him. "I don't know nothing about it."

Daddy later went over there and put tin over the windows to keep the rain out.

## MARCH 1945

One of the most significant things to happen this month was the news that Daddy shared at dinner one Saturday night. He had been to the store and came in with that telling sad look on his face. He had found out that Estell and Leman got into a fight shortly after they moved to New York. Estell stabbed Leman to death, and she was sentenced to life in prison without parole. Of course that was a grown-up conversation, and I knew better than to even try to become a part of it. I was in disbelief though, and inside I was sad, for both Estell and Leman, but especially for Estell. This was the first person ever that I was so familiar with who got into this kind of trouble.

## APRIL 1945

I don't know who brought them to our neighborhood that day in early April, but Aunt Kathy and Aunt Erlene walked down to our house from Uncle Jack's.

Aunt Kathy liked to wear nice pants, so that's what she had on. But Aunt Erlene? She was usually dressed up every day, even during the week. And this was on a Saturday. She had on a fancy-looking dress, with a matching flowery straw hat. They came in, greeted everyone, and began a discussion with

Mother in the dining room. I couldn't hear all that was being said, but I did surmise that they were planning a trip to Snow Hill. Mother went and asked Grandpa to watch the children (that included me), then she came my way.

Before she got there, I had a request. "Can I go? Please?!" I said, probably a bit too excited.

She turned to Daddy. "What do you think, Namon?"

"He'll have to ride in the back," he told her, and headed out the door.

We all piled in that Ford. Mother and Daddy were in the front seat, and I was cramped between my two aunts. But I didn't care. I was going with them. I guess part of the reason I was so excited was because I hadn't been to Snow Hill since we lived there back in 1941. As we drove away, there was a warm breeze that seemed to make everyone relax.

I think Daddy was showing off though, because he kept speeding up until Mother told him, "You need to slow down!" Aunt Kathy was enjoying it, but Aunt Erlene seemed to tense up. However, once Daddy slowed down, Aunt Erlene relaxed. That is, until an extra gust of wind came by as Daddy was rounding a curve. Aunt Erlene reached for her hat as she screamed, "EEK!" Of course that startled everybody.

"What's wrong?!" Mother asked, turning around. We all looked back and saw Aunt Erlene's hat still sailing in the dust. It landed near the curve that we'd just gone around.

Daddy brought the car to a halt and just sat there as the women discussed the situation. Then my dear mother had the answer. "Junior, you run back there and get your Aunt Erlene's hat."

I climbed out and headed back down the road. I didn't want to, but I had no choice. And I still had my thoughts, but I was smart enough to keep them to myself. *Why did I have to go get her damn hat? Why couldn't she go get it? It was hers. Better yet, she should've held onto it.*

And it might not have even been that far, but it seemed like an awful long distance to me. Then again, maybe it seemed like a long distance because I made it a point not to run and not to hurry. I was pissed! I retrieved the hat and returned to the car without a smile, and we were on our way again.

When Daddy started using the mules, he discovered that Kate was ideal. But Tom was a special case. In other words, Tom had a personality that was less than agreeable. Sometimes when Daddy would be trying to get Tom to go left, Tom would go right. If he tried to get Tom to go right, he'd go left. If Tom felt like resting, he'd lie down in the field. Tom had a mind of his own. Mother said that he had more sense than the men who worked him.

If Daddy had a need for only one mule, he'd usually choose Kate. But I suppose he determined that he had to make use of both mules and get his money's worth. Consequently, often he'd have to hitch Tom up and put him to work.

Grandpa would do the same as Daddy did when he needed only one mule. He'd hitch Kate up and get the work done. But one day he decided to give Kate a rest, so he hitched Tom up to the tobacco truck, without any issues.

Then Grandpa climbed on the tobacco truck and headed across the road to the field. When he got to the road, Tom stopped. Grandpa lightly tapped him with the reins in order to get him to continue. Tom didn't budge. So Grandpa tapped Tom again, and said, "Get up!" Still Tom didn't move. By this time, obviously Grandpa was fed up with Tom's shenanigan. So he angrily hit Tom across the rump with the reins. Wrong move.

Tom made a U-turn and took off at full speed. In the process, Grandpa went sailing through the air. Mother heard the commotion and ran out of the house, hollering, "Pa! Pa!"

Fortunately, Grandpa landed in a sitting position in a clump of grass. He just sat there looking bewildered. Mother went over to him and asked, "Pa, are you okay?" He didn't answer. She looked at his forehead. He had an abrasion, but otherwise he seemed okay. "I'm allright," he finally muttered. As he got up, he looked around to see where Tom was. Tom had continued running, and stopped at the stable.

My sisters and I thought that was the funniest thing we had ever seen. Fortunately, the only thing that got hurt was Grandpa's dignity. He relinquished his acre of tobacco, and I would never see him drive a mule again.

## MAY 1945

Daddy bought me a brand-new pair of brogans, but told me that I couldn't wear them until school re-opened after the summer. That was okay because May was barefoot time anyway.

For weeks, we students had been looking forward to getting

our summer break. That last day finally came. On our way to school that morning, we were extra excited. Personally, I had been looking forward to this since my December ass whipping. But other than that one major clashing with Mrs. Matthews, I'd been pretty successful at staying off her radar. And it sure took a lot of effort. I figured that all of us students deserved some time away from her. And I wouldn't even mind the farm work.

But hold up. That reliable plan of "continued avoidance" only lasted half the day this time. And I wasn't bothering a soul. I wasn't talking or anything. I was just sitting there, doing my work.

Mrs. Matthews was scouting the classroom as she always did; front to back, back to front, side to side. Then she came my way. She stopped right in front of my desk. "Moses," she intoned, and paused. I figured she got so dramatic just to make sure that all the other students heard her and concluded that I was scared. I was. Then she continued. "You need to see me after school today," she said, in her most frightful voice.

"Yes, ma'am," I replied.

That did it for me. The rest of my day was done. I hadn't seen her write my name down, and I knew for a fact that I had not broken any of her stupid-ass rules. But it must've been something. For the rest of the day, I tried to psych myself up for the whipping that was coming.

Then near the end of the day, she was talking to the class about summer vacation and the next school year. It was typical Mrs. Matthews talk. Nothing positive was said to the class. She mainly talked about coming back to school.

When the bell rang, I sat there. Mrs. Matthews stepped outside the door and ushered students toward the road. There seemed to be no urgency for her to get back to me, as she and the other teacher stood out front and talked for several minutes.

Finally, she returned to the classroom and sat down at her desk. I knew she couldn't have forgotten that I was there. I wanted to go ask her why I was still there, but I was scared to move. Finally, she said, "Moses, come here." I got up with my notebook and headed toward her desk. I just stood there, knowing that I dare not speak. Instead of reaching for the switch that she'd just deposited in the corner when she came back in, she reached inside her desk drawer and pulled out an envelope. That's when she looked at me, dead in the eyes. I felt like going through the floor. Then still staring at me, she came out with the bad news. "Moses," she began, "you're not going to second grade next year." She paused, and I sank deeper into my misery, wondering what I had done to fail first grade. I knew that if I had failed, then all the other kids surely had failed. I began to feel sorry for all of us.

"Give this to your mother when you get home," she said, handing the envelope to me. "When you come back from summer vacation, you'll be going straight to third grade." She still hadn't changed her expression.

"Yes, ma'am." I said. I took the envelope, and out the door I went.

I wasn't sure how I was supposed to feel. I was pleased that instead of a whipping, I had received good news. But how she did it was what bothered the hell outta me. I was a total wreck. I wondered if how she handled that was another way she got pleasure from intimidating students and simply making them miserable. If I hadn't realized it before, I did now. *It's not just the whippings she administers to students that make her happy; it includes whatever it is that she'd just done to me.* I wondered if there were other methods she had up her sleeve. At any rate, I was truly relieved, and when I got down the road, a couple of my friends were waiting. "What she want?" they asked. I told them, and my walk into summer vacation was nothing but good!

## JUNE 1945

One morning after school closed for the summer, we were eating breakfast when we heard an urgent knock on the back door. "Mr. Namon! Mr. Namon!" the man yelled. Daddy answered the door; it was a neighbor, Mr. Bridges. "I just came by your stable," he began, "and Tom was leaning against the rail, dead." There was a silence of disbelief. Mr. Bridges said that he went inside the fence to get a closer look, and discovered that Tom wasn't breathing. He and Daddy went to the stable and double-checked. Sure enough, that's what was found. In about fifteen minutes, Daddy returned and said that Mr. Bridges went back home. Mother was washing some pans as we children were finishing our meal and Grandpa was getting his second cup of coffee.

Obviously, there was nothing to be said, and a sad

atmosphere settled over the room. "I'm going to do some chopping," Daddy said. "Then I'll come back and we can take care of Tom. Pa, how 'bout telling Jack; I'll figure out where to bury Tom, and we'll get it done before the day is over."

Daddy got some tools and went on to the field, and we sat around. Grandpa later went and told Uncle Jack what had happened and what the plan was. Daddy returned to the house a little before noon. He said that he'd gotten Mr. Bridges and another neighbor to help him dig a hole down in an adjoining field to the one he'd been working in.

Apparently word had spread in the community beyond the two men who had helped him dig the hole, because about five other men and a couple of women met at our house. The pall hanging over made it feel like a person had died.

We made our way to the barn, where the men put two chains around Tom and hitched them to Kate. Then they carefully held Tom as Kate moved forward, ensuring that Tom would be gently lowered to the ground.. From there, with everyone walking slowly behind, Tom was dragged to the field where his grave had been dug.

Once there, Daddy directed the effort to get Tom in the hole. And when he was satisfied with how Tom was positioned, he got down in the hole and removed the chains from Tom's body. One of the men handed Daddy a bag of lime to sprinkle on Tom's body. When he had finished that, he climbed out and turned around, facing the grave. He stood silently, as we all did, looking into Tom's grave. Grandpa's eyes had already swelled with tears. Daddy turned to the men holding the shovels and said, "Go ahead."

Then with one on each side of the grave, they began to toss dirt onto Tom's body. And it was not just the two men holding the shovels that filled the grave. I know that this process was not rehearsed, but it appeared that it had been, because all the other men in attendance took turns shoveling..

All things considered, Tom's burial could have easily been mistaken for a human burial, because in addition to our families, there were at least another dozen friends and neighbors in attendance. And while there was no biblical content or church-type ceremony, it was the atmosphere that qualified the characterization of this occasion as one that was so very touching.

Grandpa wiped away tears, as he was the last one who lingered behind when everyone walked away.

But being in the farming business, even devastating losses have to be handled and let go of. That must have been how Daddy dealt with losing Tom. Work had to go on. Daddy started his search for a replacement mule immediately. He got numerous leads, and he followed up on most of them. However, he found what he called the perfect mule at a farm in the Goldsboro area. That was the one he returned home with one Wednesday afternoon. We called him Don.

In the past, I had become aware of how women get together and talk about a variety of subjects. They would talk about how to raise children, what recipes to use, and about other folks. The only place I had seen men come together like that was at church and on visits to each other's houses. Even though Daddy would bring news back whenever he went out alone, I never imagined that there was a gathering place for men to share information. That all changed once I was old enough to go to the store without my parents. I discovered that menfolk gathered at the corner store. The first thing I paid attention to was their behavior, both white men and the black. The white men would be gathered on the inside, and black men would be outside.

Then there was one particular thing that especially caught my attention. When white men would leave the store, some came out with a soft drink that they were drinking. They would take another swallow, then place the partially filled bottle on a stump or a drink crate. As they were walking away, they would say, "Here you go, boys. One of y'all can have the rest of that." Some of those black men would be almost running over each other, trying to get to that bottle. The white man would smile with joy.

Another thing that I noticed was that community news was passed along at the general store, and I could understand that. Even though black men and white men gathered in different places, I imagined that there was some similarity in both groups. Whether it was called "menfolk gossip" or not, it amounted to neighborhood news.

As I had noticed some time ago, whenever Daddy would go to the store, it was rarely a quick errand, and when he returned, it would be with more than what he'd gone to purchase. He would come back and share the latest news with Mother;

I would listen, sometimes pretending that I was busy doing something else, but I always listened intently.

I discovered that most of the news was nothing bad, just regular stuff, like who had a new baby, or who got another car. Of course, some opinions would be sprinkled in, along with who said what about whom. And sometimes, there would be devastating news, like a neighborhood death. I'll never forget the one that struck home with my family. It seemed like everything came to a grinding halt. It was on a Sunday morning that Daddy returned from the store on one of those rare quick trips. It seemed like he must've gotten the news and hurried back home to share it. When he got out of the car, he appeared to be in a daze. I was in the yard. He walked past me without saying a word. I followed him inside to find out why the errand was so brief, along with why he was not acting like himself. He pulled a chair from the kitchen table and sat down. Mother came in and noticed that something was out of kilter with him. But she didn't say anything; she just looked.

"Amos got killed last night," he said. "He was over at Trad Hall's farm, at that gambling house. He wasn't involved in the dispute that took place, but the fellas he went there with were. They were in the living room gambling when the argument broke out. Amos was in the kitchen, laying on a bench, drunk and asleep. When the disagreement got heated, his friends ran. Amos woke up and asked, "What's going on?" The woman who runs the place told the men that were arguing with Amos' friends that "He was with them." Daddy paused as he stared into space, then went on to share. "They said that big woman picked Amos up and slammed him back down. Then her husband and the others used a bush axe to behead him."

Mr. Amos was a pillar in the community, not only as a friend, but also such a good neighbor. His funeral was held later in the week. Mother and Daddy attended, and another couple, along with two older children, came and rode with them. Of course I had to babysit the girls.

## July 1945

It was Sunday, July first, 1945. I was on a "play break" late that Sunday afternoon. I was in the yard. Daddy came out of the house, puffing on one of those cigarettes. He blew a couple of smoke rings, and headed toward the stable. "Come here, Junior," he called to me. I stopped what I was doing and caught up with him, as he never missed a stride.

"Yes, sir?" I asked.

"Tomorrow, I'm gon give you another job," he said.

I had no idea what other work I could do, nor when I would have any extra time to do another job. I was already babysitting my sisters. I had transported the tobacco plants back in the spring. So as far as I could tell, there was nothing else that I could do.

"You ain't never done this before," he said when we arrived at the barn. He reached up and got the reins off a hook. "Come on." He headed toward the stable. "You seen me drive these mules before."

"Yes, sir," I said, still oblivious as to what was going to be said next. This was Sunday, and this day had always been one of churching and resting.

"Well, I think you're big enough to drive a mule."

Even though I was confused, I was somewhat excited that he thought I was growing up, but I wasn't too sure about the task he was presenting. "Yessir," I said.

I crawled through the fence behind him. He put the bridle on Kate and led her out to the path. Now I was really floored. This was Sunday, and as I'd heard from him and many other grown ups, this was the Lord's Day.

"I know you can do this, because I know how much you pay attention to stuff," he said. "I just want to show you this to make sure you can do it."

My usual response here, "Yes, sir."

"You know, it's easy." He then put a harness on Kate, and we were now behind her with the reins in Daddy's hands.

Out in the path, he clucked to the mule: "Click, Click. Get up," he said as he lightly tapped the mule with the reins. The mule started forward. "Whoa," he said as he pulled back on both reins. The mule stopped.

He turned to me. "Now, let me see you do it," he said, handing the reins to me. I repeated what he'd just done, but when I tried to stop the mule, it didn't immediately happen. I had to pull extra hard to get her to stop. As it ended up, I was dragged to a halt. "That's good," Daddy assured me. He took over the reins. "That was the hard part," he said. "The easy part is gittin' them to go in different directions."

Again, he demonstrated. "Come on, git up," he instructed the mule as he again lightly tapped her with the reins. "Gee," he said when he tightened the right rein. The mule turned right and kept going. He then said "Haw" as he pulled the left rein, and the mule turned left. Of course, I was now wondering which behavior caused the mule to go in different directions? Was it what Daddy said—"Gee" and "Haw"? Or was it what he did with the reins? I was betting that it was the latter, and had nothing to do with what he was saying.

"Here, you try it," he told me. I didn't dare test my theory in front of him though. So I said and did exactly as he had, and successfully passed his test for learning to drive a mule. But I still didn't know what this had to do with me having a new job assignment.

Daddy continued to talk to me while he put the mule back in the stable. "I wanted to make sure you knew all this 'cause you'll be trucking tobacco for us—starting tomorrow," he said, sounding gleeful. I didn't know how I felt, but it damn sure wasn't gleeful. As a matter of fact, I was unable to form a thought even distantly related to what he had just told me. Of course, I said the usual "Yes, sir."

On the way back to the house, Daddy explained to me what the initial steps would entail in preparing the truck for the croppers to put tobacco on. I would unfold the burlap curtain that wrapped the eight "truck rounds" (long, thick, wooden, peg-like pieces with nails in the top) and insert each in one of the metal attachments on the sides of the truck. Finally, I would open the burlap curtain and attach it to the nails on the truck rounds.

It was about time for dinner when we finished, so instead of going back to play, I went on in the house. Apparently Daddy and Mother had already discussed this new assignment for me, because when we reached the house, the first thing he said to Mother was "We got a new truck driver." She smiled just like he did when he informed me. So I knew it had to be a grown-up-parental conspiracy. All I could do was say to myself, *Okay, we'll see how it goes.*

In addition to me becoming a part of the workforce, Daddy informed me that the croppers would be him, Uncle Jack, and two men from the community. At the shelter, the workers would be Mother, Aunt Ada, Aunt Mabel, Grandpa, and five women from the community.

But there was a brighter side to all of this. It meant that I wouldn't have to be responsible for two baby sisters. With the mules, it shouldn't really be a problem. What could go wrong? I could avoid those ass-whippings. Plus, it did make me feel kind of proud, being assigned something that was so important. I guess I was really glad that Daddy had this kind of confidence in me. I couldn't wait for tomorrow to come so I could tell Uncle Jack.

The next morning, I got up on my own. At the table, Daddy looked at me, still with excitement in his eyes, and said, "This is it." Then he began to give me additional instructions. "You'll go to the field with us, and once we get the first load, you'll be on your way. It's just taking a truck of tobacco to the shelter and leaving it, getting an empty truck and bringing it back to the field, getting the truck that we'll have loaded, and taking that one to the shelter. And sometimes, you'll be told to bring some water to the field."

By now I figured that I knew what the routine would be, but I didn't say anything. Daddy and I finished breakfast and headed out the door. I was very excited because there was something new that was about to happen with me. And I knew that Uncle Jack would soon be along, and I could tell him about my new job.

Sure enough, he was coming up the road; I even went to meet him. Before we reached each other, he yelled to me, "You ready to drive that truck, boy?" My heart sank. I realized that all of them had gotten together on this. Everybody knew but me. I simply gave the right answer: "Yes, sir."

So it wasn't just a parental conspiracy; it was a total grown-up conspiracy. Uncle Jack continued, with laughter, "I guess you think you're 'bout grown now, huh?" He laughed some more. "But don't worry," he said. "We gon work you like a man."

Uncle Jack walked on to the tobacco field. Daddy hooked the mules up, and we each drove one. I followed, sitting on the curtain-covered truck rounds just like he did. The other croppers were already in the field when we got there.

The men put the curtain up on the truck that Daddy drove, and started cropping the first load of the season, my first load as a truck driver. And like Daddy had instructed me, while they were cropping, I put the curtain up on that second truck so it would be ready for them to start loading when I left with the truck in front. It wasn't long before they'd finished loading their truck; tobacco was piled so high that they put a cover on top to keep it from falling out. "Come on, Junior," Daddy yelled to me. This time there were no more instructions. All he said

when I climbed onto the front of the truck and took the reins was: "Be careful."

I was on my way. I thought of a lot of stuff as I drove back to the shelter with my first load as a truck driver. This was huge. They trusted me to deliver this and follow the routine that had been drilled into me.

As I neared the shelter, I heard one of the women say, "Here comes the truck." They realized that I was a part of their workforce, and they smiled and commented that they were so proud of me. But I'm sure that Mother and Grandpa enjoyed those congratulatory comments more than I did.

In reality, I wanted to go play. But at least it was something different. It was definitely different from changing diapers and toting plants from the plant bed to the fields in buckets and tow sacks.

The first trips went smooth enough. I guess I had my mind on what I was doing. But in the afternoon, my mind seemed to go blank. I couldn't remember a thing. The croppers requested jars of water twice that morning, and I delivered. The afternoon was a different story. After I forgot the water the first time, Daddy simply said to just bring it the next time. The next time, I forgot it again. That's when it all hit the fan. Daddy told me that if I forgot one more time, he was going to have something waiting for me that I wasn't going to like. Guess what? I forgot it again. I didn't remember until I had turned onto the rows that they were cropping. I was about twenty-five feet in the row, with no room to turn around. Of course, I panicked!

I turned the mule to the left, across several rows of tobacco, and went back to the shelter and got that water. When I was returning to the field, the closer I got, the more I heard Daddy. He was livid. I turned into the field and I could see him. He was ranting and I was scared. "Look at these four rows!" he screamed. "Look at them! This is money I can't afford to lose!" He was behaving like the other croppers weren't even there. I didn't want to go any farther, but I knew that I had to. The other croppers were quiet as they allowed Daddy to fume. When I was almost where they were, Daddy hadn't settled down, but he wasn't as loud as he was before. I didn't say a word. I stopped the mule and headed for the loaded truck. "Wait a minute" Daddy said to me camly. I was shaking, big time, because I figured that he was going to knock the hell out of me. I thought that this was so egregious that he wouldn't get a switch to me, but use his fists instead. But he stood there quietly, looking eerily calm. "Why did you destroy them rows?" he asked.

"'Cause I forgot the water again," I stammered.

He said, "Okay," and went back to work.

The other two croppers seemed to put forth great effort to not pay attention to what was going on. But Uncle Jack was at least halfway encouraging. He got the reins and handed them to me when I climbed on the truck, and said, "You be careful now."

The next morning, Daddy didn't mention the previous day. It was apparent that he had discussed it with Mother, as she informed me that I would go back to my babysitting gig. Daddy had hired a new truck driver named Lewis. I figured that his staff was set for the remainder of the summer. Plus, I also took it to mean that Daddy had forgiven me.

In spite of the difficulties that came with my babysitting job, at least it was familiar. I only had to worry about two other people—little people—and they didn't make demands of me like them damn grown ups did.

With me out of the way, Daddy began to work with a smile on his face.

The week's work was completed shortly after noon on Wednesday. I didn't know if it was Daddy's way of celebrating the fact that he had a full and reliable crew or not, but instead of moving to the next task, Daddy announced to Mother that he was going to the store in Hugo. And I was absolutely astounded when he invited me to go with him.

Hugo consisted of a fairly large general store and a sawmill. The proprietor of this establishment was Buddy Smalls. Black folks called him Mr. Buddy. Buddy Smalls was an olive-complexion man who stood about five feet at the most, and he was very muscular. He had a head full of black hair and also had thick black hairs on his arms. Daddy and I were in a line where people were buying ice cream. When we got to the counter, Mr. Buddy was scraping the bottom of a deep ice cream container. By reaching to the bottom, he had ice cream matted in those hairs on his arm. He tapped the ice cream scoop on the side of a cup to dislodge it. Then he used his fingers to wipe the scoop clean. Next, he deposited that in the cup. Finally, he said to me, "Here, boy, you want this?"

I said, "No! I don't want that!"

I saw a look of consternation like I had never seen before come over Daddy's face. He frantically said, "Take it, Junior! Take it! It's good. It's real good." Reluctantly, I accepted the cup of ice cream. Later, Daddy told me that whenever white folks offer you something, accept it whether you want it or not. Based on that experience, I later realized that Daddy was only teaching me how to survive in the unfair and racially prejudiced environment in which we were living.

Seemingly Daddy's bad luck didn't end with the truck driving debacle. On Monday, two of his handers informed him that Wednesday would be their last day working for him, because they had gotten jobs closer to their homes. This definitely put Daddy in another bind. He had to find somebody to take their places, starting the following week.

He asked around, and eventually found two men to fill those vacancies. Both of them were mentally challenged. One was named Altondo Kane, and the other one was a friend of his, J.T. Mayes. At the end of their first day, Daddy raved about what good workers they were, that these were two of the best workers he had ever hired.

But on the second day, Altondo did not show up, and J.T. only worked about two hours before he abruptly walked off. Naturally I, a seven-year-old, was pressed into service. If I could have disappeared, I would have, but I was stuck. However, I only had to do this for the remainder of that day, because the next morning, when I was preparing to go to work, Mother informed me that Daddy had hired two women.

One of the women looked like an older version of Estelle. I noticed her too, but I definitely didn't stare at her like I had done with Estelle. However, for some reason I did notice her in particular. Her name was Flora Mae. I'm not sure if Grandpa knew her from somewhere in the past, but it was obvious that he took a liking to her. Flora Mae was about half Grandpa's age. She was a tall, light-skinned woman who dipped snuff and wore ragged sneakers. Sometimes there would be traces of brown wet snuff stains on her mouth.

I was sure that I didn't know how grown-ups thought, but I couldn't figure out why Grandpa was interested in her. I also noticed that after Flora Mae was hired, Grandpa stopped using his walking stick when he was around her.

Wow! How strange!

## MID-JULY 1945

On this particular Thursday, the crew finished putting in tobacco about mid-morning; therefore, the remainder of the week was free. Of course Daddy and Mother went on to the next farming assignment.

Grandpa took a bath, put on some dressy clothes, and was ready to go visiting. But first, he got a dozen eggs and a small slab of bacon from the kitchen and put those in a brown paper bag. Next he reached in the corner and got his derby from the hat rack and went up the road to visit Flora Mae.

Much later in the day, I was out near the tobacco field,

throwing clods of dirt, trying to hit some cans. I looked up the road and saw Grandpa returning. Daddy was at the barn. I could hear him sharpening hoes, as he always insisted on having his tools ready to use on the spur of the moment.

Since I had known Grandpa, he had always walked slow. But on this particular day, he seemed to move even slower. And it didn't appear to be the hot weather that had him walking like that. His condition was so noticeable that I stopped playing and headed to meet him. When I got closer, I also noticed that he looked awfully tired. His shirt was fastened in the wrong button holes, and one shoe was untied.

Usually when he would come home after any of his visits, he'd have something to say to me. Not this time. Daddy was noticing too. I looked down where Daddy was, and he had stopped filing. Now he, too, was standing straight up, also focusing on Grandpa. Since Grandpa didn't seem to know I was even there, I went back to throwing dirt.

I was still at it when Daddy came along on his way to the house. "Did you hit anything yet?" he asked.

"Not many," I told him.

"Your granddaddy looked awful tired, didn't he?"

"I reckon so."

"Yeah, he looked beat," Daddy continued. He reached in his shirt pocket and got that pack of Camel cigarettes; then he pulled one from the pack. I thought he was just going to watch me throw and maybe tell me how to be more accurate.

Instead, he continued talking about Grandpa. He struck the match and cupped the flame, lit up, shook the flame out, and tossed the match aside. "Boy, your Granddaddy is tired! He's real tired!"

I said, "Yes, sir." I was focused on my throwing, and already knew that Grandpa was tired, which meant that Daddy didn't need to keep telling me. But he continued anyway.

"Do you know why he's so tired?" he asked.

"No, sir," I answered.

"He's tired like that 'cause it's been years since he's been with a woman." Daddy smiled, puffed the cigarette, and headed on to the house. Of course I still had no clue as to what he was talking about.

## AUGUST 1945

More than a new school year was about to begin. This time, it would be two of us heading off to school. Yep, Katie would be going. She had been quietly excited, as was her nature. As a matter of fact, she never even talked about it. She always just took things in stride.

The night before school opened, the first thing I did was get the shoes that Daddy bought me at the end of last school year. I pulled them from under the bed, still in the box, and blew the dust off. This I had been looking forward to, because they were basically brand-new! I got a rag and dusted them; sure enough, the original shine and smell were still there.

The next morning we all got up early. Katie was in one room dressing, and I was in another room dressing. Marie kept going from room-to- room to see who would finish first, like it was a contest. The last time she came to my room, she said:

"She beat you." Of course there was no race going on between us, but my progress had been hampered by some freak accident of nature. I was fully dressed, except for my shoes. They were now too small.

I went to Daddy, holding a shoe in each hand, and told him what the situation was. He insisted that I try to put them on again so that he could see for himself, I guess. I did, and couldn't get much more than my toes in them. He looked on in disbelief. My feet had grown about two sizes during the three months we were out of school. He told me that I would have to go barefooted, and he would get me another pair later.

I put my shoes back in the box and gave them to him. Meanwhile, it was time for breakfast. Mother made us some sausage and egg biscuits, and gave us a glass of milk. When we finished eating and it was about time for us to leave, Marie began pleading with Mother to let her go with us. Mother tried to explain to her that she was not old enough.

Then Mother turned to Katie and me. "Let me see how you look," she said as we prepared to go out the door. Katie had on one of the two new outfits Mother had bought her from Dalton's General Store. And I had on a pair of my new overalls and a blue shirt. "Okay," she said, after looking at us up and down, and straightening Katie's collar. Out the door we went, and merged with my group of friends, who also had some new sisters and brothers.

School was now in session, and here I was in third grade. Some of the kids who I was in first grade with the previous year thought I was in the wrong place when they saw me with third graders. Most of them were in the second grade group, but a few had missed the boat (were still in first grade). Of course what grade I was in did not remain the focus very long. In no time flat, Mrs. Matthews was her old self again. She was teaching all three grades, taking names, and whipping ass at the end of each day.

Not only was school back in session, but Bilbo seemed to go through a personality change. He began chasing kids in the morning and afternoon as they passed by our house, going to and coming from school. Daddy decided to tie him to the porch. To do this, he bought a fifty-foot chain.

## SEPTEMBER 1945

On the second Sunday in September, since there was no church service, my parents could get some rest if they chose to. For my sisters and me, it would be extra playtime.

Around ten o'clock, Grandpa announced that he was going down the road to visit Uncle Jack for a spell, and he invited Mother to go along with him. She accepted his invitation and said that she would take the girls. Before I could even consider accompanying them, which I had no interest in, Daddy told me that I couldn't go because he and I had to feed the mules and possibly mend a fence.

We all left the house at the same time. It took Daddy and me about thirty minutes to get the feeding done. Then we went and checked the chicken coop for holes; fortunately for me, there were none.

As we were returning to the house, we saw a black sedan

speeding up the road, with dust flying everywhere. We stopped and looked, trying to figure out what the hurry was, and who was driving.

When the car got near our house, it slowed down. Then it turned in to our yard. "Somebody must be turning around," Daddy said, as if he needed to explain. But the only thing wrong with that explanation was that the car didn't turn around. The driver saw us and sat there and waited. We had no clue as to what this was all about. But we both at least knew that it was some white folk, because no colored folks had nice cars like that down this way. By now, we had reached the edge of our yard. Not only did we see that it was white folks, but it was a carload of white folks, white men, to be exact.

The dust was still settling when we reached the yard. We could see that the men inside were carrying what appeared to be shotguns or rifles; all I could determine for sure was that they were long guns. I didn't know what to expect, but I wasn't scared. Daddy seemed to be at ease too. The driver had on a white T-shirt, with the sleeves rolled up and a pack of cigarettes tucked beneath the left sleeve. On his head was what looked like a crumpled Stetson hat. He seemed to be the leader.

"Hey, boy," he said to Daddy. "All you coloreds need to stay home 'til we catch up with Altondo Kane. He killed a white woman last night." Daddy never said a word; he just nodded, acknowledging the communiqué.

Then some of the other men in the car began to talk amongst themselves. "We gon git him," one said.

"Ain't no way in hell he gon git away wit it," another one volunteered.

The car backed up, turned around, and headed down the road. "Maybe they won't kill him," Daddy said. "And maybe he didn't do it," he continued hopefully.

We had been home about fifteen minutes when Mother, Grandpa, and the girls returned. Mother said that they saw the car racing down the road and turning in to our yard. "Who was it?" she asked Daddy.

"A car full of white men," he told her. "I didn't recognize none of 'em."

"What did they want?"

"They said for all colored folk to stay home 'til they catch Altondo," he said.

Grandpa then joined the inquisition. "What did they say Altondo did?"

"It must've been something awfully bad," Mother interrupted.

"They said he killed a white woman last night," Daddy told her.

Mother was momentarily speechless as she stood there staring at the wall. "Oh my God!" she finally exclaimed. "Everybody knows that he's a little off, but he couldn't have done that."

Daddy assured her with a final remark: "They said he did."

I think Grandpa saw that he couldn't get any more questions in because of Mother, so he just listened.

"Did they say who the white woman was?" Mother asked.

"No, they didn't mention that."

As Mother talked, she began preparing our lunch. I went

outside for a while, thinking about what would happen when those men caught Altondo. I must've lost track of time because it seemed like as soon as I got outside, Mother was calling us to come and eat lunch. Daddy, Grandpa, and I washed our hands in the basin after the girls had finished. Then we all sat down to eat. Daddy blessed the food, and before he said "Amen," he asked the Lord to "keep Altondo Kane."

The next morning, as we were getting ready for the new week, we were about to sit down for breakfast when we heard someone in the yard calling for Daddy. As he was heading to the door, the rest of us went to the window to see who it was. "Mr. Namon!" the man yelled. It was our neighbor, Mr. Lawson, the sharecropper from the adjoining farm. Daddy went out on the porch and greeted him. He seemed to be out of breath, so Daddy invited him in. "How y'all?" he asked. Mother and Grandpa said "good morning" to him. Being children in the group, we knew not to answer.

He finally began to breathe easier. "Did y'all hear 'bout Altondo?" he asked.

"Yeah," Daddy said. "We heard about it yesterday when a car load of white men came and told us that coloreds need to stay home 'til they caught him."

"Yeah, they came by my house too," Mr. Lawson said. "But later on, a couple of fellows from across the creek came over. They heard that Altondo might've killed a white woman, but it must've been an accident."

"Did they say who the white woman was?" Grandpa asked.

"It was Mr. Roy Harris's wife," he said. "You know where

they live, right up the road." Mother began to shake her head as she put her hand over her mouth.

Mr. Lawson continued: "They said that her husband paid Altondo to scare her, to just beat her up a little, said his wife found out he was going with a younger white woman in the neighborhood. And when she asked him about it, he got really mad and got in his car and sped up the road…but if Altondo did kill her, you know he didn't know what he was doing though. And if Mr. Harris paid him, you know he didn't pay him much."

Daddy seemed to measure his remark before he responded. "Yeah, but if he did pay him, whatever it was, he won't get a chance to ever spend a dime."

Mother got us back into the kitchen to eat while Daddy, Grandpa, and Mr. Lawson continued their conversation.

Two or three days later, Altondo was apprehended at the county line. Authorities said that he was trying to flee.

From that point on, Altondo Kane was the major topic of discussion. And I figured that this was all a part of keeping up with what was happening in regard to Altondo's legal situation.

## NOVEMBER 1945

While the focus was on Altondo at school and in the community, there was something else that served to help me not worry about what Altondo's fate would be. For one thing, November was pretty cold. Consequently, we had a fire in the fireplace on a regular basis.

And being barely literate, Grandpa was very impressed

with my ability to read so well as a seven-year-old. He would ask me to read to him at least twice a week.

My sisters and I would gather around the fireplace, and I would read to the three of them. On this particular night, Grandpa arrived a couple of minutes late. My sisters and I were already sitting on the floor. We were roasting peanuts and baking sweet potatoes in the ashes when Grandpa eased into his rocking chair.

Right as I started to read, Grandpa pulled out a plug of tobacco and cut a chew with his pocketknife. He continued to listen as he returned the plug and knife to his pocket. Meanwhile, the girls were watching Grandpa. Within a few minutes, Grandpa began to periodically spit into the fireplace. Those red embers would sizzle and fade. Then they would return to their original glow.

After the third spit, Katie said: "Grandpa, you spittin' on our tatos!"

He replied, "Oh hush up, child! You ain't gon eat the peelin'."

The very next time that Grandpa asked me to read to him, we were all in our usual spots. He pulled up his rocking chair, but this time, he had a tin cup to spit in. That really showed me how thoughtful he was.

On this particular night, he asked me to read something out of my North Carolina history book. I began reading and when I looked up, I noticed that Grandpa seemed to be listening more and more intently. "What's wrong, Grandpa?" I asked.

"Just keep reading, boy," he told me. I obeyed and continued reading. And when I read a passage about how happy the slaves were, I was shocked at Grandpa's reaction. He said, "Let me see that book." I handed the book to him, and he angrily hurled it into the roaring fire. He said that his mother had been whipped so badly, so many times by her slave master, that her back resembled a washboard.

### December 1945

After a few months of school, things were going as smooth as could be expected, both at school and at home. Marie had reconciled that this was her new reality, being at home during the day while Katie and I were at school.

Grandpa had really settled in as a part of the family as he, Mother, and Daddy kept very busy with harvesting the crops. The one negative was the situation with Altondo.

When all of the crops had been harvested, I knew that we'd had a good year because I heard Daddy bragging about the corn overflowing in the barn, and the pounds of tobacco he had sold. Plus, he had three bales of cotton that he was waiting to sell the following spring instead of this fall.

For me, Thanksgiving had also been a nice-enough short break from the monotony of school, and once I returned for the stretch before Christmas, I felt rejuvenated. But the last day before taking that Christmas vacation, it happened.

Class was in progress. Mrs. Matthews was teaching her primary class, as the other two grades were doing the work that she required when she was with another group. About midway through her lesson, she came all the way across the room, book and ruler in hand, and stopped in front of my desk. I didn't look up because I was afraid to. I could feel the other students looking at her, and at me. "Moses," she began, "when school is out, you need to stay in your seat, and see me."

I said, "Yes ma'am." But to myself, I said, *She's at it again. She needs to beat my ass at least once more before we get out, maybe to take her through the holidays.*

At recess, I told Katie to go on home without me and to tell Mother and Daddy that Mrs. Matthews wanted me to stay for a few minutes after school.

When the bell rang at the end of the day, I sat and waited as Mrs. Matthews ushered students out the door. At no time had she wished anybody a single pleasantry like "Have a good Christmas" or "Have a safe Christmas vacation." And at no time did she smile or pretend that this was a joyful time for anybody.

When she came back into the classroom, she came directly toward me. I pretended to be busy reading from a textbook. "Moses," she began, "here's a letter for your mother." She pulled an envelope from the notebook she was carrying. "It says that when you return from Christmas vacation, you will be going into fourth grade."

Again, I was flabbergasted! But maybe more than anything, I was relieved. I couldn't figure out what kind of person Mrs. Matthews was. This seemed like a reward; then again, I knew that she didn't reward anybody, for anything. I was convinced all over again that she had a real disdain for children. The only other conclusion I could arrive at was that in some kind of way, I had earned it. Maybe the whipping that she gave me was simply because she had a need to whip somebody who was NOT giving her trouble. I coulddn't ever figure her out, so I stopped trying.

After she told me that I could leave, I walked home alone. There was no other student to be found. But I understood. On the last day of school before a long holiday, you wanted to get out of that place. But this was good for me. I got a chance to be by myself and think. This was a nice Christmas present. I would be out of Mrs. Matthews' class, away from her switches and rulers, away from being subject to her punishment.

I also thought of how much I had learned in her classroom. There was so much more than the academics. In spite of all the bad, I was pleased.

When I got home, Mother, Katie, and Marie were waiting in the kitchen. Mother had that look on her face that said, "What did you do this time?" which also meant "I got another ass-whipping waiting for you."

I smiled. When I did, Katie smiled too, a smile of relief on my behalf, because she knew firsthand what a beating was like at home. I went on to share the good news as I was handing Mother the letter. She read it and stuffed it into her apron pocket, and as far as I was concerned, it was time to start Christmas vacation.

On top of the good news from Mrs. Matthews, I remembered that Mother and Daddy had let us pick out toys from the Sears and Roebuck catalogue. I was looking forward to this particular Christmas. And yes, things fell into place for us in 1945, because when Santa stopped by our house, we got everything that we had asked for.

Something else happened during the holiday break. Christmas was on Tuesday. Then on Friday, Mother's baby brother, Leon, and his wife, Addie, moved into Uncle Bob's old house. Other than the fact that this was Mother's baby brother, there was no significance to me, mainly because they didn't have any kids, so there would not be an addition for me to babysit.

### DECEMBER 31, 1945/JANUARY 1, 1946

A few days before New Year's Day, Daddy told me that he wanted me to help him barbecue a pig for the holiday. I was tickled to death that he asked me, because in my mind, he was no longer treating me like a little boy. Besides, I had just turned eight years old and had been promoted to fourth grade, so I thought that I was just about half grown.

On New Year's Eve, Daddy killed a pig, dressed it, and laid it out for the upcoming ritual. We collected some dry hickory limbs, and later in the day, we dug a pit and laid some wagon rods across it for a grate to hold the carcass. Then Daddy borrowed four long, slender poles from a neighbor. These would be used to flip the pig over after it had finished cooking on one side. The way that this worked was to push two poles beneath the front and back legs on both sides of the pig. Next, the other two poles would be placed the length of the pig above the first two. There would be one person at the rear and one person at the head. They would grasp the two poles in the left and right hands. Finally, they would flip that pig over by crossing either left over right, or right over left, depending on which way the pig was turned.

Daddy and I put the pig on the pit at about ten o'clock that night. He showed me how and where to shovel the hot embers. Then to my surprise he went in the house and stayed a long time. He only came back out for the New Year celebration. He and a couple of neighbors flipped the pig over, and before going back inside, he asked me if I wanted to go to bed. My response was an emphatic "No siree!" There was no way I was going to miss barbecuing my first pig.

We finished barbecuing about eight o'clock in the morning, and to this day that was the best barbecue I ever ate.

## January 1946

The day after the New Year arrived, Uncle Leroy and Aunt Addie were blessed with a baby boy. They named him Leroy, Jr. Of course we visited, and I vividly recalled having welcomed Johnny Wayne in that same room two years earlier.

Christmas vacation was over, and it was time to return to the grind of getting educated. Since New Year's Day was on Tuesday, our first day back to school was on that Wednesday. In a way it was like a first day for me all over again. I was a bit nervous about going to my new class, where the other kids would be older and bigger than me. But I wasn't scared otherwise, because I knew that I could hold my own in the learning sphere.

However, I did realize that it would feel rather awkward

arriving at school with my friends, all from Mrs. Matthews' class, then me going to a different classroom. I had thought about it over the holidays, and I knew that this was the way it would be. At least I knew what to expect, formally and informally; plus, I knew some of the kids in that other class.

Even though I didn't know Mrs. Woodard, I had heard about her. And all reports were good. As a matter of fact, rumor had it that she wasn't nearly as mean as Mrs. Matthews. That was the beautiful part.

When my friends came along, Katie and I were standing by the road waiting. Knowing that we would no longer be classmates, eventually the conversation turned to my now being a fourth grader. I tried not to show my nervousness by pretending that I was looking forward to my new situation. "Ain't you a little scared?" one of them asked.

"Naw," I replied. Thinking how Daddy would probably respond, I recalled his quotes from General MacArthur. "Being scared is for cowards," I told them, and that seemed to do the trick, as the conversation shifted back to how our holidays went.

Once my friends and I arrived at school, they went into their classroom, and I pretended not to be too nervous as I departed and headed to my new class. When I walked in, there were several boys and girls already there. They all stared. The teacher was sitting at her desk off to the side of the door. I went over and handed her the envelope with my information from Mrs. Matthews. Without even opening it, she said, "Good morning, Moses." She placed the envelope in her desk drawer and said, "Mrs. Matthews told me to be expecting you. I already have your seat right over there in the second row," she said, pointing to that particular seat. "That's my fourth grade section." I thanked her and went and sat down.

Even though I knew some of the other students in this class, they still stared, probably because they couldn't believe that they had such a small student in their midst. But they were all nice to me, and as time passed, most of them would prove to be very helpful in general. Early on, there were no attempts to pick on me, and there were no slights because of my size.

In addition to my perceptions of these new classmates, I also considered the new teacher, Mrs. Woodard. She was probably in her mid-forties, heavy-set, with dark skin. She also had a high backside and somewhat skinny legs. And her upper arms were flabby. Although she kept switches in the corner near her desk, I was told that she rarely used them.

A couple of weeks after I had been in her classroom, I had an experience that verified all good things that I had heard about her. One day I accidentally spilled some water on the floor. I was scared to death that I would get a beating, because at home Mother would have either beat me or slapped the living shit out of me. Seeing me trembling and crying, Mrs. Woodard wrapped her arms around me and said, "Moses, that's okay. It was an accident." I came to absolutely love that lady.

The Altondo Kane trial got underway in Kinston. Black folks from Lenoir and surrounding counties showed up. Most of them were convinced that it was unfair. However, in the end, Altondo was found guilty, and sentenced to death. But with the verdict being appealed to the State Supreme Court, there would be no action until the High Court could render a decision.

Meanwhile, life had to go on. Being in a new situation at school, my focus had to be on adjusting to that. But in spite of the goodness that I was experiencing in my new class, not all was peaches and cream. One of the first students I met when I reached fourth grade was a boy named Zeb. He was a twelve-year-old. Yep, he was a big twelve-year-old. He was one of those kids from Cottington Farm, which meant that he was tough and mean. At least that was the reputation they had, and a few of them lived up to it.

Cottington Farm was about a mile from where we lived, and when approached, the first thing to come into view was all of those shotgun shacks that the workers lived in. During the summer they partied and fought. I knew two people who were murdered there.

Zeb didn't say a lot. But when he did speak, he meant what he said. Most of the time his speaking consisted of ordering us smaller kids around. He would make a younger boy tote his books in the morning, and find a different one in the afternoon.

One day as we were leaving school, Zeb and some of his friends had stopped in the middle of the road. My friends and I went around them and kept going. After we had gotten a few yards past them, Zeb turned and said, "Junior, you wait. Come here." I couldn't imagine what he wanted. He'd never really said much to me before. I stopped, but I didn't go back. "Get over here!" he demanded. "It's your turn to carry my books!"

I refused. "I ain't carrying your books!" I told him, and started walking again.

By now everyone had stopped talking to each other and become spectators. I was quick to realize that things weren't going in my favor. When I continued to walk away, Zeb broke off a switch from a nearby tree and attempted to strike me with it.

I ran and he chased. Home was about three-tenths of a mile away, and as we approached my house, we both were barely jogging, but he was closing in on me.

When we ran into my yard, as he was reaching for me, I said, "Git 'im, Bilbo!" Ole Bilbo bolted from under the porch where he was napping and latched onto the back of Zeb's thigh when he tried to reverse direction. The only thing that saved Zeb was the fact that after a few feet, Bilbo reached the end of his fifty-foot chain.

As a reward for Bilbo protecting me, Daddy took the chain off. After he did, Bilbo was altogether different. He got along great with the other two dogs and the children in the neighborhood. He even confined himself to the yard. A few days later, we noticed that Bilbo didn't show up for lunch or for supper. We never saw Bilbo again. He had vanished, just as mysteriously as he had appeared.

It was the last week in January that I began to pay more attention to how Mrs. Woodard handled discipline. Two boys had gone off school grounds during class time. She found out that they did so in order to avoid her math class. That resulted in their being whipped with one of her two switches that she kept in the corner.

While it was not so rare for Mrs. Woodard to whip a student with a switch, what was refreshing to me was that she was not brutal in doing so. I think the most important difference between her and Mrs. Matthews was that she was fair, and not vicious. Also, in order for her to mete it out, a violation had to be perpetrated after numerous warnings had been issued, or the act committed had to be outlandish.

As for me, in order not to experience negative consequences, I always monitored my behavior very closely. Going into February, my second month in fourth grade, by my own estimation, I continued to be a model student. I believe what helped us as a class, more than anything else, was that Mrs. Woodard mixed her strictness with love and fairness.

Another thing that impressed me in my new class was something that I witnessed a couple of times. On each occasion, girls had gotten into trouble to the extent that whippings were warranted. The so-called boyfriends of those girls told Mrs. Woodard that they would take their punishment, and each time Mrs. Woodard honored their requests. Oh, by the way, Zeb and I had become friendly to each other.

Mother had chosen to prepare desserts this Sunday. Her two cakes were in a large cardboard box, and the three pies she had prepared were inside of a cooking pot. As usual, we arrived at church about fifteen minutes early. This gave everybody time to greet other parishioners and chat for a few minutes before service started. The women would always go inside while the men remained outside to talk. Of course on this particular morning, the men were talking about Altondo's conviction.

My cousins and I talked for a few minutes; then we went in and took our seats. We never sat together though, because we had a habit of getting in trouble by talking and not paying attention.

As for me, I had my personal "optional seating arrangement." This was a function of the temperature outside. In other words, how cold it was outside determined how hot the men would have the stove inside.

Plan A was my warm weather plan. This meant that I would sit somewhere near the center of the church. Plan B was my cold weather plan. This meant that I would sit near the door.

For this to make sense, one has to understand how the heating system was set up. The church was heated by a coal stove. The flue was held in place by a strand of haywire that extended from the ceiling. There was a lot of play in the wire (it was loose), and when people *got happy* and started shouting, the flue would start swaying, back and forth. When this happened, that flue looked as if it would fall any second. Thus, this was my reason for sitting so close to the exit, so I could escape if it fell.

I particularly hated it when Grandma Mary and Aunt Rudy shouted, because they were violent shouters. It seemed as if they would be trying to stomp a hole in the floor. On those occasions, not only was I worried about the flue falling, but also whether or not the whole damn church would cave in and burn down!

Other than my concerns about the heater, it was a regular quarterly meeting church service, and I survived again. There were testimonies and singing, prayers and singing, shouting and praying, sweating and hollering, and another prayer before church was over. We had our meal and went home.

## FEBRUARY 1946

February the third brought a new addition to our neighborhood. A few houses down the road, Uncle Jack and Aunt Mabel added a second son: Roger Hayes.

Also a couple of weeks later, we had the first hog killing that I can remember. When hog-killing time came around, numerous neighbors participated. Daddy and several other men killed four or five large hogs, some weighing as much as three hundred pounds.

As the men were cutting up the hogs, the women were digging holes in the ground so that they could empty the feces from the hogs' intestines; then they would pour hot water through the intestines, with one person holding the end of the organ open as another one poured. Even as an eight-year-old, I knew that the water was not hot enough to clean those things. Finally, they would start cooking several wash pots of chitterlings at a time. The stench was almost unbearable. To this day I do not eat chitterlings.

This ritual started in the morning and continued until it was almost dark. After the chitterlings were cooked, the women would use the same wash pots to cook meat skins and crackling. The men cut the meat for curing: ham, neck bones, hog heads, pig feet, pig ears, pork chops, and pieces for the women to grind up for sausage.

This was like a community party when families came together like this. Uncle Saul was a part of this hog-killing ritual. At first he bragged about his skills at butchering, and the other men took it as a joke. But then he started talking about how he was also an expert hunter. That part of his talk caused the laughter to diminish, but they still got some laughs in. Then what caused all the laughter to stop altogether was when he started talking about how good he was at training his hunting dogs. As I understood it, training hunting dogs was his passion. He had a reputation beyond the neighborhood as always having the best hunting dogs. I never did find out how he was able to have such capable dogs. But according to him and others, he was THE expert hunting dog trainer.

Daddy liked to hunt too, but he rarely had time for it. Maybe it was that conversation that motivated Daddy to make some time for himself and go hunting. Uncle Saul had a prized hunting dog that he adored. His name was Chase.

Daddy asked him if he could borrow Chase. Reluctantly, Uncle Saul agreed. He brought him over on a leash and told Daddy to be careful with him, because sometimes he might be so close to the prey that he could end up in the line of fire. Daddy thanked Uncle Saul, and assured him that he'd take good care of his dog. Additionally, Daddy told him that he was going to keep him inside a fence separated from Mac and Arthur. Daddy headed around back with Chase as Uncle Saul was walking out to the road.

Daddy had the opportunity to make use of Chase after breakfast Saturday morning. He had a big smile on his face, and he seemed so excited about this particular hunt. According to him, he'd never had access to a highly rated dog like this one. He usually had sub-performing hounds that were described as lazy at best.

Daddy got his gun and was off to the woods with Uncle Saul's prized hunting dog. He went to the thickest area at the end of the field, directly in back of our house. For about an hour at least, shots could be heard coming from down there.

When Daddy returned, he appeared to be even more gleeful than he was when he left. He had his gun slung over his shoulder, and four rabbits, hooked on a stick. Chase followed behind. "That's some dog," Daddy bragged. "I ain't never seen a dog that can do the things he can do. You talking 'bout flushing out rabbits? He's the best!"

I was happy for Daddy, but I had my own matters to attend to. So over the next few days, I forgot about Daddy's intrigue with and use of Uncle Saul's dog. I hadn't seen Chase, so I figured that he was still inside the fence or that Daddy had returned him to Uncle Saul.

When Uncle Saul came to the house several days later, Daddy told him that he had put the dog in the fence, but when he went to feed Chase one morning he was gone. He told Uncle Saul that he'd looked high and low, but had not been able to locate his prized dog. However, he said something that I thought was quite touching. First, he sincerely apologized to Uncle Saul. Then he promised Uncle Saul that he would replace his dog.

Needless to say, Uncle Saul was not happy about what he was being told, but he didn't make a scene about it.

## FEBRUARY 1946/ LAST WEEK

As well as virtually any kind of music, Daddy enjoyed listening to the news. I think that's what he depended on to stay abreast with not only what was happening locally, but also with what was going on across the globe.

On more than one occasion, I had heard him and some of the other men in the community having discussions. What I noticed was that when there was a discussion about local matters, they were all involved. But when the discussion moved beyond things local, Daddy would be holding court. And when they had questions about worldly topics outside of their regular discussions, they would seek out Daddy. I never could figure this out because he only had an eighth grade education.

And on this Wednesday evening, Daddy came in with an arm full of wood. He put most of it behind the stove, into the wood box. The few remaining pieces he inserted in the heater, which already had flames dancing about. He then tempered the grate so as to calm the flames and thus lessen the heat.

My sisters and I were scattered around the room, sitting on the floor, reading school books. Grandpa was outside somewhere, and Mother was in the kitchen. That's when Daddy went to turn the radio on.

I knew that Mother was baking cookies, and I figured that they ought to be ready about now. So, I closed my book and put it on the floor before heading to the kitchen. Katie and Marie saw what I was doing and followed.

When we arrived in the kitchen, Daddy had just gotten our battery-operated radio station to come in. Country music was blaring some Hank Williams music, my favorite. He turned it down a tad as I was asking Mother if the cookies were ready. But before she could answer, the music suddenly stopped. The announcer said, "We interrupt this program to bring you an important news bulletin." Everybody saw Daddy stop and get quiet; then he put his finger to his lips and got all of us hushed. The announcer continued, saying, "Altondo Kane has just been scheduled to the gas chamber in April of this year. I repeat: Altondo Kane has just been scheduled to the gas chamber in April of this year. Now, back to your local programming that is in progress."

The music continued; except now it seemed like a dark cloud had just settled overhead. I heard Mother ask Daddy, "Is there any way he can avoid being put to death?"

Daddy was slow to answer, but finally he did: "Yeah, but it ain't likely to happen. His case went all the way to the state supreme court, and they agreed with the lower court. So, that's pretty much it."

We all got cookies and returned to our studies.

The next morning, on our way to school, that was all we talked about—Altondo being sentenced to death. A few kids had no idea what the rest of us were talking about.

At school, after we did our devotion and before Mrs. Woodard started class, she asked, "Did any of you hear the latest news?" Most hands went up. "Okay, who can tell me what that news was?" A few hands remained up.

She called on a girl a couple of seats in front of me. "They gon send Altondo Kane to the gas chamber," the girl shared with the class.

"That's exactly right," Mrs. Woodard confirmed. "Thank you."

Then we went on and had a long discussion about what happened, and how it led to this. Surprisingly, only a few children did not know about the case. Over the course of the next few weeks, Mrs. Woodard not only taught us readin', 'ritin', and 'rithmatic, but she also taught us a few things about the law, including legal procedure.

And not to be overlooked was that after each day's teaching, Mrs. Woodard would encourage us to go home and "pray for Altondo."

As for me, I would also rush home from school each day and listen to the radio, hoping to hear that some of our prayers had been answered, and for some reason the powers that be had changed their minds about putting him to death.

### MARCH 1946/FIRST WEEK

Both at home and at school, our lives were pretty much consumed by Altondo's situation. But in those settings we also had our normal routines that served to distract us from becoming so invested in Altondo's circumstance that we were negatively impacted.

When March arrived, so did some warm weather. This

meant that we could walk to the store during recess and buy lunch if we had some money. I didn't have any money, plus Mother always made me a molasses biscuit for lunch. But what I would do on my way to school was toss it in the woods, because I knew we'd be going to the store, and students who had money would share with those of us who didn't. We would get nutritious snacks like Mary Jane candy, cookies, cupcakes, and Royal Crown colas.

But one Wednesday, as our daily routine was progressing, we were walking down the dirt road, headed to the highway where the store was on the corner. We were in two groups, acting silly and having fun. A group of girls was in front, skipping merrily along. My group of five boys was about twenty-five feet back.

Normally, only a few slow-driving cars came on this road. And when they did, the worse thing that happened was that they would kick up a lot of dust. But on this particular day, there came a car speeding down the road. Apparently, my group heard and saw the car and moved to the side. The girls obviously didn't hear it.

The car passed us, and merely brushed two of the girls. But it ran smack dab into Lisa Prince, tossing her high into the air. When her body hit the surface, it made such an indescribable sound. Crying and screaming had begun. Folks came running out from nearby houses while we kids gathered around Lisa. As she lay on her back, she turned side to side twice. Then she relaxed, with her eyes open.

In the midst of all of this, Mr. Grady Harmon arrived and

shooed us kids away as our teachers were arriving. He then covered her body with his jacket. Mrs. Matthews ushered us back to school, and Mrs. Woodard and several other grown ups attended to the injured. Our fun scene had turned into tragedy.

When we got back to school, needless to say, there was no playing and joking. We were all in shock. After about an hour, Mrs. Woodard returned and confirmed the worst news imaginable. Lisa didn't survive. The people who came in the ambulance had made it official. So now we were dealing with duel issues, Lisa's death and Altondo's situation.

It took us several weeks to accept what had happened to our classmate. In our classroom discussions, it was obvious that it deeply affected all of us. Of course we had to move on. Again, part of our therapeutic behavior was the matter of getting back into routines, at school and at home.

Then, there was one particular off-the-cuff bit of information that Mother shared with Daddy one evening at the dinner table. While we were eating, we heard several dogs running into the woods, barking.

Apparently that reminded Mother of some information about Uncle Saul's prized hunting dog that he loaned Daddy. I had forgotten all about it. I knew that Daddy had replaced Uncle Saul's dog some ten days ago, but that was all I knew. Mother went on to tell Daddy about a report she'd received from Aunt Kathy concerning the replacement dog.

According to that report, Uncle Saul took the dog out hunting, and they saw a rabbit. Uncle Saul tried to sic the dog on the rabbit. The rabbit made a turn and seemed to be coming toward them. The replacement dog turned and ran. Grandpa looked under-eyed as he loudly sipped his coffee. Daddy never offered a response, though he did seem embarrassed. He acknowledged that he heard what Mother said by simply nodding his head.

Mother told me later that Daddy had sold Uncle Saul's dog.

## April 1946

Having gotten our lives back to being somewhat normal after Lisa Prince's death, along came April. That threw us for another loop, even though we knew it was coming.

This was the month for Altondo's execution. During the first week, the radio stations would give several reports during the day. The next two weeks, reports were more frequent. But in the final week, it seemed like they were in countdown mode. They would inform their listeners of how many more days Altondo had to live. And on the last few days of his life, the radio stations gave hourly reports.

Finally, on the day before his scheduled date with the gas chamber, there was even more reporting. Those reports included what time he got out of bed, what he had for breakfast, what he ate for lunch, which preacher visited and prayed with him, and what he had for dinner. The time of death was set for ten o'clock the next morning.

We were out of school the next day, which was on a Friday. Mother was at home with the girls, and Daddy delayed his appointment in the fields, as he was determined to be at home so that he could keep up with the news on Altondo. I was sitting in the kitchen reading and listening to our battery-operated radio. It was on WFHT, with the racist host Harold Simms. He was doing what amounted to "blow-by-blow." About nine thirty, I was joined by Mother, Daddy, and Grandpa. Then two neighbors came.

This time, WFHT brought on the "Last Report" before death was due. The announcer told about Altondo's slow, nervous walk to the death chamber, and how he was strapped into the chair. Finally, a few minutes past ten o'clock, the announcer said: "Altondo Kane, from Lenoir County, was pronounced dead."

Nobody spoke for several minutes. Then they all filed out of the room, silently.

For a long time, what happened to Altondo lingered with me. I recalled some horror stories about the lynching of black men and boys, but those had been things that happened in distant places, even as far away as South Carolina and Georgia. This was a person from our community. Altondo was one of us, handicap and all. It made me think about Nigger Head Swamp and that the story I heard most often was probably true. I had heard horrible stories about the reasons that black men and boys had been lynched. And most of those had nothing to do with committing crimes. They were lynched for not saying "Yes, sir" to white men, for not showing "proper respect," and for "looking" at white women.

I had been around Altondo, and had seen him in the community; but for one exception, his handicap, he didn't seem to be any different than the rest of us. I had been around other handicapped people too, and none of them were bad people.

They were just a little different. Everybody accepted that. But to know that Altondo, who'd worked for Daddy, had been executed was not easy to make sense of.

Of course, I was not the only one who had to deal with this rotten feeling. At school, Mrs. Woodard again was doing all she could to help us get through what had happened. For the next several weeks, there seemed to be a void in her classroom because that trial and execution, plus Lisa's death, had taken up so much of our discussions.

However, as life goes, the school and the community pulled together and moved forward.

## MAY 1946

It was on Saturday, the first weekend in May. Daddy and I had gone to the cornfield to pull some weeds. We had worked a couple of hours when Daddy told me that I could go back to the house. That was music to my ears.

As I neared the house, I saw Mother at the clothesline. Her basket was almost empty, as she was finishing hanging out clothes. When I got closer to the house, I could hear voices. It was Katie and Marie. It was apparent that they were not having a friendly conversation. They were in the midst of a heated argument. The loudest voice I heard was Marie's. Then the verbalization stopped, and there was the sound of banging and thudding. Before I could get to the house, Mother, obviously hearing the same sounds, stopped hanging out clothes and was going in the door right before I arrived. She grabbed each of my sisters by the neck, giving them a tongue-lashing.

"You both know better—just stand right there," she said, as she motioned each of them to a neutral corner (opposite sides of the room). Mother headed out the door to get a weapon (a switch). Of course I knew what that meant. They were about to get the whipping of their lives.

When Mother re-entered the room with that angry look on her face and the switch in her hand, I thought back to the times in Mrs. Woodard's classroom when those boys valiantly stood in for their girlfriends. Out of nowhere, obviously without even thinking, I said, "Mother, I'll take their beatings for them."

With the look of anger replaced by one of shock, she responded, "You will? Are you sure?"

I said, "Yes, ma'am."

I stood there as the girls looked on; they too were in disbelief. Standing next to me, and facing the opposite direction, Mother gripped my left wrist with her left hand, and with the switch in her right hand, she commenced to beat the hell out of me. It seemed like that whipping went on for at least five minutes. When she finished, she was tired, and I was tired, sweating, and hurting.

Needless to say, in the midst of my pain and agony, I made a decision. As much as I loved my sisters, from that moment forward, they would be on their own. Being mindful of my ass getting lit up for taking my sisters' punishment, I think I subconsciously stayed away from them as much as possible for the next several days. I actually found myself spending more time with Grandpa.

A week later, my sisters and I were on better terms. We were playing out near the woodpile when Grandpa came out the door with a small paper bag with some items in it, and an empty shopping bag. We didn't notice anything special until we realized that Grandpa had put his bags down and had begun to try to catch one of the hens inside the pen. He went inside the enclosure and shut the gate. He continually tried to sneak up on any hen that was near him, but each time the hen would escape. Grandpa got exhausted. He'd wipe sweat from his brow and try again. My sisters and I just stood and watched as we laughed. But Grandpa appeared to be impervious to us. Finally he gave up. He got his walking stick and the smaller bag and headed on up the road.

Later in the afternoon, Mr. Jones stopped by to see Daddy. I overheard him tell Daddy what his father-in-law's visit looked like when he went to visit Flora Mae. He said that each time before he got in view of Flora Mae's house, Grandpa would go into the woods and put his walking stick behind a tree. Then he'd come back out and continue to Flora Mae's house walking real spry-like.

The very next week Grandpa and I were sitting on the front porch, him in a rocking chair and me on the steps. We heard some noise, like something running through the field. Closer inspection revealed six or seven half-grown hogs running and oinking.

They came through our yard and went into the woods behind the house. "Somebody's got their work cut out for them," Grandpa said. "I wonder if they even know that them pigs got out."

About twenty minutes later, we saw a man coming up the road. He looked tired. He saw us sitting there and made his way into the yard. Neither of us knew him.

"Good mornin', suh," the man greeted Grandpa. "I live down on Jimbo Road," he continued. "Six or seven of my pigs got loose when I was in the field," he said, as he seemed to be bewildered for some reason. I didn't understand that because pigs always escape if they can. "Suh, did you happen to see them come through here?"

Grandpa didn't answer the man's question. He sat there silently as if he didn't hear what the man had said. But he finally leaned forward, and a look came over his face, as if he was in deep thought. Grandpa said, "Wait right here." He got up and went in the house. After a couple of minutes, Grandpa returned with his pocket watch and a ball of twine. He pulled his chair closer to the edge of the porch and sat back down. The man was standing there, obviously spellbound. Grandpa placed his watch on the porch to his left. Then he slowly put his left foot closer to the watch, loosened some string from the ball, and measured the distance of the watch from his left foot. Then he broke that length of string and placed the remaining ball equidistant from his right foot. By now, the man's eyes had gotten bigger and his jaws had dropped. Grandpa seemingly had everything in place, so he pinched the string between two fingers in his right hand. Then he began to slowly make circular motions above the string with his left hand. As he did, the string began to move.

The man seemed just as speechless as I was. I didn't know

if the wind was blowing the string, or if Grandpa was blowing it. But I was certain that it was not his hand movement above the string.

Apparently the man was sure that Grandpa had some kind of weird powers. He excitedly asked Grandpa, "Whatcha got? Whatcha got!?" Grandpa didn't answer; he just kept his concentration on the moving string.

When the string stopped moving, Grandpa cupped it in his free hand and folded it into the palm of his right hand, placed it about midway between the twine and the watch. Then he slowly moved each of those, placing the ball of twine on top of the string, and the watch on top of the twine. Then he looked the man straight in the eye. "You'll find your hogs in the woods," Grandpa told the man, pointing exactly to where we'd seen the pigs enter.

"Thank you, suh!" the man said so graciously. "I sho thank you." The man went on into the woods, and Grandpa sat there and laughed. "He thinks I got special powers," Grandpa said. I smiled, and told Grandpa that I was going to play. Of course that was not the first time I'd seen Grandpa pull a trick like that, but it was the first time I'd ever seen that one. And I would see a few other ones in the future.

It was two weeks before school would let out for the summer. After devotion that Monday morning, Mrs. Woodard announced that we would have a "school closing" program on the night before the last day of school. She said that students from both classrooms would be selected to participate. She wrote down the names of students in her room who wanted to participate, and said that Mrs. Matthews was doing the same, and the two of them would get together and assign parts.

Two days later, Mrs. Woodard assigned parts. Some were speaking parts and some were not. For over a week, rehearsal was held for an hour after school.

On the Thursday evening of the following week, it was Show Time! And due to the fact that we didn't have electricity, the presentation was by candlelight. The play was presented on a makeshift stage in our room. Mrs. Woodard was also the piano player at Heath Chapel Church, so she was our musician for the program.

Chairs were rearranged for the audience (parents and families and neighbors). The overflow had chairs in the hallway; plus there were those who had to stand.

While Mrs. Woodard directed from the piano, Mrs. Matthews had a seat next to the stage. They had also enlisted a couple of parents to assist in keeping the program flowing.

The students who sang were standing on the stage throughout the program. Those who had speaking parts were called to the stage, where they spoke or recited and returned to their seats. Some other students were dressed up as certain characters. They made a brief walk across the stage when they were referenced in a reading or in a song.

Then it was Alton Jones' turn to recite his poem. He didn't budge. He just sat there smiling. He must've been enjoying the program so much. Mrs. Matthews looked across the room at him. And he didn't respond to her "Psst, Psst!" She got up and walked to the other side of the room; then she slapped the living shit out of him. She motioned to Mrs. Woodard to continue the program without that particular part.

As for me? I was selected for a non-speaking part. And I was absolutely delighted. I had my outfit on, and was wearing a big grin. This was an absolute crowning moment for me! I was Little Black Sambo.

The next day, we were in for another surprise. After we had our devotion, Mrs. Woodard took some students out to the teachers' cars and brought in boxes and boxes of food. We had barbecue, potato salad, corn bread, slaw, beans, and drinks. It reminded me of Tobacco Tyings.

I don't know what the motive was for our teachers in doing this. And I never questioned it. But I do know that a number of older boys were stealing barbecue to take home.

## JUNE 1946

It must've been a family rule that I was unaware of, that all of us children must be in attendance when services started. (No, I don't believe it was a church rule.)

Normally, we'd get to church early enough that we'd have the opportunity to chat with folks we hadn't seen in a while. But on this particular Sunday morning, we were running late. So I was spending a few minutes with my other cousins, Big Bo, Li'l Bo, and Thomas. Evidently time slipped our minds because as we were still talking, we looked around, and nobody was still outside but us. Big Bo said: "We can ease in while they're doing the prayer." When we got to the door, we could hear Grandpa's voice. He was putting down a piece of praying. We peeked inside, and could see that Grandpa had done his usual when he had a long prayer for the day. He'd turned one of the wooden chairs upside down, and he was kneeling on it, praying his heart out. "…and oh Lord, I know you been good to us. You been better to us than we been to our own selves, and I wanna say thank you, Lord…" We knew that Grandpa would be there for a while. And with praying souls in the congregation having their eyes closed, we decided that it was the perfect time to sneak in without being noticed. So, here we go, tiptoeing, as Grandpa was still praying, "…and oh Lord, we take you at your word; we wade in on your promise that all things will be…" About that time, it happened! Mother jumped up and started beating me, and Aunt Della jumped up and started beating her three boys. Grandpa never missed a beat. "…and Lord you been good to us…"

## AUGUST 1946

There was the usual hustle and bustle around the farm, and the summer seemed to go pretty fast. In no time flat, I was thinking about my return to school.

Last year, it was Katie joining me for the opening of school. This year, our baby sister would be joining us. While Marie was excited, Katie dreaded having to go back to Mrs. Matthews' room. Not only would she be there again for third grade, but our baby sister would now have to contend with Mrs. Matthews. That would mean going through what we both had experienced. From that perspective, this part was truly depressing.

Mother understood how Katie and I felt, but Marie didn't have a clue. She had seen us head off to school as she would be the only child left at home, and she could hardly wait until she was old enough to go with us. And I understood that this was such a milestone in her life.

When school started, a couple of kids told me, "Your mama gon have a baby." `

I said, "She ain't gon have no baby; she's just picked up some weight. Plus, the doctor bring babies." What did I say that for?

"You 'bout one dumbass mutha fucka!" one of the kids said. "Babies fall out cha mama's pussy." (My first sex ed class.)

## SEPTEMBER 1946

I continued to think about what my friends said about Mother having a baby, but there was too much other stuff going on for me to continue worrying about them. Hell, they were always saying stuff, just for the heck of it. And in spite of how crazy things could get around my house sometimes, I felt like I was in a place where people really cared. That counted for something. I even had some nice interaction with Daddy. For example, one day in the fall, I was returning to the house from across the field where I had been shooting my slingshot. Daddy was sitting on the front steps, smoking and reading a newspaper.

"Hey, Junior," he yelled as he closed the newspaper. I didn't say anything. I just looked in his direction to acknowledge that I had heard him. "I know y'all got a day off from school tomorrow, so how would you like to go with me to sell some 'bacca?" he asked, with a look of childish excitement.

However, I figured that the look of happiness had nothing to do with taking me with him. I concluded that it was because the crops were doing so good this year. Of course I caught the excitement too, but mine *was* childish due to the sheer thought of making that awesome trip. "Yes, sir!" I said, trying not to sound over enthused.

We were up early the next morning. Nobody had to awaken me, as I had gone to sleep thinking about this day, and I woke up with it very much fresh on my mind.

I was dressed and in the kitchen before Mother had even gotten halfway through cooking breakfast. "Good morning." Mother gleamed, seeming to have some of the excitement that was going around. "Aren't you so lucky today."

Daddy came in with some wood to put in the cook stove, to get it even hotter, before Mother finished making biscuits to bake. "I see you're ready," he said to me, "but we gotta eat breakfast first."

It was about twenty more minutes before breakfast was on the table. Grandpa and the girls came in and washed up; Daddy said the grace, with a "Thank you, Lord, for this great day. Amen!"

We finished eating some sausage and eggs on a biscuit and headed out the door. It was me and Daddy on our way to Kinston.

When we got there, I figured it would be crowded, as I had heard Daddy and other men talk about selling tobacco. We parked about two blocks from the warehouse, and walked from there. I had never seen such a cavernous building. I was fascinated by all of those cars and trucks parked in the warehouse, and as far as I could see, there were hundreds and hundreds of piles of tobacco.

I never imagined that the highlight of my day would be one of the first things I encountered. But such did become the top of the day for me. It was the chant of that one-handed auctioneer. I had only heard tobacco being auctioned on the radio, but this was the real deal, including the smell. Once the auctioneer got started, I stopped in my tracks and turned my attention to him. It was like he was talking directly to me even though I had no idea what he was saying. I guess it was just the rhythmic voice that auctioneers use. "herewegodownon-thefirstpilewegotagradeadaprimegoingfortwodaollarsapound!"

I watched.

I smiled.

I shook my head.

When he'd finished that session, I walked away, trying to mimic him in my mind.

No luck, but I continued to smile. What an art.

Meanwhile Daddy had told me that I could walk around, just not to leave the warehouse. So I wandered from one site to the next. After about two hours, I saw him when I turned a corner. He had two Pepsi colas and two packs of peanut butter Nabs in his hands. He gave me one, and we sat down on the edge of a low cinder block wall. We sat there and ate this as our lunch. Daddy said that he'd just completed taking care of his tobacco and was ready to go home as soon as we finished eating.

As we were preparing to leave, I noticed a man sitting on a pile of tobacco. What drew my attention to him was the fact that he was keeping his eyes on us. But I figured it must be my imagination. When we turned the last corner before the exit, I asked Daddy if he knew that man back there. "What man?" he asked.

"The one sitting on the tobacco, off to the side," I told him. He turned around and went back to see who I was talking about. When Daddy spotted the man, he acted like a starstruck teenager. He went up to the man in question. They looked at each other, up and down; then they shook hands for about a minute, still looking at each other.

From Daddy's reactions you would've thought this guy was a rock star or a long-lost relative.

I was standing back, waiting for Daddy to finish talking to the man so we could go on home. Instead, Daddy said: "Hey, Junior, come here. I want you to meet somebody!" As I was walking back over to where they were standing, Daddy had begun his introduction of the man. "This here is Frenchy Gibbs! He used to be the baddest nigga in Greene County!"

This "nigga" was about five-foot-two and was wearing a pair of ragged bib overalls and an old beat-up felt hat. I could tell that Frenchy was one of those old niggas who apparently used to be high yellow in his younger days, but became darker and developed a few wrinkles as he grew older.

While Daddy ran down this nigga's resume to me, Frenchy was giggling, as he continued eating a pack of square Nabs and sipping on a Royal Crown cola. "One night I saw him hit a nigga so hard, it knocked the side of the building off!"

Frenchy had a scar on the right side of his face that ran from the crown of his head to the bottom of his chin. His nose was slightly off-center, and the three teeth he had left looked like they had never been brushed.

I vowed to myself right then and there that I would definitely not grow up to be a "bad nigga."

## NOVEMBER/DECEMBER 1946

The next several weeks were inconsequential. Thanksgiving was nothing special, and I anticipated that Christmas would be likewise. Then something happened in my life that was significant. What my friends said to me at the beginning of school was about to happen.

The thirtieth of November 1946 was an unusually warm day. It actually felt like spring. This was on a Saturday. We had already eaten dinner, and I was reading a book as my sisters were playing some kind of singing game.

Mother was napping because she wasn't feeling well, and Daddy had gone to check on the livestock. He came back and went to see how Mother was doing.

After about ten minutes, he hurriedly came where the girls and I were and told us to stop what we were doing.

"I'm taking you younguns over to your uncle Jack's to

spend the night," he announced.

"What for?" Katie asked.

Without hesitation, Daddy had the answer. "So you can wait until the doctor brings the baby," he said. I didn't say anything because I had been educated by my friends a few months earlier.

He got a few clothes and gave them to us; then he walked us down the road to Uncle Jack's. When we got there, the family was just finishing dinner. Looking at their two babies in action, I was reminded of what was in store for us. Both of them were crying at the same time as Aunt Mabel struggled to comfort them. Additionally, I noticed that she was also getting kind of fat in the stomach. I said to myself, *Uh oh*.

After Daddy left, the girls and I went out into the backyard and played for a while. Then we wandered around in the woods where we had never been before. We all enjoyed our little trek. Probably the only reason we went in as soon as we did was because we heard Uncle Jack calling us. He had come all the way across the field, to the edge of the woods. "Y'all come on in," he said. "It's getting dark, and your aunt Mabel done fixed dinner for y'all."

We followed Uncle Jack back to the house, and it seemed like a long ways. I hadn't realized that we had gone so far from his house. Sure enough, Aunt Mabel had cooked chicken and rice with gravy. Plus, she had made some hot biscuits. It seemed like Sunday to me. We ate good! And I slept very well that night.

The next morning, Daddy came to get us. He put our

clothes in a large paper bag that he brought, thanked Uncle Jack for letting us spend the night, and we were on our way home.

"Dr. Carson left you a baby brother!" he shared as we walked down the path.

I was almost ten years old, and I got really pissed at him and Mother all over again for lying to me about where babies come from.

We got home and rushed to see the new baby. The first thing Katie said was: "Look at his head; it look just like Daddy's." Mother said that she would name him after her father. Thus, the name "Best" became official.

That Sunday morning, there was a rare winter thunderstorm. Of course there was not the usual quiet that was the norm at our house during a storm. And the reason was that brother Best was screaming at the top of his lungs.

That morning we had a breakfast of Grandma Molasses and fatback meat.

A few days later, some classmates found out that Best had been born. They lined up at our front door to come in and see the newborn baby. The reaction that I remember most vividly was the student who had called me that bad name back in August. He sort of repeated himself: "I told your dumb ass that your mama was gonna have a baby; that little long-headed mutha fucka looks just like your goddamn daddy."

Christmas for us was only a pipe dream. It consisted of a shoe box with an apple, an orange, three or four English walnuts, and two butter nuts.

## January 1947

If signs from 1946 were an indication, 1947 would probably be worse. There were no celebratory gunshots at midnight to bring in the New Year. It came in pretty much unnoticed, seemingly by design. Even though the previous year started out fairly good, looking back, it had been downhill at least by mid-year when there seemed to be one setback after another. I think the highlight of that year was on December first when the baby was born.

This year would prove to be different in a lot of ways. For one thing, I would have another baby to take care of, but then again, Katie and Marie were older. As a result, there would be less supervision required for them. Plus, they were old enough to help me take care of our little brother. That understanding was worth a lot to me.

But the things that had become routine as farm chores didn't seem so routine anymore. I was unable to determine where the feeling of uncertainty was coming from, but I could feel it. I could see it especially in Daddy and my uncles. None of them seemed as jovial and as confident as they had been the previous years. That observation didn't permeate my thoughts, but it did seem to hang around like a warning cloud.

The winter months were filled with all that was required to make the farm go. The notion that things were negatively different was not a good feeling. However, we got through the winter months and geared up for spring.

**APRIL 1947**

During this time period, we were not yet communicating by telephone. In any emergency, contact with each other had to be done via telegram. We were re-setting tobacco on a clear sunny Thursday in May when a car came to our house with the horn frantically blowing. Daddy rushed to see what the driver wanted. He was delivering a telegram from Aunt Rudy, in Goldsboro. The telegram read, "Mother had a stroke. Hurry!" Daddy gathered us up, and we were in Goldsboro within two hours. She was in Wayne Memorial Hospital. When Grandma Mary fell ill, she was on her knees, scrubbing a white woman's floor.

For the next three days, we traveled back and forth. We would go home to feed the livestock, and return to Goldsboro, sleeping in the car at night. But Daddy insisted on being there.

Grandma Mary died early that Sunday, on the twenty-fifth. The funeral was three days later, with the wake being held at their house. Her body was transported to St. John the next day for the funeral, and she was buried at Townsend Cemetery in Greene County.

The morning of the funeral, several young mothers had their babies lying on the bed on display while they were getting dressed. There was one six-month-old baby that family members didn't have to ask who the daddy was. It was my brother, Best.

Something else happened back home while we were attending Grandma's funeral. Uncle Jack and Aunt Mabel had a baby girl "delivered" to their house. They named her Renetta.

## May/June 1947

Right after school ended for the summer, a severely sullen atmosphere began to permeate the community. It seemed as though working the crops was more like going through the motions than what I was used to. In past years, the grown ups operated in an air of jubilance when doing any aspect of the farming. Now it seemed to be drudgery.

This was also the month that our baby brother was officially added to my list of responsibilities, and it was a permanent addition. But as I had already anticipated, my sisters were now old enough to help me out with this additional responsibility.

And even now, when I think back to how we treated him in those first few months of his life, I still get chills down my spine. For example, when both parents had to be in the fields, we would play games with him. We had seen in the comic books where Superman would catch people who were thrown from windows of tall buildings, so we would take turns throwing a five-month-old baby off the porch, and the sibling who played the role of Superman would catch him just before he hit the ground!

Whew!

But as the days and weeks went by, I came to understand the negative feeling, that uncertainty by which my parents and uncles were consumed. It wasn't just my family; it was most, if not all, black folks who were in our lot.

During that period of time, due to the return of veterans from World War II, black people were leaving the South in droves. Our school lost over a third of its students, mostly from

Cottington Farm. According to the story, one Monday morning shortly after school closed, Old Man Cottington walked down to his shacks. Lo and behold, they were empty. All of the occupants had relocated to New York City.

## SUMMER 1947

During the summer I became more and more convinced that our functioning was anything but typical. I was not in on grown up conversations, of course, nor was I ever able to eavesdrop and get a wisp of what their thinking was. But again, I could more or less sense the lack of surety in my parents and some of the other grown ups. But the demeanor of pending negativity still was not able to stifle the determination, nor the sheer will to keep pressing on in my parents and others.

And that was the case for sure in the months to come.

## AUGUST 1947

A new school year was about to begin. I was going into sixth grade! I guess that was my excitement for the year.

## SEPTEMBER 1947

Then in the fall during tobacco selling time, there were people showing up in town from all walks of life. They were in competition for the farmers' dollars. Some were honest people, and some were just plain old predators. My first awareness of this type of occurrence was on a Friday afternoon, about two o'clock.

We were sitting on the front porch after we had finished

our work for the day. I noticed a black panel truck slowly approaching. When it drew closer, we could hear muffled sounds coming from the huge speakers atop the truck. When it reached our house, it was barely creeping. There was a decal of a scantly clothed dancing girl on the door. Above her head, there was a sign that read, "Silas Green, from New Orleans." The Silas Green show was in town.

This was a Negro tent show that traveled throughout the South. It had been in existence from about the beginning of the nineteenth century. They were letting the black farmers know that the shows would commence on Friday night and end on Saturday night. Daddy's eyes lit up like a Christmas tree. But Mother was not at all amused. Several neighboring black men stopped by our house with giddy grins, inquiring if Daddy had heard about the show. The men who didn't have cars made arrangements to ride with someone else.

Of course when they would return from their entertainment, they would tell of their experiences. Of all the stories I ever heard about people who were a part of this, the ones that stood out were the magicians. I had heard Daddy and his friends talk about two black magicians in particular. One was called Nigga Devil, and the other one was Tricky Sam. They said that one time at the warehouse, Tricky Sam asked a woman what happened to her drawers. With the spotlight on her, she was embarrassed at the question. But when Tricky Sam reached in his pocket and pulled them out, she ran from the warehouse crying. He would also let a car loaded with adults, park on his body. One man declared that he could feel the car moving up and down as Tricky Sam breathed.

Nigga Devil's specialty was that he could be in two places at the same time. For example, he had the sheriff lock him in a jail cell, then send a deputy to the local pool hall, where he said that he would be shooting pool. Sure enough, the sheriff locked him up. Then he sent the deputy to the pool hall. And when the deputy arrived, there was Nigga Devil, shooting pool. The deputy then phoned the sheriff to report what he had found. The sheriff told him that Nigga Devil was still locked in his cell.

There were also traveling musicians who were mostly black. A couple that I heard of were Blind Boy Fuller and Sonny Terry. They started out playing the warehouses in eastern North Carolina. Also, there was Tar Hill Slim. The only female entertainer I can recall was a lady known as Georgia Peach. Finally, there were the Gypsies. The story on them was that they would tell your fortune and pick your pockets at the same time.

Outside of the entrance to the tent there was a small stage, and several minutes before Showtime, the emcee would come out dressed in a zoot suit and wearing a red necktie that dragged on the ground. The bass guitar would be thumping while the lead guitar would be wailing. And those half-naked high-yellow gals would be twisting and bumping to the music.

As the music reached its crescendo, the emcee would abruptly bring all of this to a halt. Then he would announce, "That's enough! If you want to see more, get your ticket at the booth." Those country hicks couldn't get to their money fast enough.

Over that weekend, the Show Girls went through those Negroes like a hot knife going through a stick of butter.

My cousin Allen Grant, the father of five minor children, was one of the suckers. At church that Sunday, his wife Eliza said to Mother, "One of them New Orleans strumpets got all of Allen's money." A lot of wives in Jones, Lenoir, Greene, and Pitt counties were fit to be tied. They wanted to raid that Silas Green camp. When the show left town, it had to leave under police protection. I never heard of them appearing in that area again.

## December 1947

Under a clear-sky afternoon two weeks after Thanksgiving, when we arrived from school I observed Daddy and several white men at the stable. The white men were looking at the bottom of the mules' feet. They were also looking in their mouths. When we got to the house, Grandpa was putting wood in the stove, and Mother was staring out the window, looking at the scene that had befuddled me.

"Hey, younguns," Grandpa said. Katie and I spoke and headed for the kitchen. Of course that's where Marie had already gone. Mother had left her position at the window and came in the kitchen where we were, with a faraway look on her face. The only thing she said was "We're moving." That information didn't seem to mean anything to Katie and Marie, as they continued getting their snack. But for me, it took my appetite. I went outside to the corner of the house, where I leaned against the wall, trying to process this devastating news.

But the longer I thought about it, the more I realized that our stay here in the Hugo area was over. When I finally went back inside, Daddy was there, talking to Mother and Grandpa. I knew that there was nothing he could tell me that would make a difference. Therefore, other than not getting a snack, I just kept with my after-school routine.

For the next couple of weeks it was frantic around our neighborhood. Daddy and my uncles spent very little time together. Whenever they talked, it seemed to be about anything else but what to be done on the farm. I realized that they were busy making plans for moving elsewhere. At the same time, I knew that Christmas was coming, and we always celebrated Christmas in some fashion. So, I wondered what we'd do about that, especially since we would all be moving.

We all did celebrate Christmas together, but it was uneventful, and by the thirtieth of December, we were off Harriet Townsend's farm. We left on Monday, the twenty-ninth. This was after Daddy and my uncles had only received a fraction of the value of their livestock and farm equipment. But they all found new residences right after Christmas.

I don't know which was the biggest hurt for me—the fact that we were leaving or that Mac and Arthur were not going on this trip with us. Daddy said that when he sold the mules and equipment, he included Mac and Arthur as a part of that package.

I don't know exactly when Uncle Jack and Uncle Leroy pulled out, but it was after we did. Daddy hired a neighbor, Mr. Benny Jamieson, who was moving the following week, to take our furniture to our new location on his pickup.

That morning about eleven o'clock, he arrived. The few things they couldn't get on the truck were packed in our car. Grandpa got in the truck with Mr. Jamieson, and the rest of us rode in our car. At that point we were on our way to a new home!

# MOVING ON

## *1947–1956*

MOTHER AND DADDY talked all the way. Katie, Marie, and I looked out the windows at the scenery. When Daddy stopped talking and began looking from one side of the road to the other, I knew we were just about there.

We were going to live on Mr. Preston Martin's farm… somewhere near a place called La Grange.

Sure enough, it wasn't much farther until Daddy turned left, into a short dirt path. He stopped the car as the pickup pulled in behind us.

The small white frame house was off to the left. There were also a lot of woods behind the house and on the side. Plus, there was a path into the wooded area. On the right, there was a fairly large two-story building, which I figured to be the pack house. Next to that building was a stable and a fenced-in area.

Daddy got out and closed the door. I took that to mean that we were to sit there until further notice. Of course I had to ask, "Mother, can we get out?" She told me to wait and see what Daddy and Mr. Jamieson were going to do. Daddy went back to the truck, where he and Mr. Jamieson talked. But Grandpa had already gotten out. He got his knife and cut a piece off of his plug of tobacco and deposited it in his mouth. He chewed a few times, spit, and began to walk around.

After what seemed like ten minutes, Daddy returned to the car. "Sarah, take the younguns in the house; me and Benny gon unload the truck and then we'll get things set up." Mother got out and raised the seat for each of us. She got Marie by the hand to keep her from running, because she liked to be first everywhere she went.

When we got inside, Mother realized that she'd left the blankets in the car. They were definitely needed to wrap the girls in because it was cold in there. I had on a fairly heavy jacket, so I was warm enough. We looked out the window and watched Daddy and Mr. Jamieson unload the truck. Finally, the last item was on the ground. Daddy paid Mr. Jamieson, and they shook hands.

Daddy brought the heater into the room where we were. "You 'bout through?" Mother asked.

"Yeah, it'll be another twenty minutes or so," he told her. "Junior, you can come with me. I need for you to go to the woodpile down by the barn, pick up some kindling, and bring it in."

I was on it immediately. When I returned, Daddy was still trying to figure out how he wanted the heater to be situated. Instead of having to run the pipe to the ceiling, it went directly into a fitting on the wall. This meant that getting heat would be quick, and Daddy got to save some stovepipe as well. He stuffed the wood in the heater and lit it. We were all smiles as the room began to get warm.

Then it was off to the kitchen to get the cook stove in place. But the piece of stovepipe that Daddy saved actually made things work out perfectly, because the kitchen stove took up the rest of the "saved" pipe, except for the elbow.

Meanwhile, Grandpa had finished his outside tour. He came in and surveyed Daddy's work. "Namon, you did a good job on that," he said, as he jiggled the pipe to test its stability. Daddy pretty much ignored him, and went on about the business of getting the house set up.

From there, it was back to the living room, where Mother and the girls were. The whole house seemed to be getting warm.

Daddy gathered everybody around and announced that he would now give us a tour. All of us, including Grandpa, followed him. The first stop was in a bedroom. Daddy smiled and said, "Look-a thar," as he pointed to the string hanging from the ceiling.

He pulled the string, and the bulb lit up. A pull of the string also seemed to make Daddy's own smile a little bit brighter. This was the routine in each of the five rooms. But only two of the bulbs worked. The others were obviously blown.

The tour was over in about ten minutes.

For some reason, as usual, based on the size of the house and the layout, I already felt some familiarity. As I had figured it, there would be a room for me (and Best, if he'd sleep in there); the girls would share a room, while Mother and Daddy would have the other room. Grandpa would probably sleep on the dining room floor, rather than on the floor at the foot Mother's and Daddy's bed like he did back in Hugo.

While I had our sleeping arrangements pretty much figured out, there was one burning question that I just had to ask Daddy. He had assured me that the move here would be made easier because we would be living close to kinfolks on his side of the family. I got the opportunity to ask him about that right before bedtime.

He was drinking out of the dipper when I walked into the kitchen. I waited until he put the dipper back in the water bucket, and then asked. "Daddy, which house does Uncle Chad live in?"

As he reached in his shirt pocket and pulled out a pack of cigarettes, he said: "Oh, he lives about a mile and a half from here."

That was not what I expected to hear. I respectfully responded: "But I thought you said we'd be on the same farm..."

Daddy interrupted me. "I said we'd be living on a farm that was owned by the same man that own the one that your Uncle Chuck live on." He paused. "But we'll be working together during the summer. We just ain't next-door neighbors." He lit the cigarette and took a long drag, then blew the smoke toward the ceiling.

I said, "Good night," and went to bed.

## DECEMBER 30, 1947

Everybody was up early the next morning. Katie and Marie played with their tea sets from a Christmas past, while Mother cooked. Grandpa was out taking a walk. And I just idled around, as I could hardly wait to get breakfast so that I could go outside.

When Mother finished cooking, we had to wait for Daddy to come back from the pasture. We had fatback, molasses, and some buttermilk biscuits. Of course I was the first one to finish. I excused myself and announced to anyone who cared to listen, "I'm going outside." Nobody questioned what I was going to do once I got outside, or why.

I first made another trip to the two tobacco barns down the path. They were in the edge of the woods, on the left. There was nothing special about them. Then there was the henhouse; I checked that out. There were no hens in it, but the smell was proof enough to vouch for what it was.

While I was down there, I rambled through the woods a bit. I was searching for the perfect branch, to make a bow. I considered several branches on a number of trees, mainly oak. Then I came upon the one I wanted. It was actually growing out of the ground beside a dogwood tree. As a matter of fact, it was much better than what I had in mind.

I started pulling it up, but it refused to cooperate. So, I ran back to the woodpile and got the axe. I knew this would do the trick. After a few blows, the stubborn stick gave in and fell to the side. I was very pleased. I was like Daddy was with the light string; I could feel myself smiling with satisfaction.

I then dropped the axe and inspected my potential bow. When I returned to the woodpile and put the axe away, I began to work on my project.

Daddy came out and asked if I wanted to walk down to the fields with him. I said that I did. I put my bow aside, and we made that tour together. There was nothing exciting about it, but we got it done. When we returned to the house, Daddy continued in the other direction. I'd done that already, so I went back to making my bow. I'd been working on that thing for about an hour when I took a break to get a drink of water. I was priming the pump when I looked up the road and saw a black boy who appeared to be about my age, riding a bicycle. I saw him looking at our house as he approached.

When he got to the path, he turned in. I stood there and looked as he rode toward me. "Hey," he said. "What's yo name?"

"They call me Junior," I told him.

"They call me B. J.," the boy responded.

"Where you live?" I asked.

Still straddling his bicycle, he turned and pointed to the house up the road, and back in a field. "Up there," he said. "Me, my two brothers, my momma, and my daddy live there. How many of y'all is there?"

"I got a baby brother, two little sisters, a momma, and a daddy," I responded.

"Do your sisters go to school?"

"Yeah, we all go to school."

"Well, y'all be going to my school," he said.

His bike was blue, with a white stripe on the side of the spoke cover. It looked fairly decent, but I could tell that it wasn't new. He sat there on his bike as he talked, keeping his hands locked on the handlebar grips. He was dressed in a pair of blue overalls, and wore a red and blue plaid shirt. Plus, he had on a black pair of new leather brogans. He must've gotten them for Christmas because I recognized that new leather smell. I was introduced to that when Daddy bought those bridles and reins for our mules, way back in 1942.

"How far is the school from here?" I asked.

"Not even a mile," he said. "Me and my brothers usually get there a little ahead of time, 'cause if you wait 'til the last minute, you might be late. Then most of them teachers will break out the switch."

"Yeah, I know about the switch," I assured him.

"What school did you go to before?"

"We went to Heath Chapel." I sensed that he didn't have any idea where that was, so I volunteered the rest of the information. "That's on the other end of Lenoir County," I said. "It's almost to the Greene County line." Then he still looked puzzled, so I told him, "It's a pretty good ways from here." That at least removed the question mark from his face.

For no obvious reason, B. J. said that he had to leave. "I gotta go," he said, "but I sure would like to see that bow when you get it done." He was riding off as we finished the conversation.

"You can try it out," I yelled to him as he rode on back up the road.

## DECEMBER 31, 1947

New Year's Eve was on Wednesday. Mother and Daddy told us kids that we could stay up until midnight to usher in the New Year. Grandpa jokingly asked, "What about me?" Of course they ignored him altogether. However, I took them up on it. Katie went to sleep early, but got up right before midnight. Marie was in no way interested in any of this celebratory stuff. She went to bed and slept right through the night.

## THURSDAY/JANUARY 1, 1948

This time around, bringing in the New Year was much different than what I had grown accustomed to. There was not the yelling and gunfire by Daddy and friends. Then again, everything was different this time. I was reminded that I would have to accept the fact that things change; situations change. So here we were in a new community, with new people, and I had not yet gotten to really know either. However, there were the exchanges of "Happy New Year" to each other in the family.

## FRIDAY/JANUARY 2, 1948

I didn't get my bow like I wanted until Friday. I was out by the woodpile testing it when again, I looked up the road and saw two boys riding bikes this time—a black boy and a white boy.

When they got closer, I recognized the black boy as B. J.

The two boys turned in to our yard. "Hey Junior," B. J. said when they stopped. This time, he got off his bike and put the kickstand down. "This here is Tim," he said. "He live farther up the road. His daddy own the farm we live on."

Tim was riding what was obviously a new bike. It was white with a tan frame, and there were reflectors on the pedals. Big time! Tim was a tall, redheaded kid, and he had freckles on both cheeks. I guess I stared at him, trying to see if those freckles were evenly divided on each side, because it sure looked like they were.

Tim didn't have on a jacket even though it was quite chilly. And he had that inquisitive look in his eyes. "What grade you in, Junior?" he asked.

"I'm in sixth grade."

His eyes widened in disbelief. "Sixth grade? Sixth grade?"

"That's what he said!" B. J. interjected, to put a stop to Tim's small rant.

"You sho little for sixth grade," Tim concluded.

"What you got there?" B. J. asked.

"I just finished making my bow," I told him.

"I don't need to make no toys," Tim said, sounding real arrogant about the whole idea.

B. J. again changed the direction of the conversation. "Let's see who can hit them cans," he said, pointing to several cans lying near the woodpile. He picked up a couple clods of dirt and put a few cans on the ground away from the wood chips. Meanwhile, I picked up a few clods of dirt too. Tim reluctantly dismounted and put his kickstand down. We threw at a few cans, but nobody was having any luck. "Maybe we could do better if we got them off the ground," I suggested. B. J. agreed, and got some pieces of wood and made a bench-like base to set the cans on. Our accuracy still didn't improve a whole lot, but at least the targets were easier to see. We threw for about thirty minutes, with no winners being determined.

"I gotta go," Tim announced. "I'll see you boys later." He got on his bike and rode off. B. J. and I threw some more.

Then B. J. wanted to see the bow that I'd made. "Tim's got a lot of toys," he said, "and he got three bikes! He got cap pistols, air rifles, and all kinds of stuff."

B. J. seemed to get excited just talking about all the things Tim had. But I guess I was getting excited too. I knew that I didn't have all that. Shit, I didn't even have a bike.

### Saturday/January 3, 1948

This particular Saturday was somewhat of a lazy day. I couldn't believe that Daddy was staying around the house. Normally, he would be down in the fields. If not working, he'd be checking on his crops. And from what I knew, there was no such thing as a weekend. There were just Sundays. But no matter what Daddy was doing on Saturdays, come rain or shine, he would make his trek into town on Saturday afternoons.

But that was just an observation. I went on about doing what I was interested in. About mid-morning, I made my first visit to B. J.'s house. I was introduced to his whole family before we went outside to play. They were: Miss Maureen (his mother), Mr. Aaron (his dad), and his two brothers, Buddy and Jake. Tim also came over and we played in the yard and through the fields for a couple of hours.

At home, things were going as well as could be expected here at our new place, but I sure missed having Mac and Arthur around. Evidently Daddy was missing them too because that afternoon, Uncle Chad stopped by and picked him up, and they left for about an hour. When they returned, Daddy had a pretty brown, black, and white German shepherd puppy, and a huge grin on his face. He said that a neighbor of Uncle Chad gave it to him. He named him Brownie. This one event caused me to feel more at home in our new place.

### SUNDAY/JANUARY 4, 1948

Sunday came. It was a typical Sunday morning. Mother was cooking breakfast, with the radio playing spirituals. Grandpa was sitting in his rocking chair on the porch. Daddy was engrossed in the newspaper he had gotten yesterday. Katie and Marie were playing in their room, and the baby was playing and sleeping in the box that served as his crib. I went outdoors to play and explore.

After breakfast, we continued our normal Sunday routines when there was no church. But about mid-afternoon when I was outside, a black car pulled into our yard. Of course I was looking real close because it looked like a car full of people; but I didn't immediately recognize it. However, when it got closer I realized who it was.

Uncle Chad got out. "Hey there, Junior," he said, as others crawled from the backseat. Uncle Chad had brought his whole family. There was Chuck, Bobby Ray, and two girls who appeared to be maybe a few years younger than Bobby Ray. Also, there was Uncle Chad's wife. She had a baby in her arms, and a little girl was holding onto her dress.

His wife started talking, and kept on talking, nonstop. Uncle Chad still managed to introduce everybody. I had already spoken to Chuck and Bobby Ray, and I was still able to hear his introductions. "This here is your Aunt Cora," he said. I don't think she knew she was introduced, because she was talking to Katie and Marie at the time. But Uncle Chad continued.

He next introduced the girls, "Rena and Nancy," he said, as he gestured to the older girls. "That's Bertha, holding onto her momma, and the baby is Katherine."

I invited Chuck and Bobby Ray outside. We went and played until it was time for them to leave. It was so much fun having these new cousins to play with; and Chuck being my age made this something really special..

They left, and it was time to get ready for the week ahead.

## MONDAY/JANUARY 5, 1948

Finally, Monday morning was upon us, January fifth, 1948.

Grownups recognized the beginning of the New Year on the first of January. But to me, the beginning of the New Year was my first day going back to school after the holiday break. Everything before that was the "holiday season."

This morning was a little exciting and a little scary. Mother got breakfast ready, fed us, and ushered us out the door. Marie's perkiness was toned down noticeably. She was even quiet for a change.

Of course, Katie had that serious straight-ahead demeanor about her. I knew she would be okay, but I wasn't so sure about Marie. "Are you ready for our new school?" I asked her.

"Yeah," she said, with the response sounding a bit shaky.

Looking up the road in the distance, I could see B. J. and his two brothers waiting at their path. When we reached them, B.J. greeted us and introduced his brothers to the girls. "These here my brothers, Buddy and Jake," B. J. said to Katie and Marie.

"And these my sisters," I replied. So, up the road we went.

I guess it took us about twenty minutes to get from our house to the school. Along the way, B. J. and I walked ahead as our siblings followed. He informed me that this school had elementary and high school students, but that they were separate.

The school was situated barely inside the city limits of La Grange, affectionately known by locals as the Garden Spot. It was surrounded by farmland and small frame houses.

While cars and buses turned on the paved road and went around a sharp curve to get to the front of the school, we turned off the paved road and went through a field. This enabled us to end up on the backside of the school. This place was huge compared to Hearth Chapel.

When we reached the school grounds, B. J. said, "I'll show you where the office is." Then he instructed his brothers, "Go on to your classrooms." He took us inside a building that appeared to have several classrooms. This sure was a far cry from what we had at Heath Chapel. There seemed to be so many people, mostly children. And it was not just women here who were teachers. There were also several men! B. J. told me that they were all high school teachers.

A few doors into the building, B. J. stopped. "This is the office," he told us. "Just go in there and wait. Miss Thomas will do what's needed to get y'all in class, and I'll meet you down by the field after school."

With that, B. J. was on his way. My sisters and I went in the office and had to wait, as the lady was busy with children who were ahead of us.

Meanwhile, a heavy-set, well-dressed man with medium dark skin and glasses was in and out a few times. I figured him to weigh about two hundred pounds. He was maybe five feet, eight inches tall. He would go into an office in the back for a few minutes and return. He seemed to be in charge of the school. I just put my curiosity on hold, as I was sure that B. J. could tell me later.

Miss Thomas finally got to us and was very pleasant. She asked us quite a few questions; then she told us to wait a few more minutes as she went out the door. It wasn't very long before she returned, accompanied by a tall, slim high school girl.

"This is Marlean," Miss Thomas said. "She'll take y'all to your classrooms."

Marlean led us out the door and down the hallway. My room was the first one that we got to. She stopped and turned to me. "This is where you'll be," she said. "This is Mrs. Kramer's room." Marlean politely knocked on the open door to get the teacher's attention. And when we were acknowledged, Marlean continued down the hallway with my sisters.

Mrs. Kramer came to the door and welcomed me as I gave her the papers that I had gotten from the office. Of course, there were the stares that I received from students already in there.

And oh yeah, all of them were bigger than me, including the girls. There were also a few comments that I pretended not to hear. "He sure is little," I heard a girl whisper.

After looking over the papers that I had given her, Mrs. Kramer introduced me to the group. "This is Moses," she said. "He comes to us from Heath Chapel School. Does anybody know where Heath Chapel is?" she asked, and waited for an answer. None of them had one. She went on to tell them pretty much what I'd told B. J. "Heath Chapel is near the Lenoir County line," she said. "…almost in Greene County."

With that being taken care of, she turned to finding a seat for me. There were several vacant chairs, but she seemed to mull over which one would be more suitable for me. Finally she moved a female student from near the front to another seat and assigned me to the one that the girl was sitting in. She didn't say why she did that, but I guessed that it was because the student she moved was tall, and had she assigned that seat to me, I would have been hidden by the student who was in the seat in front of that girl.

Mrs. Kramer, was a slim, middle-aged woman. She wore her hair pulled back and tied in a bun. With that physical appearance, she reminded me of Mrs. Woodard.

As it turned out, my day went so fast that it was like a whirlwind. The routine was new, but the subject matter was no different than what it had been at Heath Chapel. The biggest difference for me was that Mrs. Kramer was only teaching one grade. This part was really nice.

When the school day was over, my sisters were waiting for me outside of the building. The three of us went to the edge of the field as prearranged. B. J. and Jake were already there. "We need to wait for Buddy," B. J. said. In about five more minutes, Buddy came. So, off we went down the road to our houses.

On the way, I asked B. J. about the man I'd seen in the office. "That's the principal," he said. "Mr. Fields… He's the boss man here… He runs the whole school, but a lot of his job must include chasing kids that cut class, 'cause he sure spends a lot of time doing that. He lives right across from the school." My curiosity was more than satisfied.

We had been in our new school for a couple of weeks, and were beginning to get used to our new environment. Naturally, this being a larger school, things were drastically different. Whereas at Heath Chapel, in Mrs. Matthews' first through third grade class, once we got inside her classroom, we knew to immediately get into learning mode. And in Mrs. Woodard's upper grades, we would sing a couple of songs to get our day started. However, here, in the morning we would have a school-wide devotion in the auditorium. There, Mr. Fields would be in charge. That would last about thirty minutes, as there would be the pledge of allegiance, the singing of a patriotic song, a prayer, and announcements. Then all classes would orderly return to their respective rooms.

I don't know what went on in other classrooms here, but

once we returned to ours, Mrs. Kramer would read passages from the Bible to us. Then we would get started with our lessons.

For some courses, there were not enough books for each student, and we could not take them home. For those courses, we would pull our desks together and share books. And whenever there was homework in those courses, Mrs. Kramer would write it on the board, and we'd copy it. In courses that did have enough books for each student, we were allowed to take them home.

Those were the worst books I had ever seen. They were dirty, dingy, ragged, and a bit smelly. We put book covers on them, to make them look halfway decent. Brown paper bags were the most durable material for this. However, some students would use newspapers as their book covers.

But as bad as things were, we made the best of it. Teachers taught, and we learned. Unlike at Heath Chapel, where we had two female teachers who taught multiple grade levels, here the elementary teachers (all female) taught only one grade level; but the high school teachers (men and women) taught different grade levels per period. And probably best of all, these teachers seemed to be influenced from a helping approach rather than one of punishment.

Also, a noticeable difference was that at Heath Chapel, we were a part of the community and all that went on in the community. However, here there was a coming together of several different communities. By the nature of that, more conflict existed. In this vein, getting to know B. J. was huge. The key thing he told me was that the kids from in town thought they were better than the kids who were from the rural areas. It really never was a problem for me, but more of a bit of annoying trivia. The best I could tell, we were all in the same boat. And as far as my sisters were concerned, we were settling in reasonably well, even with Marie's tendency to let her mouth get her in trouble. I must admit that I was proud of her for exercising control. Overall, we were resilient.

Another interesting and relevant item that was in place due to the makeup of the student population. And this was due to a combination of factors. This was a larger school with more students, and the age-range of students was very wide. This allowed for more maturity of students and more independence from adult supervision. Consequently, there was more freedom amongst students to plan and engage in behaviors that were not supervised by the authorities.

This also meant that, in these conditions, there were also increased chances that such unsanctioned behaviors would go undetected and unpunished. But the only behavior that was a constant in this environment were the almost daily fights that occurred. We would get word that a fight would take place at recess; then we'd look for that fight, find it, and enjoy it.

Some fights would be pretty vicious, but nobody ever told. And in those fights, rarely would a combatant be over-matched. So, many times what a fight amounted to was two participants administering an ass-whipping to each other.

**FEBRUARY 1948**

We had been at our new place several weeks before we got to visit Uncle Chad. It was on a Saturday morning. Daddy had caught up, for the time being. I knew that Katie and Marie had been looking forward to this because I heard them mention it several times. I recalled that they had really enjoyed Rena and Nancy when they first met. Plus, the only girl cousins they'd ever been around much were Mattie, Uncle Bob's daughter, and Aunt Arlene's daughters, and they were all from Mother's side of the family.

We all climbed into Daddy's old Ford and headed up the road. After about a half-mile on the highway, we turned left at a store, onto a dirt road. Once we had gone maybe a fifth of a mile, about fifty yards off to the left, there was a medium-size frame church sitting amongst a grove of pine trees. "That's Simeron Baptist, your aunt Ada's family church," Mother volunteered.

We kids acknowledged that information, as Katie represented us kids in doing such, I guess. She simply said, "Oh."

About a quarter of a mile past the church, we came to a stop sign at the crossroad. Once we got through that intersection, Daddy turned up a path between two cornfields. Thankfully, the corn stalks had been cut down; otherwise we wouldn't have been able to see the house back there. It was a long ways. When we drove up, Uncle Chad was coming from a fenced-in area, headed to a barn with a bucket in his hand. I figured that he'd been feeding some of the animals. Chuck and Bobby Ray were running and chasing each other, but I didn't recognize the game they were playing.

Uncle Chad had a big smile on his face, which was the case the first time I saw him greet his brother. He put the bucket down and came to welcome us as we got out of the car. "Cora and them's in the house," he said. "I gotta finish feeding the goats. I'll be right back." I wanted to go in, but I also wanted to stay outside and play.

Since this was my first visit here, I decided I could go in for a few minutes, then come right back outside.

But before I did anything else, I had to begin assessing this place. My quick take was the usual. The yard was very spacious, and just like other farms I'd seen, the fields came as close to the house as possible.

The porch was extremely high off the ground. I had never seen anything like it.

After we'd wasted a few minutes looking around before going inside, Uncle Chad had finished his chores and joined us on the porch. I followed everyone inside.

When we walked in, Aunt Cora acted as if she'd never met us. She got me first. "What's your name, boy?" she asked. Uncle Chad reminded her that she already knew my name. She reminded Uncle Chad that she still wanted me to tell her my name.

"Junior," I said.

"Yeah, I know you," she responded with a smile. "I remember when you were a little bitty old thing." No, she wasn't one of Mother's sisters, but I liked her. Aunt Cora then turned her attention to my sisters, as they seemed to be standing back, waiting their turn.

Meanwhile, Uncle Chad had sent Chuck and Bobby Ray to take a bucket of feed to a few animals in another pen that was located down the path. So, as I was waiting for them to return, I thought about my newfound aunt. First of all, I was duly impressed with how clean and orderly she kept everything.

Physically, Aunt Cora was a short lady, with brown skin and shiny hair. This day, she had it rolled up under a scarf.

Additionally, when they visited us, I never did put much thought into her in comparison with Mother's sisters. There was no reason to. But as she talked, it occurred to me that she had such a powerful voice, though a bit raspy. That particular point jogged my memory, and I smiled. That strong voice of hers reminded me of the auctioneer at the tobacco warehouse in Kinston a few years ago.

Chuck and Bobby Ray finally got back, and they both motioned me to come outside with them. I did, and the fun began.

Our visit lasted two or three hours, and when it was time to go home, I still didn't want to leave.

The longer we were in our new neighborhood, the more I learned about relations between the people who lived there. Over time, I found out who Tim's daddy was. I knew that he owned the farm that B. J. and his family lived on, but I had never seen him. His name was Joe Bennett. Black folks called him Mr. Joe. I saw him one day when I was at the store. He walked in as I was leaving, and I heard Mr. Post greet him. "Good morning, Mr. Bennett," he said. That's when the light bulb came on in my head. I turned around and looked, but I don't believe I stared.

Like his son, he was tall and skinny, and he walked with a limp. Plus, he had trouble breathing. I found out that this resulted from his being wounded and gassed in World War One.

Another thing that I became privy to was the relationship between B. J.'s parents. His dad was also called Mr. Aaron, and his mom was Miss Maureen."

They had somewhat of an odd relationship.

Mr. Aaron was a short, small man who weighed no more than a hundred and thirty pounds, soaking wet. He loved to drink. Miss Maureen was a huge woman, and she weighed well over two hundred pounds. Some days Miss Maureen was as sweet as she could be, and on other days it would seem as if she was angry at the world. And on those days, she would take it out on her husband. For example, one day when I was visiting, Mr. Aaron asked her what was for dinner. She hatefully told him that she wasn't going to cook anything for him the rest of the week. When Mr. Aaron tried to protest, she stared him down, as if to say, "You know better." At that point, Mr. Aaron walked away like a defeated puppy.

Additionally, when I visited B. J., I noticed that whenever Buddy did or said something that pissed him off, or his other brother, they would call him Nut. One day when this happened, I asked what the reason was behind Buddy's nickname. B. J. explained that Buddy only had one testicle, and that was the result of an accident he had a few years earlier. He said that Buddy was using a tobacco stick for his make-believe horse. Somehow, he jabbed the stick in his gonads and badly injured his testicle. Consequently, doctors had to remove it.

On another occasion, as I was approaching the house, I heard a lot of noise, like metal hitting the wall. I thought of turning around and going back home, but decided to continue. Before I got to the door, B. J. ran out to meet me. We headed off to the fields to play, and on the way he told me that his mother was having another fit.

But grown up stuff in B. J.'s family was their business, and I understood it that way. I was just glad to have met both B. J. and Tim since we'd moved here. Plus, we kids had our own stuff to deal with. I was reminded of the time when I first met Tim, when we had that little exchange. I had suspected that he never believed I was in the sixth grade. And whenever he'd come to my house, it would be with B. J., or he would have been to B. J.'s house first, and found out that B. J. was at my house. Otherwise, he had never visited my house alone.

But one day after school, I was looking out the window and saw him riding his bike real fast. He turned in to our yard and had a satchel on his bike. I went out as he was pulling in.

"Hey, Junior," he said, getting off his bike. "I brought my school books. I wanted to see if y'all studying the same things in sixth grade that we are at my school."

When I saw those pretty clean books, I was in shock. I went like "Wow!" They looked like they had never been used. Unlike my books, his were all brand-new. If I hadn't realized it before, I certainly knew for sure now that our books were used up and dirtied up by white students before they got to us. This was more obvious by the fact that the several spaces for students' names in our books were all used up, and his book only had one name—his.

But Tim did get his answer. However, when I told him where we were in my book, he seemed quite perturbed. I told him that we were two chapters ahead of his class.

## MARCH 1948

I was really liking this idea of having electricity. When we had homework or reading assignments, it was very easy. Instead of going where the lamp was, now all we had to do was pull a string: instant light.

It was Tuesday, the eleventh of January, and I had a lot of homework. My plan was to play outside with Tim and B. J. until dark, then go inside and do my homework. When I got home, the first thing Mother said was "How much homework y'all got?" Katie and Marie told her that they only had a little, and they were going to get it done right away.

"I got a lot," I told her, "but I'm going to play first, and do it tonight."

She responded in her no-nonsense tone, "You need to go ahead and get yours done too, because we don't have no lights…the two bulbs that were working both blew today."

I stared in disbelief, speechless. Finally, with my plan for the afternoon dashed, I asked: "When we gon get some more bulbs?"

I don't think it was a pause at all, just a case of not wanting to share the obvious with me. "We can't afford to buy any more bulbs," she said.

I understood, and went ahead and did my homework.

But even with no lights, I could get my work done. I'd just have to do like I always did, do it before dark, and even if I had to use a kerosene lamp, I could still get it done.

Beyond the news that we no longer had electricity, I took it in stride with everything else. I understood how things had changed for us since we left Hugo. And at this point in time, not having any money in our household was the norm, not only for my family, but for all poor families. Therefore, the obvious option was to do the best we could in order to survive.

## April 1948

Our car stopped running.

## May 1948

It was about noon that Saturday morning, and my sisters and I were in the yard. I was trimming a stick to make a sling-shot, and my sisters were playing nearby. Daddy came out and paused on the steps as he lit a cigarette. I knew that he was on his way to town for a few hours. He came over where we were to say goodbye, I figured, and I was correct. "Okay, younguns," he said, "I'm off to town for a while."

We all said, "Yessir," and figured that was it. But he continued to talk.

"Since y'all gon be getting out of school for the summer, me and your momma arranged for you to start going to Sunday School with your uncle Chad and his family."

We said "Yessir," as Daddy was on his way.

I wasn't too excited about Sunday School, but I was about the prospect that we could spend some time with our cousins.

It was the next weekend that Mother reminded us that we would be going to Sunday School the next day. Sure enough, Uncle Chad drove up about an hour after we had finished breakfast.

The car was crowded, but we all managed. The ride to the church took about twenty minutes. We arrived in a place called Parkstown. I didn't think it was a town, but maybe it was. The houses were much closer together than they were in the country, so maybe this was a real town. At any rate, this was quite an interesting place.

The church, Saints Delight, was at an intersection, and it looked very similar to Saint John. Of course there was not a large vacant area surrounding it for parking. We got out and went inside. A few people were already seated, but they hadn't gotten started. I guess that meant we were on time. The grown ups greeted each other, and Aunt Cora introduced us, as she also seemed to be one of the people in charge. I spotted the preacher right off. He was dressed better than anybody else, and he had that aura of dominion over everybody and everything. He was cool.

This would become a part of our lives periodically, as my parents still had allegiance to Saint John, back in Greene County.

## July 1948

With the positive things that were currently in my life, I understood that it was not much in the big picture. Plus, I knew that it would not last. So, this positive time didn't change the fact that overall, we were otherwise ragged and hungry. Since this was a constant, there was no reason to be reminded of that fact. With that being said, even as a ten-year-old, I couldn't understand how my parents could bring another child into the world. I had noticed that Mother was getting fatter and fatter! At least her stomach was.

I thought back to the comment I'd received from the kid before Best was born: "You 'bout one dumb mutha fucka." Well, I had that sex education class, so I wasn't dumb anymore. It was a certainty that she was going to drop a baby, and it looked like it would be sooner than later.

But life went on.

It was tobacco-harvesting season. And just as Daddy had explained it, we got to see our cousins every week. Daddy and Uncle Chad swapped labor. We would start at our place on Monday, and when we'd finished there, we'd go to Uncle Chad's place. Uncle Chad had a car, of course. But when it was our turn to go to his place, we'd hitch the mules to the wagon and travel the two miles via that mode of transportation. However, a couple of times we were transported there by a tractor pulling us in a trailer. I don't remember the man's name who drove us though.

I was now ten years old and weighing about ninety pounds. Daddy reinstated me as a truck driver. Again, as it was in my previous stint, I had to stand on the front of the truck, because if I were to stand on the back, I couldn't see over the truckload of tobacco.

On days that we were at our place, I was the truck driver. Chuck and Bobby Ray took care of the babies. But on days when we were at Uncle Chad's, Chuck trucked while Bobby Ray and I cared for the babies.

The last week in July, Daddy bought an old ragged 1939 Chevy from Major Bennett (Tim's older brother) for two hundred dollars.

We finished putting in tobacco at Uncle Chad's about ten thirty one Thursday. Chuck, Bobby Ray, and I were glad to get the week's work over with. That meant a whole day and a half to rest, play, or do whatever we wanted to.

We were at the pump washing our hands and horsing around when Daddy and Uncle Chad came to do the same. Daddy got the pump handle and started pumping while Uncle Chad got the lye soap and began lathering his hands.

"Don't you boys run off, now," Uncle Chad told us. "We're going over to Lacey's place and help him finish up for the week. He's been a little short-handed lately."

Then Daddy gave us the good news: "And on the way over there, we gon stop and get you boys a bite to eat."

We all headed to the cars. I rode with Uncle Chad and the boys, while Daddy drove our car to take Mother and the girls home. We pulled into our yard behind them; Daddy parked and got in the car with us.

Mr. Lacey's place was on the other side of La Grange, and there was an Esso service station on the corner. When we got to the parking lot, all of us got out.

It was hot! The screen door to the service station was a little squeaky. As we followed Daddy and Uncle Chad in, Bobby Ray swung the door two or three times just to hear the squeak. He and Chuck got a good laugh out of that.

There was also a huge fan whirling in the window, blowing air all the way across the store. I opened my shirt and stood in the middle of the breeze from the fan. My shirt was flapping as I leaned my head back and took in all the coolness. Meanwhile, Bobby Ray and Chuck were looking at a display, while Daddy and Uncle Chad made purchases of drinks and Nabs. Then out of nowhere, we heard the white man who was operating the store, yelling, "Just get the hell out of here…get them goddamn younguns and go!"

Daddy and Uncle Chad quickly ushered us out. "Come on, boys," Uncle Chad told us. We got in the car and headed on to Mr. Lacey's. Not only did Daddy and Uncle Chad not bother to explain what had happened, but they didn't even talk to each other. I never did find out what happened there. And due to all of that, the drinks and Nabs weren't nearly as good as I had imagined they would be.

## August 1948

It was the fourth Sunday in August. Marie had turned seven years old the day before. There was no party, no celebration, of course. But on this day, we found ourselves at Saints Delight with Uncle Chad and his family for their Quarterly Meeting. Service was in progress, and it was time for the offering. The ushers made their way to the front of the church and got collection plates. They had begun their trek along the pews, passing the plates down one row and back up the other.

Obviously Reverend Sutton recognized that there was some downtime to be reckoned with. So he looked over at Aunt Cora, who was sitting on the front pew, rocking the baby from side to side, seemingly meditating. He said to her: "Sister Shepherd, will you play a few notes while the offering is being taken up?" Aunt Cora gently placed the baby on a blanket beside her and picked up her guitar. Then she closed her eyes again and hesitated. Apparently she forgot where she was, as she made a few slides and runs before she started playing a rhythm. All of that would've made B. B. King proud. Meanwhile, Reverend Sutton started patting his foot and bobbing his head. Then, he caught himself. He stopped and said: "Come on now, Sister Shepherd." Aunt Cora eased up, and went to a slower, more fitting piece of music. All I know is that I'd never heard anything like that, absolutely wonderful! From that moment on, I was in love with the guitar.

**SEPTEMBER 1948**

In spite of the additional grown-up-like responsibilities that continued to be placed on me, I was still a child. My friends and I continued to play together as usual. It was a hot Wednesday in September when we were getting ready to play cowboys and Indians at my house. Tim was smiling and looking unusually happy for some reason. In the midst of getting toys from his bike and handing them to us, he paused and looked at B. J. and me. Then he began: "Boys, today is my birthday." He paused. Then still smiling real big, he continued,

"I just turned thirteen." Next was the clincher. "So it's time for you boys to start calling me Mr. Tim."

B. J. and I looked at each other in disbelief; then we turned to Tim and looked at him the same way. But he just stood there, real defiant like. We both shook our heads and told him nope. Then Tim took his toys, got on his bike, and headed back home. We never played with him again.

However, I must give Tim credit for introducing me to my very first white folks prose, thus written:

(1) Oughts are oughts, figgas are figgas
    All for white folks, none for the niggas.
(2) I came to a river I couldn't get cross
    I jumped on a nigga. I thought he was a hoss.
(3) The darkies' hour is just before dawn.

## NOVEMBER 1948

Yep, B. J. and I had lost a friend, but I was old enough now to understand that nothing is permanent, especially friendships. And just like there are endings, there are also beginnings.

This very point was magnified for me when I found out that Grandpa was preparing to venture into something new. This year was an election year, and President Harry Truman was campaigning for re-election. His platform was equal rights. Grandpa would sit by the radio and listen intently every time the president was on. He would get all excited, and could hardly wait to vote for the first time in his life. He surmised that since both candidates were talking about equal rights, he would have no problem even if Truman didn't win.

When the day came for voting, Grandpa got up early. He put on his tattered blue serge suit, white shirt, and necktie, picked up his walking stick, and strutted out the door, headed up the road to La Grange to vote.

A few hours later Grandpa returned home. For some reason, he was crestfallen. Years later I learned that he was disqualified from voting because he didn't know how many windows were in the courthouse.

He never attempted to vote again.

Nineteen forty-eight was also a year of sorrow for our family. On the thirtieth of November, Mother gave birth to a baby girl. She let my sisters and I name her. We agreed on the name Janet.

There was something different about Janet. She cried continuously. It got so bad that they took her to the hospital, where she was kept for ongoing treatment. Mother stayed with her the first few days as Daddy would come home every night.

Janet only lived ten days. It was determined that she became sick because the midwife used a dull instrument to cut her cord. Upon hearing of her death, Daddy and Uncle Chad went to the hospital that night and picked her up. Daddy told us that he asked them to dress her in white. Then he brought her home in a shoebox. He let my sisters, my grief-stricken mother, and my two-year-old brother spend an hour with her before he put the top on the box and took it away. As Daddy was leaving, I asked, "Where are you going to bury her?" He never answered my question.

That weekend, Uncle Greg and Aunt Arlene brought Grandpa back home after he had spent a week with them. He and Mother were in the bedroom talking in whispers. I happened to be next door in the kitchen. I didn't hear their whole conversation, but I did hear Mother tell Grandpa, "He buried my baby like burying a dog."

## DECEMBER 1949

Needless to say, the remainder of the year was nothing but sadness. There was virtually nothing for Christmas, and we'd lost a baby sister.

## JANUARY 1949

The arrival of 1949 was not gleefully celebrated. I guess we were too deep into our miseries. In addition to all else that had happened near the end of last year, our car quit working, permanently. Daddy sold it for junk.

## FEBRUARY 1949

I started having nightmares. It got to the point where I was afraid to go to sleep at night. Mother would come to my room and console me whenever I woke up.

As the months passed, my health got better. One Wednesday after school, I went to B. J.'s house to play. I knocked on the door and waited for someone to answer. B. J. came to the door with one of the biggest smiles I'd ever seen. My first question was "What's wrong?" Still grinning, he came outside and began to share the good news that was causing that big grin on his face. "My daddy gave me some money," he said. By this time, we were down the steps, standing in the yard. B. J. pointed back to the house. "I got it in my room," he said, still excited. "I got enough money that we can go see *Tarzan and the Ape Man* Saturday evening."

I was still looking at him in disbelief. "Wait a minute," I cautioned. "I ain't never been to no movie place before. Plus, that's your money."

B. J. kept on insisting that he wanted me to go, "if your momma and daddy will let you." I felt certain that it would be okay with my folks, so I told him that I'd let him know if they approved.

On the way to school the next morning, I told B. J. that I had gotten the okay to go to the movie with him. For the next two days, all we talked about was going to the movies.

It was Saturday afternoon. B. J. and I were walking up the road to La Grange. I would now get to see my first movie: *Tarzan and the Ape Man.* Naturally, I had already asked B. J. what the theater was like, and he had provided me with details as to what I would be experiencing: the big screen, the loud sound, and how it makes you feel like you're right there with the action! I couldn't wait.

Of course, in addition to what I already knew about the theater, that it was for both white folks and Negros, B. J. had told me what the procedure was for attending this movie house. And he had been very accurate in his description. He said that since there was only one theatre in town, black folks had to sit in the balcony (nigger heaven) and breathe stale air. White folks sat downstairs. It wasn't important; with all the excitement I was experiencing, the seating arrangement would not be an issue.

When we arrived, there were several white girls and boys at the window purchasing tickets. I was behind B. J. as he bought our tickets. Then we went inside. B. J. informed me that we had to go up the stairway on the left side, and that the floor-level entrance was for white folks. I followed him. At the end of the stairs, there was an open area with what looked like indoor booths. That was the concession area. A young white boy was in charge of that. On past that, there were bathrooms. In the midst of all of my excitement, I began to make observations. It was apparent that nobody had bothered to clean up that area. There was popcorn and other trash on the floor, and the one little receptacle that I saw was overflowing.

Then we entered the movie area. The lights were still on, and I could see that the lack of cleanliness continued. There were candy wrappers, popcorn, and popcorn boxes littering the aisles and within the rows of seats. It was apparent that the colored area did not receive janitorial attention.

B. J. and I went and sat on the front row. There were some people we knew from school, and others we didn't know. But we greeted them all as we made our way to our seats.

For some reason, I was disappointed though. This was not about anything in general, but about something in particular. Looking down from the balcony, I could see how clean and neat that area was (for white folks).

However, once the lights were turned off and the movie began, I forgot all about my complaints. Boy, that was a good movie, the best I had ever seen!

And to top that off, B. J. introduced me to what he said was a favorite pastime for black children in La Grange. When the movie was over, we walked down to the drugstore and looked through that big plate glass window and watched the white kids sitting at the lunch counter consuming milkshakes and Coca-Cola floats. Of course, there were other black kids looking in there too. That was some night out!

For the next couple of weeks at least, I shared my movie experience with my sisters and everybody else I came in contact with.

## MAY 1949

On the first Sunday, around noon, Uncle Jack and his family came for a brief visit. Actually, it was prearranged, as they were going to take Grandpa to spend a couple of weeks with them.

In the midst of all of the negatives in my life, I guess that a positive came on the second Sunday in May. Reverend Dare was coming to have dinner with us. Since Grandpa wasn't there, we had a vacant seat at the table to accommodate him. Mother had been preparing and talking about it all week. She had already warned me not to do or say anything stupid, and she told all of us to "just be yourself."

That day finally arrived. She made us put on Sunday

clothes, even though we weren't going to church. But since we had to dress up like that, it felt like a church Sunday.

My sisters and I were looking out the window in anticipation. About three o'clock a black Cadillac pulled into the yard. It was Reverend Dare. He didn't get out immediately. Instead, he adjusted the rearview mirror and turned his face from side to side; then he stroked his mustache down.

When he did finally get out, he reached back in the car and got his jacket, put it on, and straightened the lapels. Then he headed for the door. When we heard the knock, we closed the curtain and waited to be summoned to the living room. We stood waiting as we heard the greetings. I could hear Daddy, as he was louder than anybody. "How you, Preacher?" he asked.

"I'm just fine," Reverend Dare said. "Look like you been doing a lot of work since you been here."

Daddy responded in kind, I think, "Yeah, a lot of hard work… and I see that you got a new suit; you look nice."

I guess Mother took it that Daddy was off-key with his remark; that's when she interrupted. She yelled for us to come in there. "Junior, you and the girls come in here and say hey to the reverend."

Obediently, we went, said, "Hey," and returned to the back room.

Of course I was still listening and peeking as much as I could.

"Have a seat, Reverend, while I get the table set," Mother told Reverend Dare. "And would you like something to drink while I finish in the kitchen?"

"A glass of water," the preacher said.

Mother got a glass of water. Daddy and Reverend Dare talked while the girls and I waited, and while Mother finished preparing the meal in the kitchen.

Mother returned to the living room and announced to Daddy and the preacher, "Y'all come on." Then she came to the back room and told us that dinner was ready.

Daddy and the Reverend Dare were on the back porch washing their hands in the basin that Mother had placed on a table. We lined up behind them and did likewise. We wiped our hands on a towel that hung on a string across the porch and went back into the kitchen.

Daddy and Reverend Dare were already seated, each at opposite ends of the table. Mother remained standing so that she could orchestrate us kids, the remaining participants. This was necessary of course, because we had a guest at the table and our usual seating changed.

"Marie, you sit here," she said, pointing to the chair next to her. "Katie, you're over there," she said, pointing to the chair across the table from Marie. "And Junior, you are right there," she said to me, as she pointed to the remaining chair. This meant that I was directly across the table from her.

We all took our places, as Mother remained standing. "Okay, Namon," she said, looking at Daddy, "we're ready."

Daddy hesitated, then said to our guest: "Preacher, would you mind saying the grace for us?"

Reverend Dare began, "Dear heavenly father…and bless this food before us. Amen."

Mother served what was not already on the table. We had string beans, rice, gravy, biscuits, potato salad, fried chicken, and peach pie. It was a good meal, and even though I didn't get enough to eat, I was glad to get as much as I did, especially considering the fact that the preacher got the best parts of the chicken.

I finished without asking for seconds, because I knew that there were no seconds. I remembered what Mother had cautioned me about. I was polite and courteous, as I had been taught, and doing what I always did when we had chicken. I said, "Mother, I've finished. May I be excused? And would you like to have my bones?"

I saw the strange look on Mother's face, but didn't know at the time that I had said something embarrassing. She later explained that sometimes instead of doing exactly what you have been taught routinely, you have to consider other things, like the specific circumstance.

I learned that lesson.

It was the fourth Sunday in June, a typical summer day. It got hot early. But in spite of that, I didn't get up until I smelled food cooking. The girls were playing in their room. Daddy and Grandpa were sitting on the back porch. Daddy was reading the newspaper while Grandpa was relaxing in his rocking chair. "Good morning," I said to Mother as I was passing through the kitchen. I poured salt into my hand to use for brushing my teeth because we didn't have toothpaste.

"Did you get enough sleep?" she asked sarcastically.

"I think so," I told her. I spoke to Daddy and Grandpa, and went on out the door.

Before I got to the pump, I broke off a small piece of a peach tree branch for a toothbrush. After I brushed my teeth, I was washing up when Mother called us for breakfast. She had that spiritual music playing on the radio. "Precious Lord, take my hand." I knew it was a live recording because I could hear the people having church in the background. I guess that was prepping us for our own church service a few hours from then.

It seemed like there wasn't much time between breakfast and our leaving for church. Mother was going non-stop. She got a couple of cakes and put them in boxes, as she directed the rest of us in getting dressed. Daddy put the box in the trunk, then came back inside to help Mother get us dressed.

Then Daddy ushered us to the car where he had parked on an incline. Sure enough, he let the clutch out and the engine caught as the car rolled down the hill. Daddy smiled as my sisters and I cheered.

The church was about twelve miles away, about six miles into Green County. We arrived at least twenty minutes before service started. Uncle Ott and his family were pulling up at the same time. Consequently, I got to visit with Big Bo and Li'l Bo.

We stayed out there and talked for a spell before services formally started. There were songs and praises as we entered. Then there was another song. About halfway through that one, I heard the door open. I looked up and Uncle Leroy and his family were coming in. The twins looked at me and I was looking at them. We all just shrugged our shoulders. We knew that often when Uncle Leroy came in late it was because one of the children was sick, but we were always glad to see him.

## JUNE 1949

Tobacco harvesting was fast approaching, and my folks were busy sewing tobacco curtains and making truck rounds. And since my sisters were older now, there was relief for me from tending to them. However, between the three of us, we took care of our little brother and did other chores around the house. We'd feed the chickens and mules. Plus, there was a cow that I milked every morning. But the best part of all was probably the fact that Brownie had grown so much. So whenever I would go somewhere on the farm, Brownie would accompany me.

## JULY 1949

Our arrangement for putting in tobacco was the same as last year. We swapped with Uncle Chad, and we were at each other's house every week. Also, taking care of the babies was the same as far as I, Chuck, and Bobby Ray were concerned.

On the fourth Sunday, when we went to church, Grandpa had his suitcase packed. After services, when it was time to return home, Grandpa had Big Bo put his things in Uncle Jack's car because he was going to move in with them for a spell. We missed him something fierce.

Of course, going to my first movie theater back in May obviously tweaked my interest. Even though I couldn't go often, I continued to think about my experience. B. J. and I managed to get a few dollars before summer was over and we took full advantage.

On the third Saturday, B. J. and I were at the movies again, cheering on the cowboys as they slaughtered Indians. We decided to have a little fun at the expense of white folks downstairs. Some of us began throwing popcorn on their heads. The police were summoned. The two city cops responded. They each came up the same aisle, from opposite directions, and met in the middle, slapping the crap out of each of us kids sitting on the front row, girls as well as boys. That ended the popcorn throwing. We never told our parents about this, because we knew that we'd be punished again at home.

### AUGUST 1949

The second week in August, summer vacation was over, and it was time to return to school. On opening day, there was a pleasant surprise. It had been rumored, but not confirmed. We had ten more new school buses. And those of us who lived outside the city limits were able to ride to school. There was also a large new classroom building on campus. Separate but equal? Not really. And there was no integration.

### SEPTEMBER 1949

B. J. and I picked cotton for Bill Post. And a couple of farmers allowed us to scrap their cornfields after they'd gathered. This meant that anything they left, we could have to sell.

## OCTOBER 1949

In early October I found out that mother was once again pregnant. I became depressed and angry. I was thinking, *Why? How could you?* I remained in that condition for probably two weeks. After realizing that punishing myself was not going to change anything, I was able to work my way out of that funk.

## NOVEMBER/DECEMBER 1949

In November, Uncle Saul and Aunt Kathy came to live with us. This was no big deal because we had gotten used to Grandpa living with us. They just moved into where he used to be. The only difference was that there were two of them instead of one. And my sisters and I loved them both; after all, they were family too.

About mid-November, after we had completed harvesting our crops, my sisters and I started talking about what we wanted for Christmas. Little did we know that our next visit from Santa would be our last decent Christmas as children. Christmas came, and the gifts were nice. I found out later that Uncle Saul had bankrolled that most joyous occasion.

## JANUARY 1950

The New Year's celebrations that Daddy used to have were a thing of the past. There was virtually nothing. Even the wishes for prosperity to each other were without emotion.

Aunt Kathy and Uncle Saul remained with us a couple of weeks into January. Then they moved to Richmond, Virginia. I don't know what the connection was that drew them there, probably an acquaintance or the prospect of a job.

A week after their departure, we had a new arrival to the family. In spite of my dissatisfaction with matters regarding Mother's pregnancy, Eugene, the new baby was very welcome. As it turned out, this was such a glorious time. He arrived on the twenty-first of January.

A few days after Gene was born, I had one of my worst nightmares. I was lying in bed about nine thirty, and I felt a throbbing on the left side of my head. I lay there to see if it would go away. It didn't. Instead, it started throbbing real fast, and I could hear it!

Then I started getting dizzy. That's when I got up and ran to my parents' bedroom. I jumped onto their bed where the baby was sleeping between them. I missed his head by only a few inches. Profusely sweating, I began clenching the headboard so hard that Daddy had to pry my fingers loose. Of course they were startled. Daddy turned the lights on and got up. Eventually, the two of them got me calmed down. Then Mother gave me some medicine. Daddy took me back to my room, and stayed up with me until I told him that the pain and fear had gone.

## MARCH 1950

While I had my health issues, I refused to complain because I knew that things could be a whole lot worse. At least I could be hopeful. I also knew that other boys and girls had stuff that they were dealing with too. One blatant item to reflect this had to do with a boy at school. His name was Josh Johnson. He was a ninth-grader. The principal came to our class right before lunch and called Josh to the hallway, where they talked. Josh came back in and shared that Mr. Fields wanted to see him in his office after school let out.

But Josh, being no idiot, got on the school bus. About five miles after we left school, Mr. Fields caught up with the bus. He got Josh off, and had him sit in the front seat of his car. As Mr. Fields was turning the car around to head back to school, Josh jumped out and bolted toward the woods. Mr. Fields stopped the car and got out and began to chase Josh. But he forgot to put the car in neutral and put the brake on. The car kept moving and wound up in the ditch. As the bus drove away, we could see Mr. Fields jumping up and down and waving his arms. Of course we kids got a good laugh out of that for a long time. And as might have been predicted, we never saw Josh at school again.

## APRIL 1950

In April, there was another episode of drama with the new baby. As if my seizures weren't bad enough, this time he almost starved to death. Mother was breast-feeding him the same as she had always done with her children, and just as most women did. But we noticed that he was crying a lot, even when he'd been fed, even when he was not soiled, and even when he had proper sleep. It was puzzling. Mother and Daddy made all kinds of adjustments, trying to get him to stop crying so much. Finally, they took him to Dr. Carson in La Grange. He did whatever kind of investigating or testing that was necessary, and eventually suggested putting him on bottled milk. That did the trick! The boy was on his way. Dr. Carson discovered that Mother's breast milk was no good.

In addition to that good news, my health also improved tremendously. I'm sure that was also a relief for Mother and Daddy, as they could get back to caring for the farm and the rest of the family.

On Tuesday, the last week in April, my sisters and I were getting ready for school, and I asked Mother why she hadn't cooked breakfast. She said that it was because there was nothing to cook, but there would be something to eat when we returned from school that afternoon.

When we got back home, Daddy had bought a half-gallon of molasses; that's what we had for dinner. The following morning, we had molasses for breakfast. We ate molasses three times a day for at least a week. When we had a bowel movement, we shit molasses. But at least we had something to eat.

Also to be kept in mind is that we knew it was not a "must" that we get three, or even two squares a day. As long as we ate often enough to survive, we were okay.

## MAY 1950

May arrived, and life continued to be typical for us. We were used to eking by, but so were other families. Therefore, there was no complaining.

Lucky for us, it was spring and there were berries to pick. I would take my sisters into the woods where we would pick briar berries and huckleberries. When we went to school, our mouths would be blue. But it wasn't a case where we stood out like a sore thumb. At that time of year, most kids who lived in the country had blue mouths.

The last day of school brought a new focus for me. It had nothing to do with the last day of school in its own right. Instead, it was about the future. As we were departing for our summer vacation, a glaring realization began to come into focus. I would be going to high school when I came back in the fall. And even with my confidence, that one thought seemed so imposing.

## JUNE 1950

In the summer, my sisters and I got the brilliant idea to collect as much scrap metal as we could find, and sell it to the "Junk Man." After two months, we had managed to accumulate almost a small trailer load.

Mother and Daddy had gone to town, leaving us kids at home by ourselves. Katie was on the back porch reading while Marie was playing in their room. I was in the yard trying to figure out how to tie different kinds of knots.

Suddenly, I heard a familiar sound, but I couldn't immediately identify it. I looked down the road toward the store. Sure enough, coming up the road was a black pickup truck with a cover on the back. I shouted to my sisters, "Here come the junk man!"

He pulled into the yard and asked if we had any metal for sale. My sisters and I happily directed him to our stash. That redneck loaded our iron onto his truck and paid us.

When Mother got home, we proudly told her what we had done. Her first question was "How much did you get for it?" We told her that the man gave us a dime.

Boy, she became livid. "That low-down dog, taking advantage of children! I just wish I had been here!" She went on and on for several minutes. Eventually she settled down, and we all went on to other matters. In spite of any misgivings though, we three children savored that dime.

I placed it on the dresser under a cloth. Periodically, I would check just to make sure that it was still there. Wow, that was a pretty coin!

With tobacco-harvesting time coming up, and not getting paid for harvesting our own, I began to think about how I could make some money for movies, hot dogs, and just plain junk. I figured I could make a little money by helping other farmers. I only wanted to make enough to go to the movies and buy hot dogs.

I knew that it wouldn't take all five days for us to get our tobacco in for the week. Therefore, there should be at least two full days when I could work for some of the farmers around the neighborhood. That was my plan anyway.

Even before the season started, I began thinking of nearby farmers who I might be able to get a few days of work with. Joe Bennett was the first that came to mind. And it didn't matter if Tim and I were no longer friends. This was all about the money now.

Of course, I consulted with B. J. to get the names of other farmers I might be able to work for. This approach worked well, because B. J. had the same thing in mind. In addition to Mr. Joe, B. J. shared some other ideas with me.

## JULY 1950

By now, I had learned to appreciate summer. This meant not having to go to school and not having to do homework. But best of all, even though it meant having to do more farm work, we would be able to eat regularly.

We got started with putting in tobacco. By now it was routine, except I had grown, just a little. But overall, the familiarity with all that I was surrounded by had rendered me pretty confident. And there was no drama during the entire season. That is, there was no drama on the farm. But there was one item in town one Saturday evening.

Also, the plan that B. J. and I had concerning working for other farmers at the end of the week had worked out perfectly. We usually didn't work for the same farmer, but we did get an extra days work every week during the tobacco season.

We mainly got work with Bill Post, Rudolph Sutton, and Jim Bennett. The drawback with working for Mr. Bennett was that he paid kids less money than he did grown-ups for the same job. But it was better than nothing.

In addition to consistently having food, summer also meant that people would have extra money to spend. And the nearest place to spend that money was in La Grange.

La Grange only had one block of businesses, and during the summer when people had that tobacco money in their pockets, that block would be teeming with people. One Saturday, there was a white woman's scream, and the town's two cops went running to see what the problem was.

The woman pointed to a black man, Ray Heath, the town drunk. Her report to them was "He's drunk; he almost knocked me off the sidewalk." One of the officers grabbed Ray by the back of his collar, and began tightening it as a way to make sure that he had control of his "suspect." Apparently realizing that Ray was not a threat, the cop released Ray's collar. "I ain't drunk, boss,." Ray told him. Then Ray made the mistake of staggering. At that point he was struck in the head with night-sticks repeatedly, by both cops. And as they began walking him that one block to the jail, his light-blue shirt was saturated with blood.

We finished harvesting the last week of the month. But before B. J. and I finished on our "outside" jobs, we made sure to talk to those same farmers about picking cotton for them, and scrapping corn.

By finishing harvesting tobacco so early, this meant that we had over a week before school started. This being the case, B. J. and I decided to do our last movie before school opened.

It was on Saturday night, the last weekend in July. B.J. and I were at the movies. But this time we didn't sit in the front row, and we didn't even buy any popcorn. Everybody's behavior was exemplary. When the movie was over, we decided to go across the street to the café (the only one in town) and get a hot dog. Black folks had to go in the alley at the rear of the building to be served. There was a little cubbyhole with a sliding door, and people would knock on that door so that someone would come and take their order. Then the worker would close the door until the food was ready.

That Saturday night, a black handicapped man named Pepper was working the window. According to information on the street, Pepper's handicap was the result of being struck by lightning. He never recovered, and his left arm hung limply at his side. And he slobbered, non-stop.

When we walked into the alley, B. J. knocked on the sliding door, and when it opened, there stood Pepper, grinning and slobbering. B. J. said, "Hell no!" and we both ran out of the alley and headed home.

On the way, we decided to stop by Earl White's Hardware Store and buy something to drink, as it was a fact that he had the coldest soft drinks in town. When we walked in, there were several white men sitting around talking. One of them asked us if we wanted some chewing gum. Free gum? You bet we did! We eagerly accepted, and walked out of there with cold sodas and free chewing gum. What a night out!

As we walked, we began to take turns running into the cornfields to defecate. That was the longest walk ever for us from town to where we lived. When I got home, I kept running to the outhouse. Mother asked me what was wrong. I showed her my pack of free chewing gum. She grew very angry. She informed me that it wasn't chewing gum, that it was Feen-A-Mint gum, a laxative. My stomach eventually settled down, and Mother's anger eventually subsided. But over the next few days, she would remind everyone of her displeasure of that incident.

The only other item of note the remainder of July had to do with my brother Best. He was now three and a half years old. One day he said that he was no longer Best Shepherd, but we should call him Shep Best instead. And we did for a while, until he concluded that it was no longer important to him.

Before he reverted to his given name, Shep Best suffered an injury of sorts. One day his eye was stung by a wasp, and it swelled to about the size of an egg! Aunt Cora, who was a very religious woman, was also a Faith Healer. She said that she would anoint his eye with some holy water. Shep Best told Mother that he didn't want that water on his eye. But Mother insisted that he let Aunt Cora go through with her effort to help.

Early the next morning when Shep Best got out of bed, he ran to the mirror and saw that his eye was even bigger. He told Mother point-blank, "Look at my eye! I knew that mess wasn't going to work!"

Also, summer was just about over, and money was beginning to dry up. But before it did, Daddy bought an old ragged '39 Chevy for one hundred dollars from Major Bennett (Tim's older brother). It took about ten minutes to get that thing started and in forward gear. Of course Daddy knew that parking it on an incline would counteract those issues.

## AUGUST 1950

Yep, school was about to open. I thought back to last May when I was focused on going to high school, and that very idea was just about frightful. Now, there were no fears of such monumental proportion. That fear I had about high school last May had all but gone. Now, I was more or less looking forward to it.

I knew that I would be going into an environment where there would be students who were older and bigger than me. And I was hoping that such a factor would not present any difficulty; after all, I had been here a few years and I knew a lot of people. But that one thought kept persisting. *How will I be perceived by the new students that I will encounter?* I was able to put that in the back of my mind and concentrate on things more immediate.

My sisters and I were ready, standing at the road when the bus came. And in spite of anything else that might be happening on this kind of occasion, one thing that stood out was the gaiety and the physical picture that was in place. It was exciting from that perspective. All the kids were dressed in their new outfits, and wearing smiles. They all seemed so glad to be in each other's midst. And this was rightfully so, because nobody had had the opportunity yet to make enemies. This was indeed a beautiful day. After a few more stops, we were at school. The bus unloaded and moved to the parking area. Teachers were out front helping us find where we were supposed to go.

I finally arrived at my destination. Quite a few students were already in the classroom, mostly standing up. The teacher was assigning seats as she looked at her roll book. I just stood there. When most of the group had been seated, there were about six of us still standing.

Then my name was called. "Moses," the teacher said, "you

get the seat right there." As she spoke, she was pointing to the fourth seat in the third row. I went to where she had assigned me and sat down. I could hear some snickering, and I could feel the eyes looking in my direction. I knew what the snickering was about, but I didn't let on. I continued to look straight ahead.

Finally, the teacher looked up. She stopped making further assignments of seats for the remaining students and addressed the distracting situation. "Moses," she said. "You come back up here, and let this student have your seat." I did as I had been instructed. Along the way, I also heard a few comments. "He sure is little," one girl said. One of the boys chimed in, "He gotta be in fourth grade." Yep, it was embarrassing. The desk that I was sitting in had all but swallowed me up. Obviously, it was a desk for bigger high school kids.

I don't know if some of the bigger students were repeaters or not. I just know that the teacher was very familiar with them. "George," she said to one of those bigger boys, "go to the office and tell them that I need a fourth-grade desk." Sure enough, George headed out on his assigned mission, and I was embarrassed enough for the entire year.

But over time, they got used to me being amongst them. And I was not distracted for very long. As a matter of fact, there was something else that proved to be so interesting. That was how things took shape as the year went on. Relative to the fact that the kids from in town prided themselves in thinking that they were better than us country kids, and in spite of all of their high-faluting airs, some of those same kids, boys and girls, would come to me and ask if they could copy my homework. Of course the answer was an emphatic NO!

But such interactions with them had no bearing whatsoever on what I thought of them, and those thoughts weren't negative at all.

## SEPTEMBER 1950

It was the last week in September when B. J. and I were able to move ahead with our other plan. We turned to picking cotton for Bill Post and Rudolph Sutton.

## OCTOBER 1950

Near the end of October, the car stopped being dependable. Consequently, Daddy pretty much let it sit except for when he had to go a fairly long distance. And on those occasions he'd make sure not to turn the engine off until he got back home. But before long that system was also undependable.

## NOVEMBER 1950

With our employment as cotton pickers coming to an end, B. J. and I verified our permission from the same farmers to scrap their cornfields after they'd finished harvesting them. We didn't make a lot of money, but we made some.

## DECEMBER 1950

The remainder of the year was nothing special. School was routine. And at home we were our usual poor-ass selves, barely making it.

A few days after Christmas, the car engine cracked due to the fact that Daddy couldn't afford to buy antifreeze.

However, there was one significant thing for me this month. I became a teenager. Yep, the big THIRTEEN!

In the bigger picture, that was meaningless.

Mother started packing our belongings Friday, before we were to get out of school for Christmas the following Tuesday, the nineteenth.

Our weekend was "regular," as was Monday and Tuesday. Then Wednesday morning, we started moving. Using Uncle Chad's car, and making several trips, we moved to another farm. This time it was to the Bear Creek area of Lenoir County. It was owned by Dallas Lane.

When I saw the shack that we were to call home, I cried. Mother called it Plumb Nearly, because it was plumb in the woods and nearly out of this world.

It had a kitchen and only two other rooms. There was a front porch, but no back porch. The front porch did not have any steps. Therefore, we used blocks of wood as substitutes. And at the back of the house, for some reason, we did not use such blocks. Instead, we stepped directly from the ground into the kitchen. There were several planks missing from the front porch, and several broken windowpanes. Daddy stuffed old pillows in the windows to keep the wind out, but the porch remained a hazard.

As much as I detested our new residence, there was no

option for me to "not" stay with my family. However, once we arrived at our new place and got settled in, I realized that Brownie was not there. I didn't know if that was Brownie's decision or Daddy's decision. What I did know for a fact, however, was that Daddy had a history of being the primary suspect when it came to missing dogs. Somehow Brownie wound up moving to Uncle Chad's house.

Maybe the one positive in moving to this area was that there were some familiar faces right down the road. This was the Watson family, Mrs. Glenda and Mr. Lewis. They had four children who were in the age range of my sisters. We already knew the parents because they were members of Saints Delight. They didn't have a car, but they did have a flatbed truck. As it turned out, we began going to Sunday School with them at least twice per month.

Also, my sisters and I reconciled that the wonderful Christmases we once had were long gone. Therefore, we treated this Christmas vacation time as just a few days off from school, nothing more.

## JANUARY 1951

And it was indeed a welcome time when we returned to school. It was sort of like returning from summer vacation. People seemed glad to see each other. Even the kids who thrived on having enemies seemed glad to get back to that kind of (unhealthy) life.

The following Monday, we were pretty much re-acclimated, meaning that things were back to normal. But when we got off the bus that Wednesday, everything felt different. The usual, normal horseplay and loudness were missing. I saw students gathered around in groups, quiet, whispering to each other. Then I saw some students crying.

I saw B. J., and before we reached each other, he said, "Man, did you hear what happened?" I had no response, as he could tell. "Robert Lee Jones got shot and killed last night." Some teachers were on duty, and they ushered us along to our classrooms.

This was so unbelievable on several levels. Robert Lee was seventeen years old, and an honor student. Whereas most of us wore ragged clothes to school every day, Robert Lee was always dressed up. He was known for wearing shirt and tie.

He was accused of prowling around a residence, attempting to break and enter, peeking into a white woman's window, and resisting arrest by slashing at the police officers with a knife. In response, the officers shot him in the chest eight times! Of course, since they were the only two cops in La Grange, it was the same two who slapped the shit out of us at the movie theater. Within three days, there was an inquest, and the officers were cleared, stating that they acted in the line of duty! Naturally, nothing felt the same at our school. And there we were all over again, having to live with this tragedy.

## FEBRUARY 1951

There was a pretty big snow. We even had sugar and milk in the house. We enjoyed making and eating snow cream. I helped cut wood for curing tobacco and for fuel at the house.

## MARCH 1951

The nearest store was two miles from where we lived. I walked there late one afternoon to purchase some molasses so we would have something to eat for dinner. After the clerk finished filling my jar, I set it on the concrete floor and it burst. Needless to say, we didn't eat that night.

## APRIL 1951

It was the third Sunday morning, and we were headed to church on the flatbed truck of Mr. Watson's. On the way we passed by Mr. Fields' house and saw a wreath on the door. When we got to the church, we found out that it was him and not another family member. I believe he was in his mid-forties.

## MAY 1951

Crops were being planted and tended. And we were looking forward to school closing for the summer.

The local moonshiner, Mr. Nate Shaw, employed my sisters and me to wash a hundred jars. He told us that he would pay us a penny per jar.

We were so excited about the prospects. Maybe this would be the beginning of something real good. But instead of heating some water and using soap for this project, we took a shortcut. We went to the pump and commenced pumping cold water on them.

After washing about a dozen, Katie came up with a brilliant idea. She said, "Let's take them to the ditch. Since the water is flowing, all we'll have to do is let the water do the washing.

We won't have to even pump it. Plus, this would mean that we could finish quicker." We all agreed and went to the ditch and dipped them in water. It was truly amazing how fast we got the job done. However, end results were not very impressive. But we left it at that.

Even though I knew we didn't do a good job for Mr. Shaw, I'm certain that he knew it too. But he paid us anyway. I think he felt sorry for us, and that was the only reason he hired us.

## JUNE 1951

Daddy informed me that I'd be joining the men in the field as a cropper.

## JULY 1951

Tobacco harvesting began. It was pitiful because the crop was diseased with black shank. The other significant thing that took place during this year was that Mother had another baby. My brother Lynwood Gerald was born on July thirty-first.

When Daddy told me that I had a baby brother, regrettably my response was off-key. I said to him, "Another mouth to feed!" I will never forget the hurt on his face.

## AUGUST – NOVEMBER 1951

We harvested what little there was to harvest.

## DECEMBER 1951

This was also the year that I turned fourteen years old.

So, in a nutshell, 1951 was a very bad year. And as I

expected, about a week before Christmas, Daddy announced that we were going to move.

## JANUARY 1952

The scene was eerily similar. We didn't have a car, but Daddy had gotten our fellow tenant, Mr. Louis Wilson, to move our belongings in his old black pickup. Daddy rode with him, and the rest of us rode in Uncle Chad's car. Our move was to the Rabbit Town area of Lenoir County, onto one of Matthew Post's farms.

When I first laid eyes on the house, I was astounded! It looked like white folks lived there! Once we got inside, my amazement continued. This house was truly a mansion compared to the shacks where we had previously lived. It had a living room, a dining room, a kitchen, and four bedrooms. It also had electricity, and the pump was on the enclosed back porch! On top of all of that, there were two huge grape harbors. Plus, there were peach trees, apple trees, pear trees, and pecan trees! I later learned that the Posts lived here before they bought another large farm and built a huge brick house on it.

The day we moved in, I decided to go to the stable and check out the mules. Unlike anywhere we had lived before, the stable was not anywhere near the house. It was up a path through one of the fields and across a hill. Even this, being so different, was also quite impressive. But before I even got to the stable, I was taken aback by the pasture itself. It was huge, about two acres. It was long and narrow. From one end to the other, it was probably an eighth of a mile.

After taking in the view of the pasture, I went on to the stable. If I thought the pasture was so great, what my eyes beheld when I reached the stable was absolutely astonishing! Standing in the stable, in the midst of the two mules, was the most beautiful black and white spotted pony that I had ever seen.

I ran back to the house and excitedly told Daddy what I had just witnessed. Apparently he saw the gleam in my eyes when I was telling him, because right on the spot, he interrupted and issued a stern warning. He told me that I was to feed and take care of that pony, but never to ride it. He went on to explain that Mr. Post purchased that pony especially for his grandkids. My heart sank as my excitement was dashed. But more than anything, I suppose, I was jolted back to reality. I should have known better than to fathom being astride such a beautiful animal.

Christmas was basically nothing. I figured that just being out of Bear Creek was a gift to the entire family!

Since this was such a beautiful and interesting place, it didn't take us very long to get settled in. My sisters and I didn't have to change schools, but we did have to ride a different bus. And it was via this new route to school that I discovered that now, a couple of my classmates were my neighbors. They were Carol Clemmons and Ada Graham.

Other than the aforementioned beauty, life at our new place was as mundane as it had always been. But I had reached a point in my life where I could look back and make comparisons. I realized how much our family had grown. And I realized how many different places we'd lived, and the many people I'd come to know.

And farm work was the same. Daddy prepared the fields, prepared the plant bed, planted corn, etc. Then the weather began to warm up. Of course, this would be my first warm-weather season at our new place. And believe it or not, I was excited.

## MARCH 1952

It was the first Saturday in March. Mother and Daddy went to town to get a few groceries. They took the girls with them. I guess the girls went because they enjoyed riding. I was invited, but I opted to stay at home, mainly because I knew that they didn't have enough money to buy me anything. And I liked buying stuff.

I heard a car drive into the yard, so I went to the door. It was Uncle Bob. "Hey, boy," he said as he came onto the porch. "Where's everybody?" I told him that they went to town. He walked on into the house, still talking. "I might as well look around since I'm here," he said, "to see if Namon bought anything new."

He looked in the bedrooms, in the living room; then he went into the kitchen. "Hot dog!" he exclaimed. "Namon bought a refrigerator! Life must be good."

Of course I was following him as he toured, and I listened to his comments because he really wasn't doing a conversation. He opened the refrigerator, and the only thing in there was an apple, a jar of water, and a light bulb. "I see Namon bought an apple too," Uncle Bob said as he howled laughing. He got the apple and took a huge bite. That was half the apple gone. He put the other half back on the rack. "Tell my sister that I came by," he said, and out the door he went.

## April 1952

Things in my life were going okay, at best, which wasn't bad at all considering how things had been and could be. And being fifteen years old now, I was feeling pretty good about myself. But I was still very much aware of where that proverbial line with my parents was, and I dared not cross. Things had been going fairly smooth from the standpoint of both school and farm responsibilities. However, there was one negative that occurred. That was in the health field.

We were at home about mid-afternoon that Saturday. I had just come from checking the livestock. When I walked into the house, the family was huddled in the kitchen. I rushed in to see what they were looking at. There was Gene, staring out into space, gagging and drooling. It was obvious though that he wasn't choking, and he was breathing okay. But he did look bad.

"Namon, we've gotta take him to the doctor," Mother said to Daddy.

"All right, c'mon," he responded as he picked Gene up in his arms and headed out the door. Mother went to their bedroom, got the baby and a sweater. She turned to the rest of us and assured us that they'd be back as soon as they could. Then they were off to La Grange to see Dr. Carson.

Marie, Katie, and Best all stood around looking sad, and I

guess I did too. But I knew that I was the one who had to ease their minds and get us through what was happening.

"Let's go outside," I told them. "We can play some games." Even though I had outgrown most games, especially ones that we used to play, I was confident that I could figure it out, and I did. We went to the sandy part of the yard, under the pecan trees. There, we competed at building things out of sand. This was something that everyone could do, even Best, a five-year-old. It was fun. But I knew that we needed to find something for dinner. So, about five thirty, I took them inside and opened a jar of peaches. There were some biscuits and sausage left over from breakfast. That was dinner.

Afterward, it was almost dark. I then took them to the front yard, where I introduced them to another (new) game that I had just made up. For this game, we used old car tires and rolled them in a line to see if the rollers' tire could be stopped by others' tires.

It was late that night when Mother and Daddy came home. They had the baby, but they didn't bring Gene home. I thought the worst. I guess the look on my face reflected that very thought. "We left him at the hospital," Daddy told us. "They gave him some medicine, and they gon keep a close watch on him."

Gene had suffered a seizure, and he stayed in Lenoir Memorial Hospital for two or three days. We were worried that he was going to die.

Mother and Daddy went to the hospital Sunday and brought us a report. "The doctors are still caring for him,"

Mother informed us.

After school Monday, we rushed home to get another report. It was the same as the day before.

When we returned from school on Tuesday, Gene was there, smiling like nothing had happened. That was great.

The third Sunday in April, I got up fairly early as Mother and Daddy were sleeping in. I fed and watered the mules and the pony, which was my responsibility. When I finished, something came over me. I put the bridle on that pony, no saddle. I jumped on that damn pony and began riding bareback. I let him walk a few yards; then I loped him to the far end of the pasture. On the way back, I galloped that pony hard. In the midst of this, there was a feeling of pure joy that I had never experienced before. Just as I was approaching the gate, Daddy came running out of the house in his long drawers, with one leg in his pants trying to put the other one on. "Junior! Junior! Git off! Git off! You know you ain't got no business on that pony!" (I later learned that the sound of the hoof beats woke Daddy up.) The two more years that we lived there, I never rode that pony again.

When the weather became consistently warm, Matthew started bringing his grandchildren over to the farm so that they could ride the pony. Whenever he brought them, my job was to saddle the pony and walk him to the gate. Then the children would take turns riding. My responsibilities also included helping the two smaller children onto and off the pony. And when they finished riding, they would hand the reins to me. From there, I would water and feed him. Finally, I would have to groom the pony. For our time there, I took better care of that pony than I did myself.

## May 1952

A few weeks after the episode with the pony, I witnessed the most hurtful verbal interchange that I had ever seen. It was between Daddy and a state trooper.

It was on a Saturday night when we were returning from visiting relatives in Greene County. There was a car behind us, following real close. Daddy commented on that very fact. A couple of miles down the road, a blue light came on. Daddy pulled over and sat there as the officer got out and came to the driver's window, which Daddy had rolled down.

The trooper told him that it was a just a routine stop. Along with Daddy, Mother was in the front seat with the two babies. The trooper shined his bright flashlight on them for a minute, then he shined it on the four of us in the backseat. He asked Daddy, "Boy, is all them younguns yours?"

Daddy respectfully responded, "Yessir, they all mine."

Then the trooper made a comment that shocked me, and totally humiliated both of my parents. He said, "Goddamn, boy, your thing must stay hard!" The officer went back to his patrol car shaking his head as he continued to mumble.

For us, there was complete silence the rest of the way home.

The third Saturday in June, when I was returning to the house from feeding the livestock, Daddy was at the henhouse. "I need to talk to you for a minute, Junior," he said. There was a tobacco truck in the edge of the field. He sat down on it and did likewise. "You going be a cropper again this year," he informed me. This was something that I expected, but he continued. "And while we're talking," he continued, "I think you're old enough to pick cotton and gather corn on a regular basis. So, you'll be missing some time out of school this year when we harvest them crops."

I obediently said, "Yessir," as we got up and went to the house together.

At the end of June, we started barning tobacco. This was when I got to meet the rest of Matthew's family, and other people who would be my coworkers. Of course, there was no kind of formal introduction. We got to know each other as we worked.

In addition to Matthew, there was his wife Sally, and their three daughters, Margaret, Veronica, and LeAnne. LeAnne was twelve or thirteen years old. Veronica was a sophomore in college, and Margaret was married.

The other people I met were the sharecroppers from Matthew's other farms. James Hamm was the white farmer. He was also Matthew's son-in-law, married to Margaret. And instead of being a sharecropper, James farmed on thirds.

But early on, I discovered that Margaret and Matthew were so different from the white folks I'd met before. Not that I hadn't known any nice white folks previously. I could recall Floyd Sams, our Snow Hill landlord, Louis Holder, and Miss Erma and her family as examples. But Margaret and James were so basic. At the tobacco shelter, our second day at work, Mother told me to go to the shelter and ask Margaret to send her a spool of tobacco twine. I did. However, when I was about to make that request, I addressed her as Miss Margaret. She put her hand out and stopped me in mid-sentence. Shaking her head from side to side, she said, "No, no. My name is Margaret, not Miss Margaret." I was shocked and didn't know how to respond. So, I didn't say a word.

An aside here is that Daddy used to call LeAnne "Miss LeAnne." And he would say "Yes, ma'am" and "No, ma'am" to her. Mother said that she ought to make him address Katie and Marie the same way.

Carl Jackson was the other black sharecropper. He lived with his partner, Angie Lou. They had three young children, James, Louise, and Jason. Additionally, Angie Lou's sister Della, and her husband Jasper lived with them.

Once we got into barning tobacco, I discovered that all of the new acquaintances were really good people, and there was a mix of individuals, in regard to who they were or what they were. I drew this conclusion based on general observations and paying attention.

Most of our hired help came from La Grange. But during that period, at the start of tobacco harvesting, people from everywhere flocked to eastern North Carolina. There were some from Alabama, Mississippi, and the Bahamas. When the season was over, they disappeared.

One worker I especially remember was the man from the Bahamas. The reason that he stood out was that he seemed to talk funny. His words would resonate and vibrate.

This particular summer there were two other relevant

workers who were croppers for us. One was Big Boot Tatum. He stood well over six feet tall, and he probably weighed close to three hundred pounds. Also, there was a short man named Claude. Where Boot was loud and wrong, Claude was quiet and mild. That's why people were shocked when Claude killed Boot on a weekend. Rumor had it that Boot whipped Claude's ass a few days earlier, so that was Claude's way of getting even. Needless to say, replacement workers were found.

One of the most memorable things that happened during this year was when we went to catch the bus on the first day of school following summer vacation. Our brother Best was now amongst us, as a brand-new first-grader.

For me, returning to school this year meant that a new phase in my life actively began. The proving point was that I recognized that I had different possibilities. With some new information, I was made aware that I was in a position to do different things, like join clubs and participate in activities other than academics.

In my first two years in high school, I was satisfied with what we did in all of my classes. Whatever material the teachers presented, I dove right in and learned. But there was one class that propelled me to think of alternatives. For example, in my freshman and sophomore years, there were my agriculture classes. For some reason, woodwork was included. It was different in that it wasn't so much academic, and it wasn't farming. Therefore, I had the opportunity to experience another kind of hands-on activity. I discovered how relaxing and beneficial that option was. I got hooked on it.

But in my junior year, I decided to try the Debate Club. This included public speaking. I figured this could be a benefit to me in the future. I had thought about what I wanted to do as my life's work. And this would surely come in most handy as a lawyer or as a politician. Of course those were extreme possibilities because I knew how unlikely either would be, but I figured it wouldn't hurt.

Daddy and I were cutting down trees in the back woods that Saturday when I told him that I had found something outside of academics that I really enjoyed. The only thing he said was "I hope you ain't wasting your time." But his comment didn't deter me, and I was certain that I would get support from Mother.

It was the following Tuesday before I got an opportunity to talk with Mother about my interest in the Debate Club. She was ironing when I got back from school. I was the first one off the bus. We went in and greeted Mother and the boys. "How was school today?" she asked.

"Fine," Katie and Marie and Best told her.

"It was great!" was my reply. While my siblings went and put their books away, I stayed to talk with Mother.

"Why was your day great?" she inquired.

"I joined the Debate Club last week, and today we had our first meeting," I told her.

"What does that mean?" she asked.

"It means that I'll get to travel to other schools and compete against teams. And I think sometimes there'll be several schools in a single debate."

With an impassive look, she told me: "I hope you know what you're doing."

Without a doubt, I was more than disappointed in her response. I was actually hurt, because not only was there no encouragement, but there was absolutely no interest shown in something that was so important to me. I tried not to show my feelings about the matter, but apparently I didn't hide it very well because Katie and Marie asked me what was wrong. I shrugged it off and told them, "Nothing."

But in spite of no support, I dove head-first into my debating interest. There was some consolation in that I was able to spend time getting myself mentally prepared for this new interest. I did this simply by thinking about the alternatives in imaginary exchanges in a debate setting.

The rest of the year was uneventful. And when the year ended, for the first time in a long while, I could say that more often than not, I had enough to eat almost every day! And for that, I was thankful.

## January 1953

Hank Williams died, and I cried like a baby.

## June 1953

Matthew came by the house that Saturday about noon. He told Daddy that he'd just left Carl's house. Then he began to smile as he told Daddy the circumstances that he happened upon. He said that Carl was outside naked, running around the house, and Angie Lou was chasing him. Every time Carl got to one corner, Angie Lou would come around the other corner and aim the shotgun at him. After the third corner, Matthew said that Carl dove between the two of them as Angie Lou was taking aim again. By getting between them, Carl was able to escape into the woods, where he was safe.

## JULY 1953

Della Ann Barnes, Jasper's wife, wasn't a pretty woman by any means, but she was outstandingly shaped. Despite the fact that she was married, two men fought over her one Saturday night. One killed the other. The following Monday morning, Della and Jasper arrived at our place as usual. But before going to the field, me and my dumb self said to Della, "I heard that Sonny Sharpe killed a man over you." Everybody got quiet. I could feel Mother's eyes piercing me, and I knew that I'd hear about it from her later.

When the day was over, she lit into me. She didn't wait until we got to the house. Out of earshot, she was all over me, finger pointing, the works. I think I would've preferred one of those beatings I used to get.

The second Monday in July, the Hamm family again was the focus regarding a matter of importance. I was fifteen years old, and their son Andy was a diaper-wearing toddler who made no distinction between his skin color and the skin color of his black playmates. This was a factor that endeared him to the black parents. One day when we had finished putting in tobacco, the children were playing in a sand pile. There were five black kids plus Andy. A white lady pulled up in her car and when she got out, she had two toddlers with her. She walked over where Andy and company were playing. She took Andy by the hand and started pulling him toward the two white toddlers. Andy snatched his hand away and ran back to his playmates.

## AUGUST 1953

School was back in session.

Things were normalizing both at school and at home. This meant that there was less and less money in our household, and we were getting into the heart of subject matter at school.

## OCTOBER 1953

The best part of the first semester was a negative. It was negative for all of the obvious reasons. But it was positive from the standpoint that it was informative. Or, it was another reminder of race relations. It was the week when the North Carolina State Fair was in Raleigh. And for those of us who were going, this Wednesday was very special for us. It was to be a no school day. When we arrived at school, there was so much excitement in the air.

We went to our classes and got the rolls checked. A few students who were not included, probably for different reasons, were sent to other classrooms. Next, Mrs. Johnson talked with us about how to behave. I didn't think we needed that kind of reminder, but we listened respectfully. Then we got our belongings for the trip and headed outside.

After a few last-minute verifications, it was time to board

the bus. We had two busloads of students on our way to the North Carolina State Fair. This was the first time most of us had ever gone more than twenty-five miles from home.

That trip will forever burn in my memory for two reasons. First, everywhere we stopped to use the bathroom, we were told that they didn't have any bathrooms for colored people. So finally, the two buses parked bumper-to-bumper in a wooded area, and the females went into the woods on one side of the road while the males went on the other side.

The second reason was that I only had a quarter to spend. That was what was left from the five dollars and twenty-five cents that a compassionate neighbor gave to me for the trip. I used that quarter on a ride, which meant that I spent the whole day hungry.

## December 1953

The remainder of the year went fairly smooth. But a few days before school let out for Christmas, there was unpleasant news. We got in from school, looking for food as usual. We rushed to find Mother because she wasn't in the kitchen to tell us what we could and couldn't have.

We heard the boys on the back porch. Lyn was lying on a pallet, and Gene was playing with a small plastic truck. I quickly noticed that Mother was wearing that distant look on her face. And I knew from past experience not to ask, but to wait for her to tell us what was on her mind. But since there was no similarity between this look and her "I'll whip your ass" demeanor, I knew we were safe. Gene pulled himself away from his playing and came to greet us. Then Mother spoke. "We'll be moving next week," she said, as she seemed to be more tired than disappointed. I was sure that like me, she was used to this by now. There was no discussion, no questions asked. My siblings and I just eased back in the house and tacitly agreed to forego our snack.

We would be moving to the Pot Neck community, onto one of Dr. Y. A. Garner's five farms. He had them scattered across Lenoir County. Two of them were rented to white tenants who were farming on thirds. The other three farms were tended by black sharecroppers.

I heard that Dr. Garner was big on education, and at one time he was State Superintendent of Public Schools. History tells us that he did a lot to improve public schools. But somehow, history left out the fact that black schools were completely ignored. Then again, that could be understandable since his tenure was early in the century.

Our parents began moving our things while we were at school on the Friday that we got out for Christmas. So when we got home, the house was mostly empty. Uncle Chad was still there, tying the last load down on a pickup truck that he had borrowed. We were there only long enough to take one final look at this place before we climbed into our car and headed out for our new residence. Surprisingly, the ride to our new place was somewhat brief. Of course it was new territory for me, but Mother had told us that it was near where Uncle Bob lived. I thought back to when Daddy told a similar story about the distance we'd be from Uncle Chad; consequently, I didn't put a lot of stock in her story.

Riding down the path to the dirt road, and seeing the bare trees and open fields was a beautiful scene, but the realization that this was the end of something that had been a positive for me was quite difficult. Then we pulled onto the highway, and that seemed to change my mood to one of anticipation. From that point, the ride to Pot Neck was a smooth one because there were no bumpy dirt roads. I took this as a positive in some kind of way that I really didn't yet understand.

I arrived with the usual mindset, a "wait-and-see" approach to drawing any kind of conclusions regarding what it might be like living here. Being children, our focus was not on unloading the truck and moving things inside. Our first priority was to give this place a visual inspection, and go from there. And I knew that this meant different things for each of us as children. My siblings were excited. They rushed about, looking as I used to do. But now I was older and more experienced at moving from place to place. Therefore, my thing was to get the mental picture of what it would mean to me in the long run, and however long a "long run" would be.

But let's take first things first. Other than the fact that we would still be sharecropping, a quick glance at the physical aspect proved not to be a downgrade. The house that we moved into sat a few feet off the highway, and it was a really good house. It was white, with a completely stone foundation. The only way to get underneath was through a wooden door on the side. The steps to both the front and back porches were made of cement.

And this six-room house had a hallway. There were no broken windows in it, and the roof did not leak! Even though there were no food-bearing trees on this property, the situation did seem at least encouraging.

Where the house was situated had significance too. That alone added a couple of positives to the mix. Number one, it was somewhat isolated from the center of farm work, meaning that we could be out of the fray of operating the farm. And number two, our livestock was located away from the house, meaning that the stable stench could not surround us with an ever-present bad odor.

This farm was located east of La Grange, and while we still had a La Grange address, we were closer to Kinston, via Falling Creek, on Highway Seventy.

It took about an hour to get all our belongings inside and halfway situated. Uncle Chad left, and here we were. Another thing that was welcome was the fact that we would be living along a highway instead of back in the woods.

Near dark, a black pickup truck pulled into the yard. It was Uncle Bob. He got out with his favorite attire on, khaki pants, a plaid shirt, and a light jacket. "I see y'all finally got here," he said to Daddy.

"Yeah, and I see you ain't changed none—getting here when the work is all done," Daddy responded. Of course Uncle Bob got a good laugh out of that.

Uncle Bob only visited a short while, and said he'd bring the family over some time during the weekend.

We spent all day Saturday at home except for a trip across

the road to the stables to feed the mules.

Daddy had previously visited the community with the overseer, but said he hadn't met any of the other tenants. When we went to feed up, we had to go through our new neighbor's yard. As we were passing by, there were two fairly tall, slim men standing at the woodpile to the right of the path.

One was of medium complexion, and the other man was light-skinned. The darker man wore bib overalls, and the other gentleman had on a pair of blue work jeans. The darker man spoke first. "You must be Mose," he said with a loud, sharp voice and a big smile. As he spoke, the two men were walking out into the path to greet us. The first man extended his hand to Daddy.

"Yeah, I'm Mose," Daddy replied, shaking the man's hand.

"My name's Mack Rucker; they call me Bird," he said, as his smile became brighter, "and this here is my brother-in-law, Ray Simmons." They too shook hands.

Then Daddy responded in kind. "And this is Junior," he said. He shook my hand with a strong grip. I couldn't match his strength, but I thought I'd done okay.

"How y'all?" Ray said, showing two gold teeth and chewing that gum, as if he was being careful to not let it fall from his front teeth.

"Mr. Redman told me you'd be moving in within the next few days… We been here a coupla years," Mr. Mack shared. Then he turned to me. "How old are you, Junior?"

"I'm sixteen," I told him. That led to his opening about his family.

"I got a boy a year or so older than you. He ain't here right now though. He's kind of wild and likes to run around a lot. But you'll get to meet him."

Then Mr. Ray put his two cents worth in. "I told Bird that he ought to send him off to the army; that would slow him down some."

"How many more younguns you got, Mose?" Mr. Bird asked.

"I got two girls, twelve and fourteen," Daddy told him. "Then I got three younger boys."

Now, it was Mr. Bird's turn again. "Me and my wife, Millie, got four girls," he said. "One lives right over yonder," he said, pointing to the house across the road, down from where we lived. "She and her husband Randolph live there. He's a preacher. They got one youngun, Joanie. Y'all will see her pulling Joanie in a wagon, because she's water-headed. The three that live here are Sharon, Alice, and Josie Ann."

Mr. Ray interrupted. "I gotta go," he said. "I'll be seeing y'all, Mose." He went on into the house.

"Well, I gotta go too," Mr. Bird said. "Good to have you as neighbors."

Daddy responded by thanking Mr. Bird. We went on to the stable and began to feed the mules.

Daddy was pumping water in the trough and I was moving hay when we heard what sounded like a truck coming through the woods. We turned around and looked toward the sound, but didn't see anything. The sound got closer. Then through the woods came an old green pickup truck. It came to a stop in the middle of the path, and a heavy-set white man got out and came toward us. He had on a pair of bib overalls and a red, white, and gray plaid shirt. Even though it was quite chilly, he had both sleeves rolled up to his elbows. The red hairs on his arms reminded me of Mr. Buck, who was dipping ice cream back in Hugo.

"Wha'd you say, Mose?" he greeted Daddy. Obviously somebody else had told him who Daddy was. "Them goddamn mules sho eat a lot, don't they?"

Daddy responded, "They sure do."

"I'm A. C. Anderson," the man said. He went on telling Daddy about himself, the farm, and how we'd be working together. Since I didn't need those details, I went on with the business of feeding the mules. After about twenty minutes, Mr. Anderson left.

Sure enough, Uncle Bob came by for a visit the next day and brought his entire family. However, his family had grown since we were neighbors in the Hugo area. In addition to Raymond, Mattie, and Wayne, now there were Gertrude, Harriet, and Donald.

I found my new community to be quite interesting. Of course the key source of this information was Raymond. But just being in the midst of all that was in the community was most informative also.

I also discovered that there was an intriguing similarity between this neighborhood and the Hugo area. There, Uncle Bob was surrounded by some of his siblings. But here, the neighborhood included some of Aunt Ada's siblings. She had a brother and a sister, Matthew Hamin and Beatrice Hoke.

Aunt Ada's brother, Mr. Matthew, lived next door to her. His family included a son and two daughters, O'Dom, Jolene, and Valerie. They were near the age of my sisters.

Aunt Ada's sister and her husband also had children near the ages of her brother's. =They were: Arlene, Willimena, Charles, Allen, and Betty.

In addition to those acquaintances, the Moores lived across the road from Mr. Matthew. They were: Mr. Leyon and Miss Carrie and their children Jessica, Felicia, Joyce, Darlene, Robert, and Michael. Those three families came to be the core of my interactions during my stay in the Pot Neck community.

It was around midafternoon on Wednesday that we met the overseer, Jack Redmon. I was at the woodpile when I saw a red pickup pull into the yard. There was a white man sitting inside. He sat there for about a minute; then he blew the horn. Apparently Daddy was in the edge of the woods. I saw him come out and approach the man, who was now getting out of the truck. He was about a half foot taller than Daddy, slim, and wearing a pair of pressed khaki pants and a Sunday-looking shirt. It was a chilly day, so he was wearing a sweater. I could hear them talking as I neared. By this time, he'd handed Daddy a couple of bags of something, and one was oranges. Then the man got back in his truck and headed up the road. "Who was that?" I asked.

"That was Mr. Redmon," Daddy responded. "He's the overseer."

I would see Mr. Redmon many other times over the years,

at least twice a week, as he'd come check on the farm and the tenants.

Then there was another white man I never got to meet, but I did see him from afar a couple of times. That gentleman was the owner, Dr. Y. GA Garner He never stopped by either of his houses. He'd drive past the houses on into the fields, just driving slow and looking. I figured he was merely checking on the progress of the farming process. Sometimes he'd get out of the dark green Studebaker he was driving and walk into the fields. Each time I saw him, he was wearing real dressy clothes.

## JANUARY 1954

Christmas vacation was over and it was time for us to start anew. Since there was only one high school in this part of Lenoir County for Negroes, Katie and I remained at Frink High School; Marie and Best had to attend Banks Chapel. This was like my first school. They taught grades one through eight. I also found out that the school had more than two teachers. Plus, they had two buildings! However, we lived so deep in the country, and the elementary school was in the opposite direction from the high school, so the ride took considerably more time. Other than that, there were no major adjustments for me. I was only riding a different bus with different children.

And at home, farm work was farm work. The routine here was the same: preparing the fields, seeding the plant bed, etc. And I was pleased that, just like the last farm we were on, there was no cutting wood to cure tobacco. I guess that kind of tobacco curing was a thing of the past. However, we still had to cut wood for fuel.

In this community, there was one local store. And for us, it was conveniently located fairly close to our house, about one-eighth of a mile. It was in a curve, next to Mr. Nathan's house. The owner and operator was a white middle-age couple, Randy and Ellen Davis. Randy was large and tall, probably about six feet, and maybe weighed a tad over two hundred and twenty pounds. Ellen was slightly over five feet tall and maybe weighed less than half as much as Randy.

They both loved to talk. While Randy was careful in dealing with people, Ellen never met a stranger. She would talk to everybody like she'd known them for years. I eventually discovered that they both were special in that their sense of humor was so unbelievable. Plus, they were both loving individuals.

It was Sunday evening, the last Friday in January, when A. C. pulled up in the yard and blew his horn. Daddy went out and talked to him for a few minutes. When he came back inside, he said, "Dr. Graham died today. A. C. gon take me and Bird with him tomorrow to the funeral home in La Grange to view the body." Daddy didn't look too enthused about it, but I suppose he took it as a part of his obligation.

When he returned the next evening, he said it was the first time he had ever seen a white man in a casket.

## MARCH 1954

I had come from school and was on the woodpile cutting wood when Daddy came from the back fields with a fresh load. I stopped and began to help him unload the wagon. Then I said to him: "My debate team will be going to Woodington High School tomorrow. I need fifty cents so I can get lunch."

Daddy didn't stop working, and he didn't look up. He told me: "You know I ain't got fifty cents."

We finished unloading the wagon; then he went to the pump and got a drink of water. Upon his return to the wood-pile, where I had continued cutting, he said, "Junior, I'm gon let you take care of the mules while I go back to the woods. There's a couple more trees I want to cut down before dark."

I said, "Yes, sir." And we got on the wagon and headed across the road to the stable. He got off and headed for the back woods, and I took the reins.

Right as I was finishing putting corn and hay out, I saw Miss Millie approaching the gates. "How you, Junior?" she asked.

"I'm fine, Miss Millie," I said. "How you?" With the pleasantries being out of the way, she went on and asked me about school. I provided her with a general update, and then I told her about my debate team and our competition for the next day.

Obviously by now, she knew that there was no money in our household. She reached into her apron pocket and pulled out a dollar. She said, "Good luck tomorrow. Here's a little something to get you some lunch." I thanked her as she went back to the house, and I headed down the path to go home.

Miss Millie was just a very dear person. With her high-pitched voice piercing the air, nobody ever had to ask her to repeat anything. But while she had such a small voice, she had a heart that was just the opposite, both in size and direction. It became my experience that nobody ever had to verbalize to her their needs. Seemingly, she could sense such and come to the rescue. With me, it was personal, because of the number of times she helped. But I was also aware that it was nothing special about me that got such attention from her. There were others in her life she displayed the same concern for. She was just that angelic.

It wasn't long after that until school would close for the summer, and for me, my education would be finished. And in spite of the fact that I had no real plans for the future, I was actually glad to see this process coming to an end. With so many uncertainties facing me, there was one thing for sure that I would be getting away from, and it was a welcome one. I knew that there were good possibilities that I wouldn't have anything to eat at home, but I definitely wouldn't have to go to school hungry. I also knew that I wouldn't have to put up with people who didn't have my best interest at heart.

## May 1954

The end of school came. However, I didn't get to participate in the formal ceremony because my folks couldn't afford to pay the graduation fee, which was only a few dollars. And needless to say, I didn't attend the prom either. So nothing took place to mark this milestone for me. Life continued into the summer, with the farming schedule being featured.

But in spite of there not being any kind of transition for me, there was obviously enough time for me to come up with one goal for myself. I had turned sixteen back in December of last year, but there had been no looking forward to getting a driver's license. There was no need to because there was nothing to drive at our house. We walked.

Now, for no particular reason, that was a goal I set: get my driver's license. I had no clue how this would pan out. I got my learner's permit the first week in May, and A. C. would let me drive his truck to the fields sometimes when he was busy doing other things.

One day he said to me, "Junior, you got your learner's permit, but you ain't got no car. If you'd like, I'll take you to town next week and let you use my truck so you can go on and get your license. Ain't no need to let 'em expire." That was a shock. I didn't know that he had a decent side! Of course, I accepted his offer on the spot. He said, "Next Tuesday."

Sure enough, the offer from A. C. went down as planned. I was looking out of our living room window when I saw him head down the path, so I went out and waited for him by the road. As we were approaching La Grange, we saw a one-arm black man walking in the opposite direction. "That's One-Arm Ray," A. C. said, surprised. "Wonder what he's doing so far from home? He lives down the road from us." By the time he'd finished wondering about One-Arm Ray, we arrived at the driver's license office. We went inside and my name was called immediately.

I was successful in taking the road test, and the officer directed me to where I was to receive my North Carolina driver's license. With that piece of paper in my hand, I stared at it as

A. C. and I headed to the truck. He congratulated me, and we were on our way back to Pot Neck.

When we got to the outskirts of town, A. C. said that he needed to go by the seed store, but that he could do that when he came back on Friday. Just for the sake of conversation, I asked him what was happening on Friday. He said that he had to put a fence up around Dr. Garner's house. I continued probing and asked why a fence was needed. He matter-of-factly responded, "To keep the niggas out." Question answered. I began telling him again how much I appreciated what he'd done for me. When we arrived at my house, I thanked him again and got out.

Yes, I had my driver's license, but nothing to drive. And this was fine with me. It was the thought of having it that was satisfying. Since I was used to walking, it really made no difference.

A couple of weeks after I got my driver's license, Daddy bought a car for a hundred dollars. He told me that if I would keep water and oil in it, the gas would take care of itself. Of course I listened respectfully, but what he'd said never made sense to me.

One night about seven o'clock, I'd been to Falling Creek. I pulled up to the gas pumps at Randy's store. He came out and asked, "What'll it be, Junior?" I told him that I wanted ten cents worth of gas. As he was removing the hose from the pump, he further drawled, "Do you want a road map too?"

"No, I'm just going home."

"I know good and damn well that's where you going."

One afternoon, Raymond and I were walking to the store,

which was on the property next door to Mr. Nathan's. As we approached the store, we saw One-Arm Ray going into Mr. Nathan's yard. I began to tell Raymond about A. C. sharing information with me as to how Ray lost that arm. Raymond laughed and said, "I'll tell you some more about old Ray when we come out of the store."

We were just there to buy some junk food, and that's what we did. Each of us got a soft drink, a bag of peanuts, and a bar of candy. Then we headed back toward our houses.

"Ray was a hustler too," Raymond began. "He hustles to get enough money to buy liquor. One night he stole and sold the same rooster four or five times." Raymond was laughing as he was telling me about Ray.

Of course I was laughing harder than Raymond. It was hilarious.

"The first person he sold the rooster to was the one that he stole it from, Miss Alma Gray. When he approached her, she saw the rooster and said 'Ray, that look just like my ole rooster.' Ray assured her that she was mistaken: 'Nah, Alma, it ain't your rooster; just give me a quarter for him so I can buy a drink.' Miss Alma said, 'Okay, Ray, here's your quarter; just take him to the henhouse.' Ray took the rooster right back where he got him from in the first place. A few minutes later, Ray stole the same rooster again. He continued to steal and sell that rooster until he got enough money to buy some liquor." By now, Raymond and I were both howling.

But at least I knew the whole story on One-Arm Ray. However, that was not the only education Raymond provided me with about folks in my new community. "Now, let me tell you about Ellen and Randy," he said.

He started with Ellen: "One day a traveling salesman stopped by the store and said to her: 'Can you please help me, ma'am? I'm lost.' Her reply: "No, you ain't lost. I know exactly where you are.' Then there was a thirteen-year-old boy whose voice was changing. Sometimes it would be alto, and sometimes it would be soprano. His dad had sent him to get a pack of Camel cigarettes and a penny box of matches. The boy said to her Ellen: 'I want a pack of Camel cigarettes' (in his alto voice) 'and a penny box of matches' (in his soprano voice). Ellen said to the kid: 'Hold on just minute, and I'll wait on both of you.'"

Randy was next. "Randy was also a town constable, a job he was not cut out for. On one occasion he had eviction papers to serve on a young black man for lack of rent payment. Rather than evict the man, Randy tirelessly rode around with the man until he found someplace for the man to move to."

Then Raymond made the comment that in spite of their humor and good deeds and intentions, deep down inside they both still had their thoughts about colored folks. He didn't give any particulars, but he was certain that they were like all the other white folks when it came to how they viewed black folks.

By that time we were at my house, and Raymond cut through the woods to go home. But I kept thinking about the last part of our conversation, what white folks think of blacks and how they treat them. Of course I thought about A. C. I had just experienced goodness from him with the driver's license thing, and I knew that he had a good heart. Yet, there was the other side of him.

But the point was that in the midst of all A. C.'s thoughts about "niggers," he did have a good heart. And his comment was not just something out of the blue.

I had heard such thoughts from him. I recalled the time when we were working together in the fields, and we were talking about the various jobs on a farm. I said to him that picking cotton was not one of my better skills. He retorted, "All niggers can pick cotton." But such thinking went further with him. He also insisted "All niggers steal, and all niggers can dance."

But in spite of what white folks thought about Negros, all any of us could do was to make the best of what was in place as far as relations were concerned. And thus far, both whites and Negros were making the best of it.

## JUNE 1954

It was now June, and we had suckled tobacco in all the fields in the back woods for the past two days. On this Wednesday, we started on fields closer to the barns. A. C. had to go to town before he could come and help. Odom and I, along with one of the Simmons boys, were well into our work, and discussing one of the many topics that were of interest to us. When A. C. finally arrived about ten o'clock, we were talking about how bad off we were as black people. "How you boys doing?" he asked and joined in and began carrying two rows as he could. But we were only doing one row at a time. Odom and I agreed that things were bad, and we also agreed that black folks farther south were probably in worse shape than we were.

A. C. listened, as he diligently worked quietly. Finally, he spoke up. "Naw," he said, and he stopped and just stood there seemingly to have everyone's attention before he addressed the topic at hand. We stopped too, and just listened. I wondered what he would know about colored folks anyway. He continued, "You boys way wrong 'bout that. Ain't no goddamn niggers nowhere in this country got it any worse than niggers right here in North Carolina!" Of course I wasn't stunned at his comment because he had always made his positions obvious about any matter, especially with his crass language.

## July 1954

Then it was July. And this summer was different for me because in the past, at this point of the year, putting in tobacco was merely a "this time of year" activity, with something better to follow in terms of less hot and tedious labor.

But now, there was nothing familiar for me to look forward to beyond barning tobacco. I had to get all of that out of my head, and I needed to focus on the people with whom I would be working. Of course we'd already met and gotten to know each other over the past few months. But now, we would be working together on a daily basis.

There were two truck drivers. A. C. was one of them; he drove the tractor. The other truck driver was Will, his son. He was nine years old and drove the mule. The croppers were Daddy, Mr. Mack, Mr. Ray, me, and a man who was hired from the neighborhood, Sonny Simmons. The workers at the shelter were: Mother, Katie, Marie, Norma, Nancy, Miss Millie, Sharon, Alice, and a lady who lived on another farm.

On Sunday afternoon, a few weeks into tobacco barning, we'd come from church and were all sitting at the dinner table. Daddy got it started; then Mother filled in the details. "Junior, you gon be going to live with your uncle Leroy when school starts back."

I had no clue what he was talking about. I knew that I'd just graduated from high school, so I didn't ask any questions. I just waited for the rest of what was going to happen. I kept on eating.

That's when Mother got started. "There's a bricklaying program at Green County Training School," she said. "We gon let you go there and enroll in that program."

I thought, *What can I do? I'm only sixteen years old, so it's still whatever they say.* But I knew that I wasn't dead-set on taking no bricklaying class. They both seemed to wait on me to say something. My sisters stopped eating as they noticed what was taking place. My brothers never missed a bite. Finally, I said, "Yes, ma'am."

Then Daddy showed his excitement, which I thought was fake. "Yeah, you gon like bricklaying," he said. "There's good money in that."

But I became convinced long ago that Daddy thought the only thing for Negroes to do was sharecrop, and I understood that thinking. I was also convinced that he wanted what was best for me, and he knew that sharecropping was what was safe enough from a large perspective. It had enabled him to survive the best that he had up to this point, and he'd managed it the best that he could.

But I had higher hopes. I had constantly thought about going into the military. However, as far as alternatives were concerned, I was not exactly sure what else might be out there. Still, I knew that it wouldn't be bricklaying, and it damn sure wasn't going to be sharecropping. Mother continued, "Your aunt Della told us about this program. She said it is real good. This way, you can learn something else besides plowing and farming."

She was interrupted by Daddy. "You can learn a trade," he said.

For some reason, they now seemed to be trying to convince me, which was not necessary. They'd already told me that I would be going, and as far as I was concerned that was it. That's what I would do.

## AUGUST 1954

The next fourth Sunday (August 22nd) when we went to church, I asked Big Bo and Li'l Bo about the masonry program at Greene County Training School. They told me that they knew some guys who had gone there and taken up that trade.

They said it was a good program, but there was not consistent work available after they graduated. So the guys they knew ended up back working on the farms.

They also shared with me that the next session would start in a couple of weeks, on Monday, September the sixth. Now, at least I knew a little something about the program, and wouldn't walk into the situation totally clueless.

## SEPTEMBER 1954

It was on Sunday, the fifth of September. My masonry class would start the next day. We all climbed in the car, as nobody had any gear but me. I had my few clothes stuffed in a shopping bag that only had one strap. The other one broke when I was stuffing my things in it. We headed to Greene County to drop me off at Uncle Leroy's house. We arrived without experiencing any kind of car trouble. That was a miracle. When we got there, Uncle Leroy and his family were just finishing dinner. They invited us to join them, but everybody declined with a "Thank you, anyway."

The visit was normal until it was time for my family to leave. Then it was strange to be saying bye to them. My sisters seemed okay with it, but my brothers looked at me like it was all unreal. I felt the same way of course. But off they went, and there I was.

Uncle Leroy lived about a half mile past Invitation AME Zion Church, near Taylor Cemetery. His house sat a few yards off the paved road. It was a simple house, but what was not usual was the fact that it was painted. There were five rooms, which were enough to accommodate me, along with his three older children who I knew, and several more I had never met since we moved from the Hugo area. The older children were Leroy Jr., who was now about eight years old; then there was Alberta, at age seven, and Manny, age five. Uncle Leroy came into the room where I was with the boys. "Junior, you gon be sleeping in here with Manny and Leroy Jr.," he said.

So for the next several months, this is where I would be.

Then Monday came and I caught the bus with the children. This felt very familiar, but strange. Other than my young cousins, I didn't know anybody else on the bus.

And they looked at me like I was an intruder, which I was. I arrived at school, went to the office, and told them what I was there for. Some man, teacher, I guess, led me to the masonry building, which was outside and about fifty yards from the main building. The man walked me around two corners. Two other rather small buildings came into view. He pointed out that they both housed cleaning equipment.

As I approached the door of the wooden building, I could hear the sound of scraping. I hesitated and took a deep breath.

When I opened the door, I paused again. Evidently those who were inside had already started. I figured that they had been there before. Then I saw an older man who looked to be about sixty years old, with a dingy denim apron. He saw me and obviously knew why I was there. "Come on in, son," he said to me. "I'm Mr. Watson. I teach this masonry and bricklaying class," he said, as he extended his hand. We shook, and he showed me around as he explained the program.

At the end of the tour, Mr. Watson assigned me to a small room off to the side of the work area and gave me some books with designated chapters to read. I did, and around lunchtime I had finished. During lunchtime I walked to the store and got a Pepsi and a bag of peanuts.

Naturally, I continued to think about my being in this situation, which was actually forced on me. But the more I thought about it, the more I began to see some possible goodness. Yes, maybe this experience would be profitable in some way other than what was explained to me. The environment was new, I was meeting new people, and my current situation wouldn't last forever.

Also, there was one other thing. The school didn't look like the one that I knew when we lived across the road from it twelve years ago. The house that we lived in was still standing, but barely. Of course nobody lived there.

During my matriculation in this program, I got to go home about every other weekend. Either Daddy would come pick me up, or Uncle Leroy would take me. And another positive was that I was spending time with my little cousins.

For quite some time, I had been thinking about my seventeenth birthday, which was coming up in a couple of months. So, the next time I went home, I asked Mother if she would sign for me to go into the Air Force.

She emphatically refused, on the grounds that if she did, and I got in and didn't like it, I would forever blame her. I didn't argue her point, but I figured that it was just a ploy to keep me at home. So, I decided to wait and go in at age eighteen, when I wouldn't need anybody to sign for me.

## December 1954

Those next two months were routine. Then in came December. On the ninth, I turned seventeen. It was nothing special, except that now I was really looking to the next one, so that I could be independent of what I determined to be unnecessary control by my parents, and I could get the hell out of there. I felt that I deserved to be allowed to have the independence I thought would come when I graduated from high school. Needless to say, that didn't happen.

But something very significant did happen two weeks before Christmas. It was a blow to me. The Ruckers moved to Kinston. But their house didn't stay vacant long. The very next week, the Hendersons moved in.

As much as I knew that I would miss the Ruckers, and especially Miss Millie, it turned out that this new family, the Hendersons, were such wonderful people. There was the mother, Miss Lavera, the grandmother, Miss Fannie, two boys a bit younger than me, and some younger siblings.

Thanksgiving and Christmas came and went, mostly unnoticed.


### January 1955

In January, I was in the fifth month of my masonry program. I only had two more weeks before the course would be over. Those last two weeks seemed to fly by, and a couple of hours after school that Friday, Uncle Leroy had me back in Pot Neck.

Winter routine was the same, as I helped Daddy cut firewood to keep us warm, and we got the ground ready for planting crops. With me being available full time as another adult, Daddy seemed to be in hog heaven. But I was miserable, not because of the tediousness of the work, but because of their selfishness of not allowing me to join the Air Force. Fortunately, I realized that I was making myself miserable by dwelling on the situation. After a few days, I was able to get re-focused on the business at hand and do the best job I could do.

## APRIL 1955

Then unexpectedly in April, I got a chance to earn some money by using my newly acquired masonry skills. Uncle Bob was on one of his regular visits to our house that Saturday morning, and I was at the woodpile, chopping wood.

Before going in the house, he came over to where I was. "Junior, since you got that bricklaying training, I got a job for you. And I'll pay you real good," he said.

I must admit I was just a little excited, and a little bit apprehensive, because this would be my first job doing something other than farm work. "What's the job?" I asked.

"I'm thinking about replacing the wooden steps to the front porch with cement and adding a few pillars underneath. Do you think you could handle that?"

It took me a minute to visualize what it would entail. "I think I can," I told him.

"Let me know what materials you'll need, and I'll get them. You can get started whenever it's convenient for you," he said, and went on in the house to visit with his sister.

Since I was out of school, if there was no farm work that needed to be done at any given time, I had the luxury of being able to work other projects into any schedule that I might have. Maybe this arrangement had some potential for me.

On that Monday morning, first week of April, I went to Uncle Bob's house with paper, pencil, and a ruler in hand. I knocked on the door. Aunt Ada came and greeted me, with the baby not far behind. She said that Uncle Bob had gone to town and that he'd be back sometime in the afternoon. I told her I was just there to do some measuring so I could tell Uncle Bob what materials I would need, and how much I would need to do the job he'd asked me to do. I spent about thirty minutes inspecting, measuring, and sketching.

I finished that part of the job, then sat down in the swing on the front porch and made out a list of the things I needed. I knocked on the door again and told Aunt Ada that the list was complete. I asked her to give it to Uncle Bob, and I headed home.

Over the weekend, Uncle Bob informed me that he had secured everything that was on my list, and I could start whenever I wanted to. That was perfect timing because I pretty much had a whole week to work on this project. And thankfully, the weather cooperated. Consequently, I was able to get quite a bit done during that "off" week. But on the days that I had farm work to do, I would still go over to his house and get as much done as I could.

## June 1955

I completed the job on a Wednesday afternoon, the last week in June. Uncle Bob wasn't there, so I just stood alone and admired my work. No, it wasn't perfect, but I thought it was pretty good. I knocked on the door and asked Aunt Ada to tell Uncle Bob that the project was finished. She came outside to look at it, and she was very complimentary. That, I appreciated.

Our visiting each other and seeing each other in the neighborhood did not change, but Uncle Bob didn't say a word about the job I'd done for him. This strange behavior went on for two weeks. He didn't say how the results were, or even mention it. And he never mentioned paying me either.

So, around mid-afternoon on a Wednesday, I finally decided to go and ask him about it. I took the shortcut through the woods. When I got there, he was outside by the field, feeding the chickens. We greeted each other, and I told him the purpose of this visit, to get paid for the work I'd done for him. He started laughing, roaring, like I'd just told him the funniest joke he'd ever heard. I was actually stunned by his reaction. He kept on laughing. I couldn't believe what I was witnessing.

So, I turned and walked back across the field on my way back home. I wasn't angry at him. But I was hurt, and maybe most of all, I was disappointed. This was an uncle not much older than me, somebody I'd looked up to all my life. This was a tough pill to swallow. But that was the cruel reality. Needless to say, the admiration ceased, and my hero image of him began to fade.

### JULY 1955

Summer was nothing but typical, as far as work was concerned. Raymond and I spent time in Kinston on Saturdays. As a matter of fact, I think most people in the surrounding communities spent time in Kinston on Saturdays. Raymond and I would walk that two miles to the main highway and catch a Trailways bus to town.

Everybody would be just hanging out or shopping. For us, of course, it was not about shopping. As much as anything else, it was a chance to visit with schoolmates we happened to see. Plus, Raymond and I did our fair share of people watching. Another favorite thing for us was walking into a crowd and doing silent farts, to watch the reactions of other people.

It so happened that this was the summer when I witnessed one of the most disturbing incidents that was actually an example of the times from a racial segregation perspective.

On a Saturday afternoon in July, Raymond and I were making our usual trek up the main pedestrian thoroughfare, Queen Street. It was jammed with people, and there were policemen stationed on each corner for about four blocks. When people wanted to cross the street, black folks would wait for the green light. If the light was still red, white folks would walk on across.

At one particular corner, as a crowd of people waited, the traffic cleared. The light was still red; all those white folks and one young black man stepped off the curb. A collective groan could be heard coming from the throats of the black people. The cop ran behind the young man, grabbed him around the neck, and slammed him against the building. The officer then did a complete search, handcuffed him, and charged him with jaywalking!

On our return trips to Falling Creek, we usually caught the 6:00 local. The only bad thing about leaving this time of day was that the bus would be crowded. Of course the seating arrangement was normal: white folks up front, and colored folks in the back. On this particular trip, there seemed to be even more of a crowd than usual. I think the driver put forth his best effort to accommodate the large number of passengers. Raymond and I knew to get to the station and get our bus tickets and get in line early enough to ensure ourselves a seat. The driver was obviously a veteran at his trade. He knew that there would be passengers who would have to stand. Therefore, he took the time to ask for those who were standing to arrange themselves in the order that they would be getting off. As the bus pulled out, people standing were holding onto the overhead bars when the bus went around curves to keep from falling. Right before the bus got out of town, around the last curve, a little white boy slid out of his mother's grasp off her lap. She was reaching, trying to get him back in the seat with her, but the four-year-old was having none of that. He spotted a little black boy about his age who was standing and holding his mother's hand. The black boy escaped from his mother's grasp, and the two boys began to play some sort of look-grin-and-giggle game. The white mother began to softly coax her son back to the front of the bus where she was. She did manage to get a little louder, and her son obviously heard her. "Come on back up here, baby…Mommy needs you." Unexpectedly, he got louder than she did. And when he responded to her, her face turned beet red. Surely she was most embarrassed. He screamed out, "Why can't I stay back here and play with the nigga?"

## SEPTEMBER 1955

Summer had gone. Raymond was back in school, and I was relegated to finishing out the rest of the farm year.

It was the second week in September, and Daddy and I

were in the woods, clearing some brush and cutting trees. He got sick and decided to go to the house. Of course this was quite unusual, because although he was a little man, he was tough. Usually when he said that he didn't feel good, he'd work through that feeling and end up staying the course. But this time was different. And I could tell by how he was acting that he needed to go to the house and get some rest. I continued to work until the usual time that we would knock off.

I finished cutting several more trees down, and loaded them onto the wagon. I went home and unloaded. Then I went across the road and put the mules up. When I got in the house, Mother was becoming frantic. Katie and Marie were home from school, and they were standing around Mother looking as scared as she did. The boys were pretty much impervious to what was happening, as they continued playing in the backyard.

We decided that Daddy needed to go to the doctor. I went and informed A. C. about what was happening. He told me to go back home and get Daddy ready, and he'd be right over. I rushed back to our house, and Mother already had him dressed. It was only a matter of minutes before A. C. was pulling into the yard. We got Daddy in the truck and he and Mother headed to La Grange.

Dr. Carson said that he'd suffered a severe stroke.


## NOVEMBER 1955

November came, and Daddy's health was not a lot better, but it had stabilized and the prognosis for further improvement was good. The longer he was sick, and I was doing all of the work, it became more and more apparent that this was how it would be for much longer than I had anticipated.

And over the next few weeks of this being the reality, I made the decision that I would postpone my going into the military. Right after dinner one day, I informed both Mother and Daddy together that I would stay one more year to help get the family through this ordeal. Then, I would be gone! There was nothing for them to argue against, because now I had some control over what I would do. Therefore, all they could say was "Okay."

Thanksgiving? We didn't celebrate Thanksgiving. To us and other poor folks, this was just another day. What was significant was that farmers stayed out of the fields so as not to be struck by a stray bullet from folks hunting.

## DECEMBER 1955

It was the ninth of December, my eighteenth birthday. This was the day I'd been looking forward to since my desire to join the Air Force was shot down by my parents. We would say "Happy Birthday" to each other, and go on about the business at hand. With this being the case, I was still extra happy. Even though my situation was not very good at the time, I was so thankful for this day!

Christmas was rough, even compared to our standards. Jack Redmon brought his usual bags of oranges and apples, candy, and a few nuts. That was all we had. Mother couldn't afford to make cakes and pies like she used to. But we really didn't mind. At least we were able to eat something the entire week of Christmas. And believe me, that was pretty special.

## January 1956

The New Year arrived seamlessly. And according to the calendar, it was time to start thinking about the accompanying fresh cycle of farm activities. Except this time, it was all on me. With Daddy being sick, I was now running the farm. The mere thought of taking on this monumental task was frightening. There were eight acres of tobacco, twenty-five acres of corn, and five acres of soybeans.

Normally January would be the easiest month of the year. But with things having changed in our household, I was certain that it would be different. I knew that Mother would shoulder as much of the farm work as she could, but that would be limited, as she had to take care of Daddy.

However, I did take the first week in January off. The second week was the beginning of my all-out assault on the new farm year. The first task at hand was cutting firewood. For two weeks straight, I cut and hauled firewood. Not feeling that I had enough for the rest of winter for heating and cooking, I continued for two more days the following week. The next day was Wednesday, the first of February. That day being the middle of the week for some reason seemed very appropriate. However, I was soon jolted back to reality by being mindful that when you sharecrop, no days, especially weekdays, have any significance! So, the next day, I had the bush axe on my shoulder and headed for the ditch bank near the back woods, before my siblings left for school around seven o'clock.

## FEBRUARY 1956

I had just gotten home that evening when A. C. stopped by the house and said that he would offer me as much assistance as he could spare, and that he was available any time I needed advice. Of course, I thanked him because I was having reservations about my being up to the task. I was definitely not a hundred percent sure in terms of each step that I would be facing.

Seeing as how Uncle Chad and Uncle Jack were so far away, I took A. C. up on seeking advice and help.

That Monday, again I was out early on my way to the ditch bank when I looked back and saw A. C. coming toward me on his tractor. He stopped and reminded me that we needed to pick out a spot for the plant bed. He shared that he thought the field across the road from where my family lived would be an ideal spot. I agreed. He also asked me about my work on the ditch bank. I told him that I thought it would take me about two and a half weeks. Consequently, we set the last week in February to begin working on the plant bed.

Even though the plant bed was not locked in on my schedule, I knew that it had to be done. For the next two weeks, this was my schedule. Each day, I would finish up about an hour before dark. This meant that I would have time to feed the mules, then go home and cut some wood.

It was the third week in February, and things were going as smooth as could be expected, farm-wise. But Daddy was not doing well at all, though he'd made significant improvement. He wasn't walking very sturdy. He would be bent over and could only go a short distance whenever he did walk. Plus, he'd gotten awfully frail. But there was nothing at all that I could do to help Daddy health-wise, so I had to focus on that which I could control.

I heard A. C. going to the plant bed site on his tractor as I was finishing my breakfast. My brothers and sisters were going out to catch the bus as I left the house. I was glad that A. C. had that tractor. By the time I got across the road to the field, he was busy cutting through the weeds. I got a bush axe and began to whack the area next to where he was cutting. When he'd finished cutting the weeds down, he went back to the barn a couple of times to exchange tools that were more applicable for the various ensuing steps in preparing the plant bed. After he had finished cutting and plowing, I went and got a mule and a raker as planned. A. C. went to do some work in some of his fields, and I smoothed the plant bed; then it was ready for seeding.

It was about ten thirty when I finished. So I took the mule back to the stable and cut down some more weeds along the road next to the plant bed. I finished that around twelve thirty and went home for lunch. Lunch consisted of two fatback biscuits and a glass of water. When I went back to work, I cut along the ditch that ran through the fields. By the time I finished, it was two thirty.

Then I went to A. C.'s house and told him that I was ready to put covering on the plant bed. He already had the mesh on the back of his truck, so I rode to the field with him. He drove the truck along the side of the plant bed and we unloaded the topping and spread it out. With him on one side and me on the other, we pulled the twenty-foot-wide cloth the length of the plant bed (fifty yards). To get the cloth on perfectly took approximately forty-five minutes. Afterward, A. C. said that he had some errands to run for his wife, so I was left to peg the entire plant bed by myself. When I finished, it was six o'clock and I was beat!

## MARCH 1956

The second week in March, I started breaking ground. I had hoped to get all of this done in one week. Unfortunately, I found myself continuing all day Saturday, and until ten thirty Monday. Of course I was tired, but pleased that I had completed that monumental task. So, I rewarded myself by going to the house. The mules and I would rest an extra ninety minutes. We did. And around twelve fifteen, I changed equipment and went right back to the field and started the planting process. Again, this was from sunup until sundown. I ran rows in the cornfield. This meant plowing on each side, then splitting them down the middle. Boy! That took some time!

I had two mules and a heavy plow that I had to walk behind and keep in a straight line! Thankfully, I did finish before nightfall the following week.

The next week, I walked those rows to sow fertilizer.

After that, I had to walk it all over again, planting corn.

By the time I finished planting corn, it was time to start preparing the bacca field.

When I finished running rows for that, it was time to plow the corn for the first time.

Guess what my next job was? Set out tobacco. I had planned to do this the last week in April, but the plants hadn't grown enough, so we had a free week. I needed the break. Of course this was not really a free week. There was plenty of chopping and plowing to do.

I found myself being envious of A. C., because he had a tractor to do his plowing with. All I had was two mules. Starting at daybreak on Monday morning, I would not finish until Saturday afternoon. A. C. would start the same time. But with that tractor, he would finish on Tuesday afternoon!

## MAY 1956

The first week in May, the tobacco the plants were finally ready, so we started setting out tobacco. A. C. took care of all the organizational details, which only included some minor hires. And Daddy was doing better; therefore, Mother was available to help. She, Norma Sue, and another woman pulled plants. I hauled the plants and water. For water, there was a ditch that ran through the back field. I used a peck bucket to dip water from it and fill the barrel on the tobacco truck. Then I hauled it to the transplanter.

We finished setting out tobacco on that Tuesday of the following week. This meant that I was on my own again, dawn to dusk. There were dual tasks staring me in the face: number one was that I had to prepare a field for soybeans. And, number two, it was time to plow the corn for the second time. At this point, there ceased to be any line of demarcation in existence. From there, I knew that it would run continuously, until it was time to put in tobacco.

Being the primary worker in our house gave me an altogether different perspective of things. When I would be alone in the fields or in the woods working, I would also be thinking about things that I'd never even given much if any consideration to. Now, I especially looked at my little brothers in a different light. Before, it was mainly about my advancing in order to better myself. But now I thought, *What about my brothers? How do they move forward in their lives?* And, I began to look at where they were on a different level. I noticed how they dressed. What they didn't have in order to be successful where they were in their lives. In particular, their clothes were a case in point. Neither of my brothers had a decent pair of shoes to wear! Before diving into the imposing tasks ahead, I had to address my brothers' needs.

I knew that every Wednesday morning the overseers from surrounding farms gathered at the Feed and Grain store in La Grange. I didn't know what anybody's schedule was after that, but I did know that Jack Redmon would be there.

I didn't even tell Mother my exact plans. I just told her that I would be up and out early the next morning, probably at daybreak. Sure enough, at five forty, I was halfway to Jenny Lind. That meant that I had five and a half more miles to go. It was now getting daylight. So far, no cars had passed. When I got a couple of hundred yards from the intersection, a pickup passed and slowed down, out of curiosity, I think. A young white man was driving. He remained at the stop sign for about a minute; then he pulled off. I figured that he was going to pick up workers.

Once I got to the main road, I seemed to get a new burst of energy. There were more vehicles on this road. None seemed to be curious. They probably assumed that I was just somebody going up the road a short distance to go to work.

I had never walked this far before, and to think that I was walking fast, I was surprised that I wasn't getting tired. It didn't seem like it took me long at all before I was on the edge of town. The streets and roads were busy with folks going to work. I saw the clock in the bus station: six fifty-five. So far, so good. The Feed and Grain store was right around the corner. As I approached, I looked through the parking lot, and I saw Redmon's pickup truck. That was a relief. I'd understood all along the possibility that he might not be attending today for some reason or other. Yeah, I was a bit nervous as I approached. But then I focused on my purpose for being there, and I felt the bravery within.

I first looked through the screen door, trying to spot him. But all I could see was the counter right inside the door. There was a woman at the desk looking through some paperwork. The way she was dressed, I assumed she must be the secretary. She wore a gray skirt and a blue long-sleeve blouse. Her brown hair was pulled back and tied with a ribbon. But I could tell that she hadn't been in the sun very much, as her oval-shaped face was as pale as a dingy sheet. I took a deep breath, preparing to walk in. That was when she looked up and saw me. I reluctantly opened the door and walked in.

"Whaddya you need, boy?" she asked as she chewed that gum.

"I need to see Mr. Redmon," I told her. She continued to visually size me up. But at this point, I didn't give a damn. I'd come too far not to complete my mission.

"Wait right here," she finally said, as she turned and went to the back.

After about two minutes she returned, followed by Mr. Redmon. He looked shocked to see me there. I secretly smiled, enjoying the look on his face. "What's wrong, Junior?" he asked.

"I need to talk to you," I said, looking him square in the eye.

"Let's go outside," he stammered as he pushed the screen door open. We walked to the edge of the gravel parking lot. He stopped and turned to me, not saying a word. I figured that he was waiting for me to tell him why I was there.

"My brothers need some shoes," I told him.

His face turned pale and went blank. My read was that he couldn't believe that I had said that to him. After several seconds of silence, he finally responded. "I'll arrange for you to get some shoes at Clancy's. He opens at nine o'clock. You just be there when he opens up, and go in and pick out some shoes for your brothers. Tell him that I sent you." He then turned and went back inside.

I was satisfied that this had worked out okay, but I still was not pleased that things were like this. I had an hour and a half to wait, then walk back home, so I walked through the town for about an hour and then I went to the store and waited for Mr. Clancy to open.

Lucky for me, he arrived at about eight forty-five, and he let me go in with him and pick out the shoes. I asked him if he had a big bag because I had to walk about seven miles with those boxes of shoes. He went in the back and brought out an empty feed sack. He put those boxes in there and tied the top with tobacco twine. He even tied some string together to make a handle. I thanked him and was on my way home.

I got back home about ten fifteen. Mother was chopping in a nearby field. Gene and Lyn were with her. I went on in the house and checked on Daddy before going to where Mother was. I told her what I had done and where I'd put the shoes. Then I informed her that I was going to hook the mules up and go to the back fields and do some plowing.

At this point, it was mid-May, and different farming tasks started to overlap. Of course I was rushed, and I knew that the beginning of summer was just around the corner. I was going from one field to another, trying to keep pace with all that was needed. But I was determined to do the best I could as long as I could.

As well as being a good advisor to me, A. C. periodically offered to lend a hand, seemingly when I needed it most. A few weeks before we were to begin barning tobacco, he approached me about working together in spraying our tobacco fields. I was sure that he had seen how I was wearing myself down. He knew that it would be all but impossible to spray my tobacco with no help because I only had a mule, a tobacco truck, and a barrel for pesticide. And he knew that I couldn't manage all those items at one time, which would include driving the mule and manually operating the sprayer.

The following evening when I was putting the mules in the stable, I saw his green Chevy pickup coming, and noticed that it was slowing down. "Whaddya say, Junior?" he greeted. "I got it all figured out. We can spray that bacca together next week. Then you'll have a break before we start cropping."

I was not about to turn that down. "I'd like that," I told him.

"Be at my house at eight o'clock Monday morning," he said as he drove off.

## June 1956

Whereas it would have taken me at least two days to spray by myself, A. C. and I had the spraying done in a day and a half! I thanked him, and we headed to the barns to put the equipment away. With me standing on the back of the tractor and A. C. driving, we headed out of the field. Since we were in the back woods, we had to go through the Hendersons' yard to get to the barns. As we got closer, we heard what sounded like somebody singing. I think we both heard the singing at the same time because we both looked in the direction that we thought the sound was coming from. A. C. slowed the tractor down to quieten the motor.

Sure enough, that was a scratchy sound we heard. It appeared to be someone singing, but they also seemed not to be singing in any particular key. It would be loud at one point, just about screaming, then there would be a slow-down and some talking in between. It was Miss Fannie, the Hendersons' grandmother. She had a hoe, chopping away in her garden, and she was singing and praising the Lord as she worked.

A. C. yelled to her, "Aint Fannie, shut up all the goddamn noise!"

Obviously Miss Fannie had seen and heard the tractor too, and without even looking up, she kept on chopping and she kept on singing, "O Lord, I wanna thank you and praise your name." She was still chopping and still not looking up. She sang "…and bless Mr. A. C. and learn him how to act better."

A. C. surely heard the prayer sent up for him, and he turned a little red on the cheek. But he kept up his onslaught. With a smile, he said even louder, "Shut it up."

Miss Fannie was also smiling when she responded, "You just go on, Mr. A. C. I ain't even studyin' 'bout you." A. C. put the tractor in gear and we continued to the barn.

Thankfully, Mother and my sisters carried their share of the workload. There was a lot of plowing and there was a lot of chopping. The latter is where they were so valuable. They did all the chopping, and I did all of the plowing. I plowed the corn for the third and final time in the first week of June. What followed the chopping and plowing was a lot of work with the tobacco. That was where we all worked together, removing worms from the plants, topping, and suckling the tobacco plants.

## JULY – SEPTEMBER 1956

Finally, it was the first week in July, and we began barning tobacco. This was completed the second week in August. From there, and into September, it was off to the packhouse, preparing tobacco to be sold.

On days that tobacco was sold, Jack Redmon and I would go to the warehouse in Kinston together. We would watch the auction, and within a half hour, we would go to the office to get paid. He would go inside for the check while I sat outside and waited. For the first four auctions, he would return from the office, reach into his pocket, and hand me a ten-dollar bill.

## OCTOBER 1956

The fifth and final time in doing this was in October. Mr. Redmon came out of the office with a check. I must admit, since we had not made anything on the previous sales, I (stupidly) was wishful that this time, things would be significantly and positively different. And they were different, but most disappointing. With the check in his hand, he looked me in the eye as he handed it to me. I looked at the check, and he continued looking at me and said, "I'm sorry, but that's all there is."

That check was for THIRTY-THREE DOLLARS AND THIRTY-FIVE CENTS.

That was our reward for laboring in those fields from dawn 'til dusk, for an entire year!

## DECEMBER 1956

December was a good month. My brother Best turned ten years old on the first. Then on the ninth, I turned nineteen. But that was just part of what made this such a wonderful month. The truth of the matter was that even though there was no money in the household, and very little food on the table, I was looking ahead. This month in particular was special because it was the last month of that wretched year. And it would propel me off to better things. I had optimism; I had so much hope.

Christmas came, but there were no expectations as to some big celebration. I made sure that my two little brothers received a couple of gifts, but we older ones got our joy from their happiness.

I had decided to leave a couple of days after Christmas, and it was quite chilly that morning. It was a few minutes after seven when I set out to walk those two miles to Falling Creek, at Highway Seventy, in order to catch the bus to Kinston. When I was about fifty yards from the highway, the bus zoomed by. "Dammit!" I stood there helpless and frustrated as I watched the bus continue up the highway. I had never hitchhiked in my life, but that day would be my first. I reconciled in my mind that I could do it. After all, I'd done such a distance before. As a matter of fact, it was closer than my trek to La Grange to get money when my brothers needed shoes. This would be only seven miles as opposed to the eight miles to La Grange.

But to my surprise, after a few minutes, a green Ford passed by and stopped a few yards ahead of me. An elderly white man yelled to me, "Come on, boy, hop in." He asked me where I was headed, and I told him that I was on my way to join the Air Force. He said that he wasn't going all the way into Kinston, but that I'd be closer to the recruiting office than I was.

When he got to his destination, I thanked him and completed the walk to downtown Kinston. The remainder of that walk was rewarding. I envisioned life as an airman, with no mules or plows in sight.

The Air Force Recruiter's office was located in the basement of the post office. When I approached the door, there was a sign that read, "Air Force Recruiting Office closed for the day." I felt like crying and headed for the exit.

Then as I was about to climb the stairs, I glanced to my left and spotted a beautiful sign that read, "Navy Recruiter." I made a beeline for that office!

There, a petty officer had me take a test. After I completed the test, he informed me that I had passed. Then he asked me when I wanted to leave. I told him that I wanted to be on the next bus to Raleigh.

"Whoa," he said. "That's a little too fast." He went on to inform me that there was at least a thirty-day delay because they had to wait until there were enough recruits to fill a bus. He also assured me that I would get a letter in the mail which would let me know when that bus would be leaving. I had mixed emotions about his response. I understood, but I had also been looking forward to beginning my new journey immediately. I thanked him and went on back out the door.

When I returned home that day, Mother and my brothers and sisters acted as if I were a long-lost child, returning home.

They too had anticipated my leaving for the Air Force that very day.

If I had not realized before, I did now. They cared so much. Knowing that it would be a few days before mail would arrive from the recruiting office, I began to watch the mailbox. That Friday, I sat in the living room and looked out the window. I saw the mailman drive past the Hendersons' mailbox and slow down when he got near ours! He kept going.

The next day I was at the woodpile chopping wood when I saw the mailman's car coming up the road. I stopped what I was doing and went and sat on the front porch steps and watched as he made his way again past the Hendersons' mail box. He seemed to be slowing down as he approached ours. This time he stopped! I was all but running across the road while he made a deposit and pulled off.

There was only one piece of mail. It had my name on it. I clutched it before I even thought about opening it. This was it. I went back and sat on the step and opened the letter. It read: "Dear Mr. Shepherd…"

### JANUARY 1957

For me, the New Year arrived with excitement. For obvious reasons, it was nothing so special for anyone else in our household.

I had roughly one month left in my current situation. Come February, I would be out of that life. I had no idea what specifics to expect, but I was truly looking forward to it. I figured that I was two years delayed already. Of course I spent time thinking about my sisters and brothers, but I knew for a fact that I could help them more by being someplace else where I could realistically get paid and send a little money home for food.

## FEBRUARY 1957

The first day of February ushered in the month of reckoning. This time, I was certain that I would be boarding that bus for Raleigh. My departure this time was unlike the first time I left. Before, I just walked out the door, not formally saying goodbye to anyone. This time, there was a formal departure, but it was awkward. After all, this was new, and it was different. I made a point to shake Daddy's hand and tell him that I would write.

Mother just grabbed me and hugged me, with tears freely streaming down her face. I hugged her tight and went on out the door without looking back.

Even though my parents were sad, they understood why I left; they realized that there was nothing for me to stay for. Another reason for leaving was that my black ass was about to starve. And although it wouldn't solve the problem, I knew that once I got in, I could send an allotment home.

According to my letter, I needed to be at the recruiter's office by eleven o'clock a.m. I left home at nine thirty, to make sure that I wouldn't miss the bus again. Of course, I was at the bus stop in plenty of time. The two-mile walk from home to Falling Creek seemed like the shortest walk I had ever taken.

After about fifteen minutes, I saw the bus coming up the

highway. I was the only one waiting. Once I boarded, I spotted a few other boys who appeared to be about my age. I could only speculate where they were headed.

When we arrived at the bus station, there were quite a few boys getting off other buses too. They were mostly white, with a few blacks sprinkled in. But based on everything I saw, I figured that we were all there for the same reason.

Then I saw some of the white boys get into cabs and tell the driver to take them to the recruiting office. I knew that the recruiting office wasn't that far away, so I never entertained the thought of getting a cab. Not only had I never ridden a cab before, but most of all, I didn't have money for a cab anyway.

It only took me a few minutes to reach the recruiting office, as there were a few boys ahead of me and some behind.

The recruiting office was very crowded, too small for everyone to get in, so the group spilled over into the hallway. Of course it helped that there were three sailors going around helping with getting everyone up to speed and ready for our next move. After about ninety minutes of the officers double-checking our paperwork, again we were all on the same bus, but this time we were headed for Raleigh. The bus was almost full. So now, I understood even more why I had to wait those thirty days.

It was mid-afternoon when we arrived in Raleigh. We four blacks were driven to the YMCA by one of the sailors. And whites were taken to the Sir Walter Hotel. We were informed that the next day we would have our swearing-in ceremony.

None of us had ever stayed at the YMCA before, and I'm

sure that we all demonstrated it by our curiosity. We were provided with a bag meal, and ate in our rooms. Two of the boys were from Greenville, and the other one was from Kinston.

The next morning, we were picked up by a limousine and taken to the Naval Facility so that we could be sworn into the United States Navy. Once we got there, we were taken to what I called a library-sized room. There were probably twenty tables dispersed throughout, and there were at least six hard-bottom chairs at each table.

Nobody told us to sit down, so some of us did, and some of us just milled around, talking, meeting each other. I guess we finally got a little too loud, because the sailor who took us to the room told us that we needed to cut the noise. And we did. We got quieter, but obviously only for a brief period. I was paying attention. After about three minutes, the noise level had risen to where it was before. Again, there was a reminder to talk quieter.

Next was the swearing-in ceremony. A different sailor entered the room with some paperwork under his arm. We sensed that this must be somebody important, so we got quieter without being instructed to. Sure enough, this was it.

Though quite simple, the swearing-in ceremony was something special, probably only because it meant so much to me. I had heard other guys talk about having joined up; consequently, I knew that this was merely another step toward becoming a sailor.

The ceremony only lasted two or three minutes, but these minutes will forever be etched in my memory. The officer told us that we were about to have our swearing-in ceremony, that he would read the oath to us, and for us to repeat after him. He went on to inform us that at the very beginning of the oath, after the word "I," we would say our own full name. He then told us to "Stand. Raise your right hand, and repeat after me…" For me, it was: "I, Moses Shepherd, Junior, do solemnly swear that I will support and defend the constitution of the United States of America against all enemies, foreign and domestic…"

Then the administering sailor said, "You are now in the U.S. Navy." We cheered!

The sailor who administered the oath got the material that he'd come in with, and he left. Then the sailor in charge of the noise level left the room also. Again, the noise level rose beyond where it was previously.

In walked a sailor we hadn't seen before. He was rather short, but he looked like he was in charge. He stood and just looked around, as if he couldn't believe what he was seeing and hearing. With one swing, he pounded the table and started letting us have it. "Goddamn it, all you sonsabitches get quiet; you in this man's navy now. You WILL obey." With that being taken care of, he turned and left the room, but we knew that starting then, we'd better get our shit together.

Before we left the naval facility, we were informed that we would be put on a bus to the Raleigh airport, catch a flight to Washington, D.C., and then fly to a naval base in Illinois.

The Raleigh airport was about seven or eight miles away. So, it was back on another bus. We young boys were excited. We were now legitimately members of the United States Navy.

I couldn't believe that it had finally happened.

Two of the sailors from the swearing-in ceremony accompanied us to the airport. En route, based on different conversations, I had discovered that for most of us, this would be our first time flying.

Once we arrived at the airport and got off, the two sailors directed us to the waiting areas. Blacks were taken to the black waiting area, and whites to the white waiting area. We were told to remain there until we were summoned.

After about thirty minutes, the two sailors returned and one of them announced that we were to follow them. Out to board the plane, my first flight! Of course, this was also my first time seeing an airplane up close. Boy, it was big, but not as big as I had imagined. We were guided underneath and to the rear of the plane. That was the entrance for us to get on. I was scared, excited, and still in a state of disbelief! As this was my first time riding an airplane, I had no idea what to expect regarding its smoothness. It wasn't smooth at all. Instead, it was like riding in the wagon with them mules loping over bumpy paths. But be that as it may, we reached our destination safely.

If I thought the Raleigh airport was something, this Washington airport put it to shame! And I didn't try to disguise my amazement. I didn't care who saw me with my jaw dropped and my eyes all big. Wow! And there was such a horde of planes, huge planes, coming and going.

When we got there, Navy personnel were waiting. These three sailors informed us that there was a four-hour layover until our flight would take us to Chicago.

Upon hearing that, our group dispersed. I searched through my pocket and found the address of Mother's half-sister, Annette. She lived on South Dakota Avenue in North East Washington.

I called and told her where I was, and that I would walk to her house since we had that long layover. She told me that she thought it was a little too far for me to walk. So that idea was dashed. After talking to her, I decided to go to the waiting room and relax for a while. But after a prolonged period of time looking for a sign that said, "Colored Waiting Room," I was informed that everyone used the same place to wait. That was drastically different from what I was used to.

The next wake-up call that I got was when I went to the drink machine to make a purchase. Soft drinks were selling for ten cents! I had been paying a nickel all of my life. This didn't make sense to me. Consequently, I took the stubborn stance and refused to buy one. I went to the waiting area where the other guys were and waited until it was time for us to leave.

Finally, it was time to go. The Navy personnel who had met us at the airplane returned and led us to the gate for our flight to Chicago.

This was a huge plane.

Once we resumed our journey, it seemed like we were riding on air, no bumping, and no jerking. The difference between the two airplanes was like night and day. Whereas we flew what seemed like a noisy, bumpy crop duster from North Carolina to Washington, this second leg was nothing but smooth. Additionally, we were in the first class section and we were fed a dinner of our choice.

When we touched down at the airport in Chicago, we North Carolina country boys thought that we were dressed for cold weather. What a rude awakening. We might as well have been naked. All of us were trembling, and our teeth were chattering. Of course we got stares from folks who were dressed for that kind of weather. But we didn't care.

When we got to State Street, none us had ever seen a building over four or five stories tall. Imagine twenty-five or thirty young men, mostly white, with southern accents, including those from eastern Carolina, with drawls, and nasal talking mountain boys.

Joe said, "By god, look-a there! That goddamn sumabitch damn near touchin' the sky."

Jimmy Lee intoned, "Hey Joe, Leroy, look! That's 'bout a tall muthafucka, ain't it?"

We caught the train from downtown, out to the Great Lakes Training Base.

"Welcome to the Great Lakes Training Facility," barked the second class petty officer who was standing mid-watch (midnight to 4 a.m.). He continued, "I bet this is the first time any of you goddamned jungle bunnies and rednecks ever been on a plane."

I smiled. I shook my head. I thought about the auctioneer, and kept on smiling. Then a tear fell. For some twisted reason, I felt like a boulder had been lifted from my shoulders. Right then and there, I knew that my sharecropping days were gone forever.

Tony BASK

E-BOOK — WWW.Otiscollin.com
$19.97

CPSIA information can be obtained
at www.ICGtesting.com
Printed in the USA
LVHW041001061020
668071LV00015B/673

9 781977 222763